Music, Cosmology, and the
Politics of Harmony in Early China

SUNY SERIES IN CHINESE PHILOSOPHY AND CULTURE

Roger T. Ames, *editor*

Music, Cosmology, and the Politics of Harmony in Early China

Erica Fox Brindley

Cover image courtesy of Bigstock Photos

Published by
STATE UNIVERSITY OF NEW YORK PRESS
Albany

For information, contact
State University of New York Press
www.sunypress.edu

Production, Diane Ganeles
Marketing, Michael Campochiaro

Library of Congress Cataloging-in-Publication Data

Brindley, Erica Fox.
    Music, cosmology, and the politics of harmony in early China / Erica Fox Brindley.
      p. cm. — (SUNY series in Chinese philosophy and culture)
    Includes bibliographical references and index.
    ISBN 978-1-4384-4314-0 (paperback : alk. paper)
    ISBN 978-1-4384-4313-3 (hardcover : alk. paper) 1. Music—Political aspects—China—
History. 2. Music—Social aspects—China—History. 3. Music—Philosophy and aesthetics.
4. China—History—Zhou dynasty, 1122-221 B.C. 5. China—History—Qin dynasty,
221–207 B.C. 6. China—History—Han dynasty, 202 B.C.–220 A.D. I. Title.
    ML3917.C6B75 2011
      780.931—dc23   2011036271

10 9 8 7 6 5 4 3 2 1

Contents

PART ONE
Music and the State

PART TWO
Music and the Individual

Acknowledgments

Many lovers of music, aesthetics, ideas, and the history of science and religion helped in the making of this book. I am indebted to their insights and thank them all graciously for taking the time to peruse parts of the work and offer their thoughts. I am most grateful to the two anonymous reviewers for this book. It is clear that both reviewers put a lot of care into their feedback. One reviewer's notes were so careful and on the mark that I have no doubt that the current version of this book is significantly better because of them. Nancy Ellegate and Roger Ames at SUNY were also a pleasure to work with and have given me many reasons to want to continue to publish in this series and with this press. And many thanks to Joseph Lam, Scott Cook, David Schaberg, and Miranda Brown for providing invaluable comments on very early drafts of material that have since been incorporated into this book.

At my home institution, Penn State, I would like to thank my colleagues, especially my amazing senior colleagues involved in Asian Studies, who have all supported the publication of this book, if merely by the power of their virtuosic collegiality. In particular, I thank On-cho Ng for being a great mentor and friend and Eric Hayot for his friendship and our many philosophic discussions about scholarly pursuits. In addition, I am grateful to Penn State College of Liberal Arts, Asian Studies, and Department of History for their funding to help defray publication costs. I also thank Ronnie Hsia, Sophie de Schaepdrijver, Tina Chen, Carrie Jackson, Jennifer Boittin, Chunyuan Di, Yuexing Li, and Michelle and Todd Rodino-Colocino for their collegiality and friendship during the period of writing and publishing this book.

I dedicate this book to my husband, Derek Brindley Fox, who never ceases to amaze me with his kindness, big heart, helpfulness, and empathic abilities. I also dedicate this book to my first-born daughter, Claire "Pualani"

Brindley Fox (Qian Yeming 錢業明), most of whose existence has covered the period during which this book was created and refined. Incidentally, Claire's Hawaiian name means "Flower of the Heavens," and resonates not only with the work I have been doing but with my husband's expertise in astronomy. And lastly, speaking of the heavens, I thank my lucky stars for my entire family, which includes the latest addition, Lia "Leilani" Brindley Fox (Qian Yexin 錢業欣).

PERMISSIONS

Parts of chapters four and five of this book were previously published as "Music and Cosmos in the Development of 'Psychology' in Early China," *T'oung Pao* 92.1–3 (2006), p1–49. Parts of chapter three were published as "Sound Phenomena: The Cosmic Power of Sound in Late Warring States and Han Texts," *Journal of Chinese Religions* 35 (2007), p1–35. The author thanks Koninklijke Brill NV and the *Journal of Chinese Religions* for their permission to reprint these articles in this book.

Prologue

The concept of harmony is central to music and musical endeavors. It also represents a foremost goal for political regimes all over the world, both ancient and contemporary. In coverage of the 2008 Beijing Olympics, for example, newscasters on NBC read from Chinese scripts that explained various musical performances in terms of the ancient value of harmony. Viewers were presented with a picture of China as a world leader that hopes to contribute to human flourishing in a peaceful, innovative, and, indeed, splendid way. A multiplicity of ethnic groups entered the stage to represent the diverse faces of the People's Republic. The message of "harmony amid diversity" resonated throughout the Olympic Stadium, and the world smiled at such a noble and magnificent goal.

The rhetoric of harmony in the People's Republic, however, is complicated, and some might claim that it does not always point to a satisfactory reality for all. Recently, dissident voices in the People's Republic have coined the term "*he xie* 和協," the contemporary word for "harmony," to point to the phenomenon of state censorship on the Internet.[1] The ironic use of this term attests to an intrinsic conflict between rhetorical uses of the notion of harmony by the state and the practices it supports. But it is important to be clear about the various definitions of "harmony" in Chinese culture. If "harmony" refers to the creation of a homogenous and unified sense of culture without serious dissent, then the state's use of "harmony" to justify censorship of "unsavory cultural content" on the web seems to be an appropriate use of the term. On the other hand, if harmony refers not merely to the conformity of similar items but to an appealing admixture of many diverse ones—as it is defined in the *Zuo zhuan*, the *locus classicus* for defining the term "harmony" in ancient China, then the state would be more hard-pressed to justify its actions—such as Internet censorship and the incarceration of dissident voices in the community—in terms of an effort to promote harmony in society.[2] This is certainly suggested by the Internet critics of *he xie.*

The purpose of this book is not to pursue how the current Chinese state employs the notion of harmony in its presentation of itself and through its policies and actions. It is also not to criticize the current regime by means of the age-old Chinese scholar-official's technique of examining the past in order to highlight current problems. Rather, I raise the issue of current uses of "harmony" to set the stage for thinking about possible political uses and implications for theories on music and harmony in ancient times.

In this book, I show how discussions of music in early China—based primarily on conceptions of harmony and balance—served as an important political and cultural tool for the state and its elite corps of ministers and intellectuals. The fact that the notion of harmony is still utilized as a tool that aids in state and social control, I think, attests to its effectiveness as something that speaks to people and resonates powerfully with Chinese longstanding political goals for state, imperial, or national unity, providing people and rulers alike with a familiar touchstone for speaking about the goal of cultural and political coherence and order at all levels of society.

For many authors in early China, music came to occupy a position of extreme importance in relationship not just to individuals and society, but to the larger cosmos as well. Around the fourth to third centuries BCE, authors of many different intellectual proclivities began to invoke metaphors of harmonious music to describe the workings of the cosmic Dao. Some authors even went beyond figurative associations to assert a primary, functional connection between harmonious music and the inherently balanced patterns or operations of nature and the cosmos. At first glance, one might not think to place too much value on such claims, since during the late Warring States and early imperial periods, assertions that referenced or invoked human connections to the cosmos were a matter of course. But upon closer inspection, one sees that music held an especially privileged relationship to the cosmos, above and beyond other elevated human activities such as the five other arts of a gentlemanly education and sometimes even ritual (though music was often later considered to be a part of ritual).[3] Indeed, while mastery of such other pursuits was integral to social standing, personal cultivation, and even—if one were a ruler—state order, music came to include and surpass these as a vital path to the highest levels of spiritual elevation and cosmic order.

Insofar as the notion of harmonious music held a special, spiritual connection to the cosmos, it comes as no surprise that it would be utilized by emerging states to aid in centralization during the late Warring States and early imperial period. The newfound cosmic implications of harmonious music placed it within a larger ontological framework, so that many aspects of music—such as instrumental pitch, its level of detail, its rhythmic movement and emphasis on timing, and the emotive quality of its sound—became highly regarded areas of expertise not merely for aesthetic purposes but for spiritual purposes that could also be utilized by the state. In such a vein, music served as a tool to maintain social order and religious authority over one's own population as well as alien others.

In addition to such lofty uses for music, the idea of musical harmony could serve as a tool for high ministers and other elites for criticizing rulers. Harmonious music often served to gauge of a ruler's level of virtue, as well as the health and well-being of his body and, by extension, the state. Such virtue was often indicated not merely through the types of music patronized by the ruler, but by his psychological, medical (or "psycho-physiological"), and spiritual health as well—as influenced by the type of music he supported and performed at court. As a measure of health, virtue, and state order, music linked to the various parts, systems, and attributes of the human body, so that the ruler was viewed as the most important recipient of its benefits and harms.

In exploring how music and cosmos are linked through the politics of harmony, we focus on two main topics of discussion, which comprise the two parts of this book: 1) music as a patterned expression of and means to state order, which includes viewing music as a civilizing force in state and society; and 2) music as a means of cultivating the moral self and maintaining bodily health, balance, and equilibrium, which includes viewing music as a boost to one's spiritual status. Through an analysis of these two areas—music and the state, and music and the individual body—we gain a glimpse of the changing roles and status of music in early China. We also learn how the spiritual belief in a harmonious cosmos made it possible for all of these areas to be thought of in terms of resonating spheres of activity. In such a way, we shed light upon why the notion of "harmony" seems to have held special cultural significance in Chinese society, throughout the centuries and up to today.

Introduction

Music and Cosmological Theory

地氣上齊，天氣下降，陰陽相摩，天地相蕩，鼓之以雷霆，奮之以風雨，
動之以四時，煖之以日月，而百化興焉。如此，則樂者天地之和也

The *qi* of Earth ascends above, while the *qi* of Heaven descends below. Yin and Yang rub against each other, and Heaven and Earth jostle up against each other. Their drumming creates peals of thunder; their pressing, wind and rain; their movement, the four seasons; their warming, the sun and moon; and so the hundred transformations arise therein. Just like this, music constitutes the harmony of Heaven and Earth.[1]

Music has always played an important role in human life and history, though the specific values it is given and the place it holds in relationship to cultural and political practices may vary greatly from one society to the next. In texts from early China, we learn of a vast array of practices and ideals associated with music and musical performance. Beginning early in the historical record, these writings describe the importance of music in a variety of contexts: as a means for rulers to express and wield power, as an integral part of ritual fulfillment and the means by which to achieve efficacy with the spirit world (through methods such as divination or sacrifice), as a vehicle for personal cultivation and health, and as sheer entertainment and public spectacle. This book will examine music primarily in relationship to one main aspect of life: the spiritual world, which was understood in ancient China in terms of the cosmos around us. We will see how authors over time began to view music as a critical, inherent aspect of the cosmos, tantamount to its harmonious patterns and idealized modes of operation, as in the quote above. We will also see how the concept of harmony—along with related notions of balance and resonance–played a crucial role in integrating disparate areas of inquiry such as music, the body, and the cosmos, into a seamless system with political, ethical, and medical ramifications.

NATURE VS. RELIGION, OR NATURE AS RELIGION?

Before we begin to characterize the relationship between music and the cosmos, it is important for us to understand the basic religious orientations that made such views possible. Greco-Roman and European traditions of thought tended to dichotomize "nature" and "religion," such that the separate study of nature, or "science"—as distinct from religion—might be understood as a natural outgrowth of such dichotomized thinking. This perspective does not do justice to early Chinese views. In early China, the spiritual character of the cosmos—including what we often designate as "supernatural" elements—was embedded deeply in the natural, phenomenal world. Indeed, people conceived of the reality around them in terms of an array of agents or agencies, without thinking of "spiritual" or "supernatural" as anything other than part of the "natural" world, and vice versa. In other words, what we today might classify as a "natural" event was often considered by the early Chinese to be imbued with sacred meaning or associated with "spiritual" agents such as ancestors or astral or earthly deities. Spiritual agents could effect changes in nature and human life precisely because they were considered to be a part of everyday reality.

Much of early Chinese religiosity is expressed through a somewhat naturalistic system that includes the agency of humans, deities, and forces as fundamental parts. More specifically, such entities and forces may include the Dao—or Way (sometimes understood as the Way of Heaven), Heaven, Earth, other astral deities, nature spirits, deceased ancestors or local spirits, deceased humans or ghosts, qi, and yin-yang. These spiritual agents or forces either govern intentionally, or they carry out actions deistically, according to regulated systems and patterns irrespective of any larger intention. However, even when the cosmos, as "nature," or Heaven and Earth, is considered to function according to seemingly spontaneous systems and patterns, we cannot simply deem this to be "naturalistic," in terms of its being "non-religious" in character. Indeed, in this book, "naturalism" is spiritual and carries religious meaning. So even though the Dao in many naturalistic traditions may seem to carry out its operations indifferent to human concerns, this does not make it a non-spiritual entity.

In short, while some scholars such as A. C. Graham have chosen to mark Chinese "proto-science" as distinct from "religion," I would suggest we collapse such a distinction and consider the two as one and the same.[2]

When discussing early Chinese views, we might wish to define nature and science (or "proto-science") not in opposition to religion, but, rather, to alter our conceptual structure so that ideas on nature or cosmos actually represent ideas on religion *par excellence*.

MUSIC IN RELATIONSHIP TO DEVELOPMENTS IN CHINESE COSMOLOGY

At some rather nebulous point in the written record (judging from texts dating somewhere between the fourth and early second centuries BCE), a new and quite prevalent discourse on *qi* (氣 material force) began to take hold in the minds of intellectuals. Causes and conditions that used to be attributed to local, ancestral, and Heavenly spirits with arbitrary, personal powers began to be explained in some circles by spiritual notions of another type: by cosmic harmony, balance, and resonance, especially as such notions related to the most basic force of *qi*.[3] As Nathan Sivin puts it: "But in that period [i.e., during the last three centuries BCE] the universe by fits and starts became a cosmos, that is, an orderly and harmonious system."[4] In keeping with the practice of viewing what is "natural" also in terms of what is "spiritual," the early Chinese considered *qi* not as a material force devoid of sacred value and strictly confined to the world of "natural science" as opposed to "religion," but as a natural-spiritual entity that acted according to certain set rules and the logic of cosmic creation and development. For this reason, throughout this book, I navigate the world of early music in relationship to the "cosmos" as a natural-spiritual entity, not as a mundane entity of exclusively scientific or astronomical interest. I therefore view the early Chinese endeavor to link music to the cosmos as a fundamentally religious endeavor—though, as we will see, political goals often appear to have fueled such a belief.

According to this new development in early Chinese cosmology, cosmic normalcy was contingent upon sets of systematic patterns defining the harmony and balance of *qi* primarily, and other forces such as *yin-yang* and the Five Phases were gradually worked into various cosmologies as well.[5] Some scholars describe this systematization of the cosmos in terms of a turn toward "naturalism" and refer to the cosmologies that developed in this vein in terms of a single cosmology, or "correlative cosmology."[6] Certainly, various late Warring States and early imperial authors did increasingly correlate disparate objects with each other, organizing their correlations according to an array of categories and subjecting the objects and phenomena of the world to a causal logic of resonance. One must be careful, however, not to assume "correlative cosmology" to refer to a single cosmology. Rather, it should probably refer to a similar method of explaining the world that subsumed many competing cosmologies. Such a method asserted that discrete objects could be correlated with each other, that correlation could be fulfilled through a causal logic of resonance, and that patterns of resonance in the world could come together so as to create an overarching harmony and balance among the myriad things in the world. Moreover, authors who presented such cosmologies chose to view spiritual agency in the world in terms of cosmic forces rather than—but not to the exclusion of—individuated or anthropomorphized spirits. Their systematization of things was therefore grounded in a logic that spiritual, vital forces exerted influence over things and acted according to predictable, resonant patterns, rather than according to an intention or will, or even a mechanistic pattern. Hence, this describes not merely "naturalism"—i.e., that which is proto-scientific or scientific *rather than* religious—but a "spiritual naturalism" that is at once naturalistic and religious.

Not surprisingly, music in early China—with its underlying emphasis on harmony and balance—was found to be a manifest ally or analogy of such a cosmos. As Jenny So puts it: "Music's role in cosmology made it an essential component of the *ganying* theory of resonance, in which things in similar categories of being were believed to sympathetically affect each other via resonant action at a distance."[7] The overarching harmony and balance of a resonant cosmos depended greatly on timing, rhythm, and attention to cyclical processes. As with music, this meant that all elements of the overall mixture should present themselves at the appropriate time. For example, random, cacophonous notes should not interfere with the mode of the moment, random rhythms should not upset the patterns or meter of a regulated rhythmic style, and random noise should not confuse the harmonic qualities of instrumental timbres. In cosmic terms, balance and harmony referred to the proper appearance and prominence of certain forces and phases—especially *yin-yang* and the Five Phases—at appropriate times of the day, month, and season. Thus, music and the cosmos were both idealized—and therefore linked—as harmonious processes. As David Schaberg puts it: "Perhaps because of the way it [music] crosses the frontier between the human and the cosmic, music became a master metaphor, with an indeterminacy and adaptability that facilitated correspondences in several intellectual realms and innumerable rhetorical situations."[8]

When one considers the relationship between music and the cosmos, Pythagoras (sixth century BCE) and his followers in ancient Greece immediately come to mind, through their notion of the "music of the spheres."[9] The Pythagorean theory that planetary bodies move and interact according to set, numerical relationships that constitute the harmonies of music seems to correspond to what I describe in this book concerning early

Chinese beliefs about music and cosmos.[10] It is not known whether the early Chinese, in believing that the movements of the cosmos produced music (or that musical harmonies were intrinsic to cosmic operations), were influenced by Pythagoras' theories on the connections between numerical patterns and music. It might have been the case, as Scott Cook suggests, that an early Chinese awareness of musical harmony and its conformity to the numerical laws of the cosmos arose wholly within the Chinese tradition itself, so that the "very cosmic order would be explained in terms of musical qualities."[11] But the possibility that the Greeks somehow influenced the Chinese on this matter, or vice versa, cannot be ruled out.

This book will not compare early Chinese concepts of music and harmony with that of the ancient Greeks. Rather, it will engage Chinese texts exclusively and leave such a comparison for further study. In the coming chapters, we will explore the manner in which music not only became a "master metaphor," but the ways in which it became understood—through its link to notions of harmony—as an integral aspect of the natural-spiritual cosmos, thereby insinuating itself into regimes of bodily cultivation and health. We will examine the many ways in which the values and uses of music changed as music took on a more prominent—indeed, even primary—role in relationship to a changing concept of the cosmos. We will also show how conceptions of human relationship to music changed as music took on such a privileged status. In so doing, we will learn how its privileged relationship with the cosmos helped justify its extreme importance in political rhetoric at court.

WHAT CONSTITUTES "MUSIC" IN EARLY CHINA?

In our contemporary society, the concept of music is constantly challenged and upended by composers, musicians, and musicologists alike. What once constituted music and traditional forms of harmony in the West has been overturned by other cultural traditions of music, as well as avant-garde experiments of the twentieth century that introduced altogether new possibilities for harmony, sonic and recording technologies, and audio-visual performances linking music with other art forms. Early Chinese concepts of music, or yue (Old Chinese: *ngrawk 樂), shared features with our contemporary audio-visual pieces, insofar as yue not only encompassed the musical performance of song and instrumental pieces, but also included dances and spectacular visual performances using flags, feathers, costumes, spears, banners, and other props. Other related terms in classical Chinese make use of the homologous graph, yue 樂, to refer to notions of "pleasure," "enjoyment," "joy," "to take delight in," etc. Authors who discussed music in early China often exploited such linguistic associations for rhetorical purposes.[12] The early Mohists suggest an even more comprehensive understanding of *yue* as a type of musical entertainment accompanying feasts.[13] Because of the broad spectrum of performances included in the concept of *yue*, scholars might choose to translate the term as "music and dance performances," or simply, "entertainment."[14] To my mind, however, the phrase "music and dance performances" is too unwieldy, while "entertainment" is too broad. By understanding *yue* as entertainment, for example, we fail to distinguish between it and other forms of public or court entertainments, such as verbal repartee, archery contests, recitations of poetry, and acrobatics or other dramatic arts.[15] What, then, constitutes an adequate translation of the term *yue*?

Throughout this book, I use "music" as a translation for *yue* despite its lack of perfect congruence with *yue* in practice. I do this not only for the sake of simplicity, but also because the core meaning of *yue* in many of the texts I examine points most directly and fundamentally to sound and the patterning of sound through a combination of tunes, rhythms, and harmonies. Intriguingly, the dancing and the other visual aspects of *yue* usually appear to be of secondary importance in many of these discussions. Of least importance to the authors making claims about *yue* appears to be the banners, flags, and props accompanying a performance, though sometimes an author will reveal an awareness that such aspects are part of the performance. For this reason, we must remain vigilant of these aspects of *yue*, despite my use of the term "music" to translate the concept. Whenever an obvious discrepancy obtains between our understanding of music and the early Chinese understanding of *yue*, I will do my best to point out the difference and how that affects our interpretation of the specific claim under examination.

There are other aspects of "music," as it is understood in certain contemporary American circles, which we will not be analyzing here in detail, since they lie mostly outside the scope of early Chinese contexts for *yue*. Such phenomena might include musical incantations used in mantic or medical rituals; drumming and clanging sounds utilized to signal the beginning of a battle or to communicate with troops; or even the use of bells and whistles as accoutrements of a properly outfitted chariot. Certainly, at times we will find it helpful to relate practices such as mantic rituals and military signals to ancient discussions of *yue* or the cosmos, especially in our discussion of the significance of sound in chapter three, or in the use of certain musical elements in maintaining health in chapter six. But for the most part, we will limit ourselves to commonly discussed aspects of *yue* in our texts, especially as centered around terms that denote sonic harmony, pitch, and musical theory, such as *he* (harmony 和), *yin* (tones 音), *sheng* (sounds 聲), and *lü* (pitch-pipes, pitch-standards 律).

STRATEGY AND AIMS

Music in early China is a neglected area of study, despite textual and archaeological records that demonstrate its ubiquitous presence in many aspects of life. Still limited to a few Chinese histories of the entire musical or aesthetic tradition—which often cover thousands of years at a time—and to a few monographs and books in Western languages, the field lacks specialized studies that concentrate on but a few aspects of music during specific periods of Chinese history.[16] One overlooked area is the role of music in political and religious (which included, according to our explanation above, "scientific") thought. As notions of harmony changed and authors began to propose intrinsic relationships between sound and nature, the bond between music and the cosmos strengthened, affecting the status and uses of music in society in ways that touch upon all of these areas.

Through a close analysis of received and excavated texts (dating roughly to 400–100 BCE), I show how music took on a privileged position as it became increasingly intertwined with notions of a harmonious and resonant cosmos. My aim is to advance a general understanding of how music served religious views on nature and the human body. At the same time, I evaluate the usefulness of music to early imperial regimes (~200–100 BCE) that wished to demonstrate their access to and control of natural phenomena, which were conceived in terms of harmonious networks of order, much like their idealized vision for the state. And I show how discourses on music often delineated a psychology and spoke to medical concerns, since bodily systems were also linked to a harmonious cosmos.

Two central questions form the basis of my discussion. Why should music have taken on a privileged relationship to the cosmos? And how did discourses on music and views of its effects on humans change as music took on such a privileged status? I respond to these questions by exploring the ways in which an emergent type of cosmology stressed the harmonious and resonant aspects of the cosmos. As a result of such a cosmology, music—which exhibited both harmony and resonance—became identified as a natural arena for conceptualizing and depicting cosmic operations and human relationship to them.

While there is some amount of Chinese and Japanese scholarship on Chinese music, little of it converges on a single theme. The secondary texts that address issues related to the period of my study are mostly general histories of Chinese music that give equal weight to many different topics and provide a plethora of sources and information on the culture of music throughout the ages. Cai Zhongde's 蔡仲德 *Zhongguo yinyue meixue* 中國音樂美學史 and Tian Qing's 田青 *Zhongguo gudai yinyue shihua* 中國古代音樂史話 are examples of such general comments on the history of music or musical aesthetics in China.[17] From an archaeological perspective, Wang Zichu's 王子初 *Zhongguo yinyue kaoguxue* 中國音樂考古學 provides an expansive history of musical instruments from prehistoric times through the Qing.[18] These are helpful references, but they offer limited insights into specific themes developed in this book, such as the relationship between music and the cosmos on the one hand, or a discussion of concepts of harmony and integrated systems of music, state, and body on the other. Their sweeping coverage of thousands of years of music history also necessarily limits the depth of their inquiry into any one historical period.

More specific studies of music during the Warring States and early imperial periods include such works as Mizuhara Iko's *Chugoku kodai ongaku shiso kenkyu* 中国古代音樂思想研究 and Zhao Feng's 趙渢 edited volume, *Yueji lunbian* 樂記論辨.[19] I have found such scholarship to be informative, but their encyclopedic, topical approach prevents them from developing more incisive conceptual schemes or claims.

In Western languages, there are several important studies of popular music and music in state ritual from Wei-Jin and Song times to the modern day.[20] Still, however, there is a considerable dearth of scholarly accounts on music in early China. A few studies focus on the *Canon of Odes*, a text of song-poems that held cultural currency among elites. Scholars such as Steven Van Zoeren and Martin Kern in particular have made significant contributions in this area.[21] Their scholarship on the *Odes*, however, while touching upon music and recognizing its importance as a primary feature of this classical text, mainly stresses the literary culture, lyricism, and other aspects of the text, rather than music and harmony per se. Clearly, the current book, which takes music and religious thought, not literature, as the starting point of discussion, has very different things to offer than literary studies of the *Odes*.

In more recent years, Kern has gone on to write about developments concerning the rhetoric of music during the Han Dynasty.[22] This aspect of his work has enriched the current study, especially in its delineation of "new music" as a Han phenomenon.[23] But its brief, summary nature and focus on specific attitudes and policies at the Han court do not generally overlap with the goals of this book. Lothar von Falkenhausen's seminal study on the chime bells from the tomb of an early Chinese marquis (Marquis Yi of Zeng) provides a focused archaeological and technical study of music and music theory in early China.[24] His work has demonstrated that exercises such as excavating the musical theory behind bell sets and extrapolating information about political culture from them are entirely possible and fruitful endeavors. Similarly, Ingrid Furniss' pioneering book discusses music in ancient China through the lens of various instruments and what their arrangement or placement in tombs can tell us about the social occasions for their use.[25] Both Falkenhausen's and Furniss' work use primarily archaeological sources, and they help shed much light upon music and musical performances through an analysis of instruments or specific sets of instruments. They significantly enhance our knowledge of the nature of early Chinese music and musical performances. But both studies rely very little, if at all, on textual sources, which sometimes presents problems. For example, Furniss' claims about the arrangement of instruments in tombs at times pits musical entertainment against music used in ritual contexts.[26] Such claims are perplexing when one considers that the two—entertainment and ritual—were not mutually exclusive, at least, as they are presented in textual sources. Indeed, yue was always considered to be a part of ritual, whether it was performed in a formal state or ancestral ceremony or for the pleasure of individuals at home and at court.

A narrower study of early Chinese music theory in relationship to the cosmos was conducted by James Hart in the early 1970s. Hart points out the relationship of music to astronomical beliefs, elaborating on an important cosmic element that is highlighted in the current book as well.[27] His study specifically focuses on a particular set of bells mentioned in a single text, the *Guo yu* 國語, and contributes to our knowledge of some details concerning astrological and musical relationships. However, it is too narrow to generate broader, historical conclusions about music and religion in early China.

Scott Cook's "Unity and Diversity in the Musical Thought of Warring States China" is a Ph.D. dissertation that provides a rich discussion of about eight different texts and their relationship to music.[28] In his discussion of music in many of the philosophical works and certain compendia of the period, Cook touches upon many themes that impinge upon what is articulated in this book. Despite its panoptic nature, impressive array of topics and high level of discursive detail, it does not discuss music in terms of a single theme. Nor does it analyze music in terms of an historical narrative, i.e., in light of political, social, or religious changes that emerged over the course of the Warring States and early imperial periods. So while Cook's dissertation is invaluable as a general resource on musical thought during Warring States China, there is still a need for other, focused accounts on specific issues, such as music and cosmology, which the present book attempts to provide.

One last work on music deserves special attention here. In his 1982 monograph on music and aesthetics from the Warring States through the Six Dynasties periods, Kenneth DeWoskin discusses a wide range of topics, mostly focusing on music performance and theory and how one might go about understanding the aesthetics of music.[29] DeWoskin takes on such thorny issues as the mind's relationship to hearing and music, music in mythology and cosmology, the culture of playing the *qin*-zither, and the empirical role of pitches and pitch-standards in musical aesthetics. Ambitiously covering approximately a millennium of China's history, DeWoskin mimics to a certain extent the Chinese scholarship on music mentioned earlier, but he goes much deeper by providing perceptive, thematic connections across such a broad range of time. Certainly, the present book draws upon many of the themes first presented in DeWoskin's account and further discussed in Cook's scholarship. In particular, it picks up on and attempts to refine the broad, historical generalizations imparted by DeWoskin concerning Zhou and Han discussions of music. Zhou discussions, DeWoskin claims, focus on music in relationship to morality and morale, while writings from the Han reveal an interest in empirical matters relating to natural philosophy and acoustical theories.[30] In this book, I acknowledge such a difference, but frame it in terms of the rise to prominence of a certain cosmological outlook. This outlook did not displace discourses on music and morality, but rather, wove musical ethics more systematically into the fabric of a proto-scientific and spiritual worldview.

My account on music and harmony in early China draws from and enhances previous studies on music in socio-political life and cosmology. I agree with Hart's, DeWoskin's, and Cook's presentation of the special, privileged relationship between music and the cosmos in many early Chinese texts. But rather than taking this privileged relationship for granted, as most of the earlier scholarship on music does, I discuss its development historically, in tandem with increasing imperial concerns about controlling the natural world and religious orientations related to such political concerns. I claim that the historical rise of the isomorphic trio of music, the cosmos, and the human body cannot be taken for granted and that connections among the three were forged at certain moments in the religious and political history of China. In such a way, I add to the work of the scholars mentioned above and ask not just what music and musical performance meant to people in society, but why certain ideas about music came about as they did and what role they may have served in the demand for an increasingly systematic and unified theory of cosmic control.

In addition to offering a sustained, historical, and systematic study of views on music in relationship to political and religious cosmology, this book provides a nuanced reading of different texts and types of texts that are not examined in the above-mentioned literature. The recent publication of excavated and unprovenanced texts from tombs has allowed scholars of early China to reconsider, add to, enhance, and alter previous understandings of Chinese culture and history. In this book, I analyze the newly excavated treatise "Xing zi ming chu [Human nature emerges from Heaven's Mandate]" 性自命出 (1993), which highlights music and has not been adequately studied in terms of its claims on how music figures into self-cultivation and moral psychology.

Scholars familiar with the main themes in early Chinese intellectual culture will notice that this book's emphasis on the importance of cosmologies of resonance that consist of various elements including *qi*, *yin-yang*, and Five Phases echoes histories of the so-called correlative cosmology of early China. "Correlative cosmologies" are discourses on the workings of nature that display a fundamental belief in the inherent harmony and relationship among certain categories of objects in the world. Most scholars use the label to refer to a very diverse range of discourses on the natural philosophy of the day. Because such a label fails to describe adequately the underlying view of causation that makes such a cosmology distinctive—namely, the view that radically different objects obtain mystical resonance with each other—I prefer to use the phrase "cosmology of resonance" instead.

Texts such as the *Mencius*, *Zhuangzi* "Inner Chapters," and fragments of the *Laozi* appear to contain more references than early Warring States texts to cosmic forces such as *qi* and *yin-yang* and to the various relationships among physical phenomena in the world. The "Five Phases" texts discovered at Mawangdui and Guodian show hints of a budding cosmological framework for *qi* and *yin-yang*, although the Five Phases in the title refers mostly to the Confucian (Ru 儒, "ritual specialists") category of Five Virtues, rather than Wood, Fire, Water, Metal, and Earth. However, the foremost thinker to have promoted what scholars now typically epitomize as correlative cosmology was Zou Yan, active around 250 BCE, who successfully promulgated a theory on the "Five Phases."[31]

Rather than focus exclusively on the details of and differences among cosmologies of resonance, I underscore the salient and recurrent emphasis in many late Warring States and early imperial texts on ideals of patterned regularity, which often imply harmonious, balanced, and resonant interactions among disparate objects. The fact that such ideals overlapped and even converged with ideals associated with music gives me reason to suggest that music was used as a convenient analogy for an emergent cosmology of resonance. In many ways, this book provides a simple elaboration of how writers and statesmen of the day established correspondences between music and the cosmos so as to tailor and refine their visions of each according to the other and to the purposes of the state. My method in inquiring into musical cosmology is constrained by the fact that I am not so much trying to uncover or depict actual performances or practices regarding music as I am trying to narrate a history of idealized representations of music and its changing values in society. I therefore do not dwell on specific details associated with instruments or orchestral instrumentation, particular dances or Odes, or famous historical performances—though I will provide basic information concerning these areas in footnotes when the occasion arises. I also do not engage many of the mathematical, harmonic relationships designated by theory that emerged in tandem with notions of cosmic music, though I include such information when appropriate.[32] Instead, I analyze theories of music that shed light upon common attitudes towards music, its relationship to individuals and ideals of government, and views on harmony and the significance of sound in society and the cosmos. Such an analysis is therefore centered on how thinkers theorized about music, rather than musical theory *per se*. Its main concern is to outline how notions of music were embedded in cosmic visions of the self and state, not to study musical practices and theory as ends in themselves.

Other limitations affect the strategic approach of this book. A chief constraint is the lack of precise textual dating and data about specific individuals and their contexts. A cultural history of music in later periods of China would be able to provide more information on the backgrounds of specific music directors and practitioners, their roles and activities as musical advocates at court, and the particular stories surrounding certain claims we find in specific texts. Unfortunately, for the early, pre-imperial and imperial periods, it is difficult to pursue meaningful inquiry into these areas, as most written accounts from the period do not provide detailed information about the circumstances that contributed to the writing of particular texts. Nor do they provide much biographical information about specific authors, music directors, and theorists of music, let alone common musicians.[33] It is also rare to know the specific year in which a text was composed or the circumstances behind its composition. In most cases we are lucky to know the date range of a particular Warring States text (often in terms of a range of two centuries) and to be able to infer ideological relationships between and among texts based on the information given in the texts themselves. Beginning with the late Warring States and early imperial periods in China, our knowledge of dates and peoples greatly improves in comparison to the early Warring States period. Thus, it will sometimes be possible to know specific dates of texts and certain details surrounding court politics at the time of their composition.

A BRIEF HISTORY OF HARMONY (HE 和)

One main aspect of this book deals with music in a way that may seem completely foreign to most modern readers: by discussing music in terms of its relationship to the cosmos. When we think of music and its uses, attributes, and joys, we do not automatically think about the sacred patterns in nature, the movements of cosmic bodies, or the ethical imperatives of Heaven. Yet in some circles in early China, music came to signify such lofty things. In its most idealized form, music came to represent the cosmos and its infinite processes of decrease and fulfillment, coming and going, heating and cooling, darkening and illuminating, etc. Indeed, music came to be associated with the harmonious patterns of the cosmos itself.

Below, I document a change in the concept of harmony that is relevant to our understanding of the idea that music could come to have cosmic implications in ancient China. It is necessary to show this change because it helps support the fundamental claim of this book; namely, that a religious change in cosmology—rooted in political concerns—affected the way in which music was thought of and discussed.[34] Such a change hints at the religious and political background of musical thought, shedding light upon why music was deemed especially useful in state government and the fulfillment of ambitious political regimes and cultural programs.

The term harmony (he 和) can be found early in the textual record in relationship to a variety of contexts. Notably, it is not until the century and a half before imperial unification under the Qin (221 BCE) that it began to be associated directly with the intrinsic and ideal patterns of the cosmos. A brief look at some pre-imperial texts will document this change and show how such a term evolved from describing a goal of humans, society, and music, to serving as the conceptual linchpin that flawlessly linked all natural and spiritual systems to each other.

In many of the pre-Warring States chapters of the *Book of Documents* (*Shang shu* 尚書), harmony is mentioned in musical contexts as well as social interactions. In the latter case, it conveys that which humans might achieve in, among, and for groups of people, whether in one's speech, at a gathering of leaders, or for the larger population. In a survey of usages for the term "harmony" outside of aesthetic or musical contexts, it serves as a human accomplishment and construct. Thus, in the "Luo Gao 洛誥," the king proclaims a wish to follow in the virtues of the Duke of Zhou, so as to "harmonize and bring constancy to the people of the Four Directions 和恆四方民."[35] Similarly, in "Wu Yi 無逸," the Duke of Zhou describes King Wen as having "applied himself to harmonizing the myriad peoples 用咸和萬民."[36] And lastly, in "Jun Shi 君奭," the Duke speaks to Prince Shi about King Wen, who was able to "refine and harmonize our regions of Xia 修和我有夏."[37] The usages referred to here occur in the pre-Warring States chapters which help make up what Edward Shaughnessy considers to be the "heart of the authentic *Shang shu*."[38] In all of these instances, the term *he* is used primarily as a verb, "to harmonize," that describes the actions of a virtuous ruler in relationship to his populace.

This does not mean that the term harmony was not also used in aesthetic contexts. Noting the special application of the term to non-musical or non-aesthetic contexts, Scott Cook argues for a primarily aesthetic, rather than social or political, use of harmony from early on: "No early Chinese text ever sets out to demonstrate the aesthetic necessity of the harmonious balance of contrasting parameters in music or cuisine by an appeal to the intrinsic nature of social and governmental operation."[39] This notwithstanding, it is significant that outside of aesthetic contexts, the term harmony was often invoked as a social or political ideal—as an enterprise rulers embark upon for their kingdoms—which implicitly likened the act of ruling to an aesthetic endeavor.

The theme of social harmony is pervasive in a variety of early texts. In the *Analects*—the earliest portions of which likely reflect the thinking and goings-on of the fifth to fourth centuries BCE—harmony appears not only as a key characteristic of proper music, but also as a standard of both musical performance and social interaction: "When the Master was singing with other people and liked someone else's song, he always asked for him to repeat it before harmonizing along with him 子與人歌而善必使反之而後和之."[40] Here, harmonizing implies both one's participation in music and the patterning of such participation through human compliance with, not disruption of, the situation.[41] As a key to patterned social integration, harmony represents a social ideal in the *Analects*. But it also remains a political goal, as seen in the passages above: "Where there is harmony there is no such thing as having a low population 和無寡."[42] This political use of the term can be found in early Mohist writings as well, which likely date from the early fourth century BCE.[43] Specifically, the early Mohists refer to the goal of achieving a state of "harmony of the world 天下之和," as well as the "harmony of the myriad people 萬民和."[44] Thus, in examples from both the *Analects* and early Mohist writings, harmony is not something that is inherent to music, society, or even the cosmos; rather, it is a socio-political and aesthetic ideal that is achieved through humans. Harmonious music and harmonious society are man-made constructions that must be achieved through effort and finesse, not natural entities that may be discovered in the cosmos.

The *Zuo zhuan*, considered by some to be a fourth century BCE text, also generally confirms a view of harmony as a human achievement.[45] A few examples from hundreds of different usages of the term demonstrate this point. In one famous example, Yanzi invokes the harmony a chef might achieve through cooking in explaining how harmonious human behavior differs from conformism:

和如羹焉。水火醯醢鹽梅以烹魚肉。燀之以薪宰，夫和之齊之以味。濟其不及以洩其過。君子食之以平其心。

Harmony is like a broth. Water, fire, vinegar, meat juices, salt, and plum are used to boil fish meat. It is cooked with firewood, and the chef harmonizes and equalizes it to taste. He adds to what is lacking and dilutes what is in excess. The gentleman drinks it to even out his heart-mind.[46]

This passage becomes the *locus classicus* for an understanding of harmony in terms of diversity and not uniformity. Significantly, harmony here is not an inherent aspect of any of the objects in question, such as the broth or the gentleman, or any one of the many ingredients. It is acquired and constructed through the human art of mixing and blending diverse elements together.[47]

Similarly, in another passage of the *Zuo zhuan*, the use of the term harmony in relationship to music most exclusively points to a quality achieved and expressed through proper mixing of distinct tones. Jizha of Wu, upon being presented in the state of Lu with music of all styles and regions, comments thusly upon hearing the Zhou "Lauds" (*song* 頌), which later became an important part of the *Canon of Odes*: "The Five Tones harmonious; the Eight Winds balanced;[48] each phrase regulated and preserving its [proper] sequence: such is the unity of flourishing virtue 五聲和，八風平，節有度，守有序，盛德之所同也!"[49] Indeed, it was not uncommon for statesmen to demonstrate their expertise in moral virtue through their musical sensibilities. One's ability to recognize harmony among sounds corresponded to one's ability to make prognostications about the harmony and well-being of a particular state and society, as demonstrated here through Jizha of Wu. Tonal harmonies in this context appear to be musical constructions that have significant implications in human life.

There are a couple of instances in the *Zuo zhuan* in which there appears to be a subtle connection between the concept of harmony and the greater workings of the cosmos. In Duke Zhuang, year 22, for example, a tortoise-shell divination reveals an auspicious sign, interpreted as male and female phoenixes flying and singing harmoniously together (鳳皇于飛, 和鳴鏘鏘).[50] While this reference to harmony directly points to the harmony of birdsong—and not to any larger patterns of the cosmos—the term for "phoenix" (*feng* 鳳) was linguistically connected to the wind, and so it connotes aspects of one's natural environment as well.[51]

In another passage, the relationship to the cosmos is perhaps even stronger. There, the Six *Qi* of the cosmos are linked to notions of harmony and balance:

天有六氣，降生五味，發為五色，徵為五聲。淫生六疾。六氣曰陰、陽、風、雨、晦、明也，分為四時，序為五節，過則為菑

There are the Six *Qi* of Heaven, which descend to produce the Five Flavors, expand to make the Five Colors, manifest themselves in the Five Tones, and in excess, produce the Six Illnesses. [These aspects of Heaven] are said to be Yin, Yang, Wind, Rain, Obscure, and Bright. They divide to make the four seasons and form a sequence to give the Five Modes.[52] If there is too much [of any one of them] then disaster strikes.[53]

Though this passage does not explicitly mention the term "harmony," it speaks of the importance of having the Six Qi of Heaven remain in balance, so that one may ward off illness. In addition, it clearly links the Six Qi to the fundamentals of music, the Five Tones and Five Modes, thereby grounding music essentially in the meteorological and seasonal aspects of the cosmos.[54] This excerpt provides us with a window on a certain conception of the cosmos as connected to both music and harmony as "balance"— one that becomes much more explicit in the transmitted literature after the fourth century BCE, and, thus, primarily after the writing and compiling of the *Zuo zhuan*.

Let us summarize our findings so far. In early Zhou texts such as the *Documents*, as well as in texts dating up to the mid-fourth century BCE, the term harmony primarily expresses aesthetic ideals, interpersonal and political achievement, and even goals for an integrated social order. When not referring to aesthetic ideals in the contexts of the culinary and musical arts, it usually refers to the goals of rulers in governing their people as well as the signs of political and social order and stability. In this sense, it belongs to the realms of human construction, achievement, and political attainment.[55] Only in a small number of passages in the *Zuo zhuan* do we find hints that people were thinking about harmony in relationship to the entire cosmos and its workings. Such instances are so few in comparison with the more mundane uses of the term harmony, however, that we might conclude that while authors of the fourth century BCE might indeed have begun to think about the cosmos in term of harmony, they did not consider such a link to be a primary topic of discussion.

At some point by the late fourth and early third centuries BCE, many authors began to formulate more explicitly a naturalistic concept of harmony, one that implied the intrinsic balance of cosmic forces in the world, in people, and in things. In general, harmony no longer referred primarily to that which individuals could achieve through music, ritual, their behavior, or good rule. It was no longer more exclusively used to describe a goal of human attainment. Rather, it became more universally regarded as a fundamental characteristic, pattern, and even structure of the cosmos.[56] This new articulation of harmony appears more prevalently in texts that can be dated from within a period starting from around 325 BCE.[57]

One of the most famous and possibly earliest examples in which the term harmony refers to the inherent workings of the cosmos occurs in Zhuangzi's passage on the panpipes of man, Earth, and Heaven:

子綦曰：「偃，不亦善乎，而問之也！今者吾喪我，汝知之乎？女聞人籟而未聞地籟，女聞地籟而未聞天籟夫！」子游曰：「敢問其方。」...泠風則小和，飄風則大和...子綦曰：「夫吹萬不同，而使其自己也，咸其自取，怒者其誰邪！」

Ziqi said, "Yan, what a good question that you ask! Just now I lost myself; do you understand that? You hear the piping of humans, but you have not heard the piping of Earth. You hear the piping of Earth but you have not heard the piping of Heaven." Zi you asked, "May I dare ask what that means?" . . . "With a gentle current, there is a faint harmony, but with a full gale, a giant harmony ensues . . . Ziqi responded [with respect to the piping of Heaven]: "It's blowing [that stems from] the myriads of different things and allowing them to be of themselves. All take for themselves—who could it be who does the sounding?"[58]

In this passage, just as the breath of humans creates music through certain instruments, the wind of the earth creates a chorus or harmony of natural sounds, and the piping of Heaven produces a diverse harmony of self-motivated life forces among the myriad creatures. The depiction of music as the way of the cosmos is so deeply embedded in this passage that I believe it makes much sense to interpret the comparison literally rather than figuratively: in other words, in terms of the workings of cosmos as a form of music, and not merely as a process similar to music. This interpretation compares favorably with Pythagoras' notions of the "harmony (or music) of the spheres," mentioned above, which claims that the planetary bodies move according to actual harmonic relationships, making music as they go. Similarly, in this passage of the *Zhuangzi*, Heavenly music is an actual performance produced or given by the various processes of life and nature, or, more simply, the cosmos.[59]

The *Lüshi chunqiu* (*LSCQ*), datable to around 239 BCE, picks up on this theme of the inherent harmonies and sounds of the cosmos to draw important conclusions about the music of humans. Rather than focus on the claim that the cosmos is music, the authors of the *LSCQ* chapter "Great Music" acknowledge the cosmic roots of sound. They do this in order to point out that the principles and building blocks of sagely music actually replicate cosmic harmonies: "When the youngest sprouts were first stimulated, they were given shape through coagulation. Shapes and forms had their hollow places, and none was without sound. Sound emerged from harmony, harmony from what is fitting. When the First Kings fixed their music, they started from these principles 萌芽始震，凝堕以形。形體有處，莫不有聲。聲出於和，和出於適。和適，先王定樂由此而生。"[60] Here, as with Zhuangzi, harmony is key to the ontology of the cosmos. The musical principles of the cosmos derive from the hollows of the world, underlying its very existence and operation.[61]

Other passages from the same chapter of *LSCQ* lend credence to this conclusion: "As a general principle, music is the harmony between Heaven and Earth, and the perfect blend of Yin and Yang 凡樂，天地之和，陰陽之調也."[62] Still later, the author hints that human music should imitate natural sounds. This resonates with a belief that harmony, in this context most certainly pointing to a sort of music, is inherent in the cosmos: "Kui thereupon made songs in imitation of the sounds of the forests and valleys, he covered earthenware tubs with fresh hides and beat on them, and he slapped stones and hit rocks to imitate the sounds of the jade stone chimes of the Supreme Sovereign, with which he made the hundred wild beasts dance 夔乃效山林谿谷之音以〔作〕歌，乃以麇对（置）〔冒〕缶而鼓之，乃拊石擊石，以象上帝玉磬之音，以致舞百獸."[63] Kui, commanded by the sage Emperor Yao, creates music that imitates natural sounds. His human creation, while producing a harmony entirely of its own, nonetheless appears as an extension of cosmic sounds. Although this passage does not directly state that harmony is inherent in the cosmos, there is an underlying sense that the cosmos (as represented through nature) constitutes an inherently musical space.

A section of the *Mozi* that is quite probably a later, post-fourth-century BCE creation also points to a harmonious cosmos that serves as an ideal for social order. The author of chapter six, "Ci Guo 辭過," speaks of the inherent "harmony of Yin and Yang 陰陽之和" as well as the human goals of re-establishing "harmony between Heaven and Earth 天地和" and "harmony of one's body [flesh and skin] 肌膚和" through sagely control of the desires.[64] Similarly, the notion that cosmic harmony can be established through the workings of Yin and Yang is also present in the *Laozi*, which was probably compiled no earlier than the late fourth century BCE.[65] In chapter forty-two of that text, the author shows how the myriad things blend or shake the energy (*qi* 氣) of Yin and Yang to create a harmonious admixture of cosmic elements.[66] While this vision conceives of the myriad things as agents who aid in the creation of cosmic harmony, such agents can only achieve such harmony by allowing the processes of the cosmos (those inherent in their own bodies as well) to occur spontaneously of themselves.[67]

Texts associated with the early imperial period most explicitly identify harmony as an intrinsic aspect of the cosmos. Take, for example, the following passages, found in the "Chuzhen 俶真" chapter of the *Huainanzi* 淮南子, which describe various stages of the undifferentiated cosmos, such as when it "upheld virtue and contained harmony 被德含和," or when Heaven "contained harmony yet had not descended 天含和而未降."[68] Such passages, couched in a more extensive cosmogonic account, shows us clearly that the term "harmony" was understood to be a primordial characteristic of the cosmos, as well as something that could be possessed within, like a virtue.

Even the "Yue ji 樂記," the foremost classical treatise on music in the Confucian tradition found in the *Book of Rites*, espouses a view of harmony as intrinsic to the workings of the cosmos:

地氣上齊，天氣下降，陰陽相摩，天地相蕩，鼓之以雷霆，奮之以風雨，動之以四時，煖之以日月，而百化興焉。如此，則樂者天地之和也

The *qi* of Earth ascends evenly [to Heaven], while that of Heaven descends to Earth. Yin and yang rub against each other; Heaven and Earth ruffle each other. They drum it [the *qi*] so as to [produce] peals of thunder, arouse it to [produce] wind and rain, move it to [produce] the four seasons, warm it to [produce] the sun and moon, and the hundred transformations arise. It is in this manner that music constitutes the harmony of Heaven and Earth.[69]

This author implicates the natural harmony of sexual relations, as represented by a masculine Heaven and feminine Earth, in a musical dance that constitutes a cosmic process. Thus, like Zhuangzi, he goes so far as to claim that the forces and interactions of the cosmos constitute music at its very core.

In the Ru text *Zhong yong* 中庸, approximately datable to the third–second centuries BCE,[70] harmony is connected to the metaphysical underpinnings of the cosmos. It represents a vital accomplishment in cosmic operations, and not merely an attainment of humans, as in the texts described above:

喜怒哀樂之未發謂之中。發而皆中節謂之和。中也者，天下之大本也。和也者，天下之達道也。致中和，天地位焉。萬物育焉

When happiness, anger, grief, joy have not yet issued forth, [this] we call being centered. When they have issued forth yet each attain due measure, [this] we call being in harmony. Centrality is the great root of the world; harmony is the world arriving at the Way. Centrality and harmony achieved, Heaven and Earth [find their correct] positions, and the myriad creatures are nourished.[71]

Here, all life, creation, and even the operations of cosmos depend on centrality and harmony. Harmony is the attainment of the Way that helps place cosmic operations back in order. Though, unlike in the other passages just examined, harmony does not describe the inherent functions of the cosmos, it does describe its idealized and proper state of being. This passage thus shares with the other, post-fourth century BCE texts an orientation towards harmony as something idealized and applicable to the entire cosmos, not merely the socio-political order.

As authors began to extend the discursive reach of harmony to the cosmic realm, they conferred on music a special role as an important vehicle for attaining such order. The "Yue ji" essentially defines music as the harmony of Heaven and Earth 樂者，天地之和也.[72] Harmony, on the other hand, is defined as "that which causes the hundred things each to transform 和故百物皆化."[73] In other words, harmony is the "motor" of the cosmos, and music is the creation that embodies, reflects, and represents such harmony. This is reinforced in other statements in the "Yue ji," which claim that music follows along with the natural cycles of yin-yang and qi, thereby mimicking the normative "harmony of Heaven and Earth."[74] Similarly, music is associated with the seasons of spring and summer: the most vibrant, life-giving time of the year.[75] It "commands the spirits and follows Heaven . . . Thus, the sage creates music to respond to Heaven, and produces ritual to match Earth. When ritual and music are clear and fully established, Heaven and Earth take their [appropriate] offices 率神而從天 . . . 故聖人作樂以應天，制禮以配地. 禮樂明備，天地官矣."[76] This comment highlights the power of sagely music not just to keep the cosmos running, but also insure that Heaven and Earth are functioning properly and according to their appropriate roles. As such, the role of music in society is paramount in helping reconnect humans to the spiritual, cosmic realm so as to influence the balance of forces in their surrounding environment.

These later texts attest that from the late fourth to second centuries BCE, harmony had become a term of cosmic significance.[77] The meaning of the term appears to have stretched so as to encompass the workings or patterns of the cosmos, while the aesthetic and social connotations of the term seem to have receded into the background.[78] This new, pronounced focus on cosmic harmony marks not merely a linguistic turn that was limited to metaphorical understandings of the cosmos; it also suggests a transformation in intellectual writings and concerns that was more ontological in nature.[79] Indeed, for many writers of the late Warring States period, harmony began to serve as the very basis for cosmic operations and existence.

THEMES AND STRUCTURE

The transformations in the meaning of harmony just described shed light upon important ideological changes that implicate music and its status and use in society. We follow these changes in this book by exploring music first in relationship to the state, and then in relationship to the individual and his/her body. Below, I briefly sketch the contours of our discussion of this status according to the primary thematic division of the book.

Part One focuses specifically on the relationship between music and the state in an attempt to show how such a relationship changed as music became more and more identified with the harmonious patterns of the cosmos. In particular, we will focus on three related politico-religious applications of music and musical sound: as a tool for ordering the state and cosmos, as a civilizing force for centralized, imperial rule and as an agent of cosmic harmony and order. Our discussion of music in Part One is primarily limited to music performed in public, official, and ritual spheres of interaction, especially as sponsored by imperial patrons and the state, but also extending to socio-political rituals of mourning, ancestor worship, and other local religious ceremonies that help promote the continuity of family lineages and communities as orderly components of the state.

Part Two takes us away from the court, ruler, and government to notions concerning the effects of music on the individual and human body. The above-mentioned change in cosmological outlook can also be sensed here, as individual bodies began to be thought of as microcosms of the larger cosmos. While some discourses on music in the fourth to third centuries more exclusively concerned themselves with music as a form of self-expression, as well as the impact of music on self-cultivation, the emotions, and psyche, this began to change by the later part of this period. As idealized forms of music became increasingly associated with the cosmos, ideals for self-cultivation also became linked to sagely achievements connecting individuals to the greater Dao or cosmos. In this section, we will examine a host of changes in the relationship between music and the individual through accounts of the music in self-cultivation, especially as such cultivation relates to the body, emergent cosmic psychologies, and notions of medicine and health.

PART ONE

Music and the State

CHAPTER ONE

Music in State Order and Cosmic Rulership

Afterwards, the House of Zhou deteriorated and became decadent; the rites collapsed and music went bad; the various feudal lords acted according to their whims and competed in the enjoyment of local practices. The tunes of Sang Jian on the upper banks of the Pu River,[1] as well as those from the states of Zheng, Wei, Song, and Zhao, filled the air and traveled far. Plugging and clogging up one's heart and ears, so that one forgot all sense of harmony and balance, throwing government into disorder, and causing harm to the people, these tunes caused extreme illness and docked years off of one's life.[2]

Music in early China was especially valued for its intimate connection to ritual and the state. As one of the Six Classics of the pre-imperial period, music was officially revered as a critical part of Central States and Zhou cultural identity.[3] Even prior to the rise of the Six Classics as an intellectual genre and course of study, music in the Zhou period was linked to ritual and the royal court in a variety of ways. First, it constituted an integral part of ritual services to ancestors and other spirits, whether in the form of sacrificial rites, divination, or worship. Second, it could be expressed in the form of the Odes (詩),—a select musical repertoire of the Zhou royal court—that garnered value for its lyrical insights into the everyday life and moral, emotional strivings of aristocrats and, possibly, commoners.[4] Third, it was considered to be one of the Six Arts in which a man of higher status in Zhou society would be educated.[5] As a critical part of Zhou education and the rites, music developed and was cherished in conjunction with them, often promoted most publicly by Confucians (more precisely: the

Ru) and other members of society invested in helping construct and maintain a sense of cultural heritage and social coherence.

The following brief summary of various ritual uses of music at court prior to the Warring States revolution in cosmological thought—ca. the fourth century BCE—should situate the reader within a context of public, and often political, musical performances that were part and parcel of Zhou court ritual. These public contexts provide the backdrop for most early Chinese discussions of music and the state. Audiences usually consisted of rulers, elites, and noblemen, rather than lower classes. As Ingrid Furniss has demonstrated in her recent book on instrumental arrangements in tombs, when Eastern Zhou ensembles of instruments appeared with bell and chime stone sets (often, in the central compartment of a tomb), this usually signified the use of music in formal ritual ceremonies.[6] Wooden instruments, when they appeared without bells and chime stones, were generally separated from ritual vessels and placed in a side compartment. Such an arrangement seems to signify their use in warfare or more private forms of entertainment and chamber music.[7]

Since Shang and Zhou times, it had been a long-standing practice in ancient China to use music to conduct religious ceremonies to appease and glorify one's ancestors and heroes. Certain forms of Zhou music, such as the "Elegantiae" (ya 雅) and "Lauds" (song 頌),[8] which later constituted parts of the Canon of Odes, were known to have been the musical standards at the Western Zhou court and were integral to various rituals involving human connection to the spirit world.[9] Through ritual procedure and proper performance of the Odes, humans could establish ties with particular deities or ancestors. They could make requests, give thanks, celebrate victories and glorious powers, and honor an array of willful and cognizant deities. For instance, in the Canon of Odes, Mao version, Ode number 274 ("Mao 274," for short), singers proclaim how they seek blessings from Zhou ancestors such as the illustrious King Wu, King Cheng, and King Kang, using the expressive potential of an imposing array of bells, drums, stone-chimes, and pipes.[10] We see here that humans, with the help of music and other ritual behaviors, could link together the social and spiritual realms, communing and communicating in a lasting way with the spirit realm.

This same function for music can be observed in the Zhou yi (Book of Changes) under the hexagram for Yu 豫: "The 'Commentary on Images' states: 'Thunder issuing forth and Earth being aroused. (These are the trigrams that make up) Yu. The former kings thereby composed their music to honor virtue, presenting it grandly to Shangdi, the high god of the Shang and Zhou peoples, and matching it up with that for their oldest ancestor 象傳: 雷出地奮，豫。先王以作樂崇德，殷荐之上帝，以配祖考.'"[11] In this hexagram passage, music was thought to have been an explicit creation of rulers to commemorate virtue and thereby please their various gods and ancestors. It was therefore a tool for ritual communion that likewise served the selfsame function as the sacrificial object presented to the spirits for their pleasure and appeasement.

The Zhou state also sanctioned official musical performances to promote harmony and continuity, not just with respect to the ancestral and spiritual realms but with respect to dynastic and cultural longevity as well. As Martin Kern states: "Its sacrificial hymns not only constitute the ritual situation and celebrate the core ideology of lineage continuity, they also, by their very linguistic structure, represent ritual coherence and continuity as such."[12] Many of the Odes found in the *Canon of Odes* mention how music might be used to express social order as well as the power and prestige of the royal court. Mao 242 emphasizes the organization and ritual layout of musical performances prepared for the purpose of appeasing the dynastic ancestors. At the same time, it impresses upon its audience the majesty and organization of the Zhou ruling house:

虡業維樅，賁鼓維鏞。於論鼓鍾！於樂辟廱！於論鼓鍾！於樂辟廱！鼉鼓逢逢，矇瞍奏公。

On the upright posts and cross-beams with their spikes; Hang the big drums and large *yong*-bells. Oh, well-ranged are the drums and bells, And merry is the Moated Mound. Oh, well-ranged are the drums and bells! And merry is the Moated Mound. Bang, bang go the fish-skin drums; The sightless and the eyeless (musicians) ply their skill.[13]

This jubilant passage glorifies the ritual arrangement of King Wen's famed "Moated Mound," named Bi Yong 辟廱. Since King Wen had set up a prosperous, continuous dynasty, it is fitting that his musical instruments would be properly arranged in ritual readiness to celebrate and express the glory of the Zhou social sphere. Not only does the name, Bi Yong, connote harmony, but the spatial layout of musical instruments signifies dynastic and far-reaching social order by pointing to an organized and impressive arrangement of resources and men.[14]

The commemorative tradition of dynastic musical performance continued in a similar vein during the Spring and Autumn (722–481 BCE) and Warring States (481–221 BCE) periods, even as more variegated stories of legendary sages and heroes began to emerge in the literature and lore of the period. In texts dating from the Warring States, we gain a sense of the state regularization and codification of certain dances and musical styles. Music gained meaning not only as a medium of specific spiritual and dynastic goals but as it became defined by stylistic repertoires with moral

implications as well. In the "Canon of Emperor Shun," a chapter of the
Canon of Documents (*Shu jing* 書經) that likely dates from the later Warring
States period, the author describes state music as a highly organized institution, requiring an official functionary, who is both specialized master as
well as innovative sage-leader:

帝曰:「夔!命汝典樂,教冑子。直而溫,寬而栗,剛而無虐,簡而無傲。
詩言志,歌永言,聲依永,律和聲。八音克諧,無相奪倫,神人以和。」夔
曰:「於!予擊石拊石,百獸率舞。」

Emperor Shun says: "Kui, I command you to codify the music and
instruct the noble sons in it. . . . Let them use poems to verbalize their
intents; songs to chant their speech; sounds to support their chants, and
pitch-standards to harmonize their sounds. The eight [instrumental]
timbres in tune with one another, none usurping another's position—
thus may humans join with the spirits in harmony." Kui responded: "Yes,
indeed! For when I strike the stones and tap the chimes, the hundred
beasts are compelled to dance."[15]

This intriguing passage highlights the various aspects of a royal musical
performance, which, it states, spans a continuum from the recitation of
poetry and speech to the harmonization of the eight instrumental timbres
with each other, ultimately resulting in dancing among all humans and
beasts. The overall effect is a harmonious and coordinated chorus of action
that joins earthly beings with spirits. Indeed, such a performance could
symbolize the state's ability to bring all beings together in organized, patterned harmony.

The role of the royal Music Master in the passage above is pivotal in
enabling the entire ritual communion to take place. Kui, as commanded by
Emperor Shun, is not only a teacher to the noble sons leading the performance. He is the mastermind who "codifies (*dian* 典)," or regulates and sys-
tematizes, musical ritual so that harmony and beneficial communication
with the spirits might occur in a consistent fashion throughout the ages.
This reference to the codification of music represents an attempt to give
justification to what was already by the time of this writing an emergent
cultural repertoire of music, including a vast array of song lyrics so admired
by members of the aristocratic and *shi* classes, including Confucius and his
followers. The reference points not just to ritual music, but to the phenomenon of officially sanctioned music that is the organized possession of the
state, as well as to the official sage-bureaucrat, or the royal Music Master,
who enables such music to be spiritually efficacious in the first place.

The *Zuo zhuan* depicts ritual contexts that reveal not only the various uses of music in society, but also its use as a tool for proper diplomatic communication. The Odes were a part of ritual performances sung at court not only to entertain and impress guests, but to convey from one state authority to another diplomatic intents and meanings in a poetic and thinly veiled manner. The following excerpt from *Zuo zhuan* 6.3.6 depicts how the ritualized interactions of two heads of state convey meaning. In it, the performance of an Ode clearly takes a prominent place alongside ceremonial behavior and speeches:

莊叔以公降、拜。曰：「小國受命於大國，敢不慎儀？君貺之以大禮，何樂如之？抑小國之樂，大國之惠也。」晉侯降，辭。登，成拜。公賦《嘉樂》

Zhuangshu [Shusun Dechen; advisor to the young Duke Wen of Lu] allowed our lord to descend and bow to the Duke of Jin and say: "When [our] small state receives the Decree from [your] large state, can we afford not to pay heed to the rules of etiquette? You, my Sir, grace us with the great ritual; is there happiness greater than this?[16] Oh, but it is the generosity of your great state that really makes our small state happy!"[17] The Duke of Jin descended, declining to accept [the polite treatment by the Duke of Lu].[18] Both then ascended the steps to the dais, bowed to each other, and sang the Ode "Jia Le [Superb Happiness]."[19]

The singing of this Ode, which confers blessings to a noble lord of upright conduct, helps consolidate the intent behind a series of ritualized interactions between the two dukes described above. The Ode extols a lord who is embraced by the common people, Son of Heaven, and Heaven alike. Such a lord is a model ruler who follows the rules and does not venture past his rank and role in society.[20] Not only does the meaning of the Ode normalize relations by highlighting the goal of fair play and ritual conformity, but the act of performing it between noblemen of different states serves the purpose of exposing one's certain, publicly acceptable desires and intentions in a conventionalized and predictable way. As a politico-religious Hymnal, the Odes offered a set and delimited form for expressing sentiment and intent—a rare commodity at the diplomatic level—so that a sense of trust between parties could be secured in a controlled fashion.

Through these select examples, we see that music, as a key element of state rituals in Zhou China, served as a vital tool in state government, interstate diplomacy, and the maintenance of court power and prestige. Musical performance and lyrics were valued for their role as ceremonial tools that helped facilitate interactions and establish trust between different political parties. Similarly, music served as an accompaniment to the ritual act of celebrating or transferring power and favor, and was performed at various religious sacrifices and rites as well. Given the aforementioned roles of music in state ritual, its meteoric rise as a form of its own that sometimes transcended the meaning and significance of ritual will seem surprising. Yet, as cosmologies of resonance became increasingly prominent in the political rhetoric and religious mindset of the day, music at court changed subtly from a celebratory, communicative ritual device to a means by which the state could verify its authenticity as legitimate heir to cosmic powers and processes. In its expanded capacity as a symbol for cosmic authority, music acquired new valences of meaning that had repercussions for how courts and their rulers should relate to it.

THE ROLE OF MUSIC IN ORDERING STATE AND COSMOS

Displacing older visions of spiritual ancestors and natural deities interacting with humans according to anthropomorphic types of interactions, a newer, more systematic cosmology sprang up sometime by the fourth century BCE.[21] According to this new type of religious vision, the world was broken down into *qi*—the life-force of the universe—which could manifest itself according to a plethora of qualities, most of which were sometimes reduced to the basic pair of *yin* (shady, dark) and *yang* (sunny, bright) traits and functions. Most importantly, *qi* behaved in the world not like human beings with arbitrary wills and different personalities, but according to causal principles that were both intelligible and somewhat predictable.[22]

The addition of *qi*-related types of cosmologies had profound impacts on almost every aspect of life. In terms of music, the impact was sensational, as music came to be considered a key ingredient allowing rulers to harness the proper configuration of *qi* necessary for bringing about cosmic and state order in the world. Below, we examine changes in the status of music at court from a cultural tool that could help insure and symbolize state order and health to a spiritual technique, the control over which would allow rulers to position oneself at the critical node between cosmic functioning and state order.

Most likely influenced by a genre of medico-religious and political writings that concern themselves with the health and well-being of the ruler's body, many early writings on music sought regulation of an individual's, and especially, a ruler's personal attitudes, habits, and psycho-physical routines in order to promote state order and cosmic harmony.[23] Such texts regarded the ruler's body as the site of potential balance in political and cosmic arenas, so that effort put into the careful, physiological maintenance of the body might translate into a ruler's control of the cosmos, not to mention the proper, worldly acceptance of his position as the central link between cosmic patterns and human affairs.[24] Indeed, as Nathan Sivin puts it: "Intellectuals bound the structure of heaven and earth, and that of the human body, to that of the state. This was not unprecedented in China, but now the links were made systematic and tight. In every instance their creators were preoccupied with political authority and its effective use. As a result, macrocosm and microcosms became a single manifold, a set of mutually resonant systems of which the emperor was indispensable mediator."[25]

Below, I will elaborate on discussions of the dual relationships between proper music and an ordered, peaceful state and cosmos on the one hand, and excessive music and a chaotic, "doomed," or "perished" state (*wang guo* 亡國) on the other. I pay special attention to the mediating role of the ruler's body as a site of virtue or debauchery and an augury of state order. In particular, I show how music was seen as affecting and indicating the health of a state and the cosmos—as seen through the physiological and psychological health of its ruler. Following Nathan Sivin's lead, I end by showing how the "single manifold" of macrocosm and microcosm that developed during the fourth century BCE allowed for a ruler, through attention to his physical body, to claim control of or access to cosmic processes as well as bureaucratic, human ones.

First, let us examine standard roles for music that link state order to the ruler's person in some way. In texts such as the *Zuo zhuan* (~fourth century BCE), the health of a state is generally viewed largely as a function of a ruler's moral awareness, which could be expressed through the music he sanctioned. Consider the following statement:

夫樂以安德，義以處之，禮以行之，信以守之，仁以厲之，而後可以殿邦國、同福祿、來遠人，所謂樂也 . . .

Now, one uses music to repose in virtue. Righteousness is used to reside in it, ritual to carry it out, trustworthiness to hold onto it, and benevolence to sharpen it. Only after [a ruler] has these qualities may he be assume his place at the palatial throne of the country, share in all blessings and emoluments, and attract people from a distance. This is what is meant by music.[26]

Here, music is one of five common, Ru components of moral rule (including righteousness, ritual, trustworthiness, and benevolence). Though clearly all five components are deemed necessary to successful governance, the specific object under discussion in this passage is music. As a means of defining correct, moral government, music serves as a legitimate means of gauging and aiding in a ruler's moral cultivation and degree of enlightened rulership. Thus, the act of performing music or having it be performed during ritual is not only of importance to the state. In passages such as the one above, music is discussed in more abstract terms—as both an educational tool for and indicator of moral virtue, which in turn is a prerequisite for state order.

In the same text, activities associated with music, such as entertainment and feasting, are depicted as rites that teach the virtues of reverence and economy. Such virtues are in turn directly related to the tasks of governing a state:

於是乎有享、宴之禮。享以訓共儉，宴以示慈惠。共儉以行禮，而慈惠以布政。政以禮成，民是以息。百官承事，朝而不夕，此公侯之所以扞城其民也。

Thus there are the rituals of entertainment and feasting. Entertainment serves to instruct one in reverence and economy; feasting to demonstrate kindness and generosity. Reverence and economy are used to carry out the rites; kindness and generosity are used to set up a government.[27] When one uses ritual to fulfill one's government, the people will therefore enjoy rest. The "hundred offices" are duly given their official business in the morning and not in the evening. This is the means by which dukes and lords might protect and defend their people.[28]

Here, the reason why musical types of entertainment are morally exalting is that they express—and therefore instruct one in—simple virtues such as reverence and economy. Musical entertainments bring welfare and protection to the state because the virtues they reinforce help insure the organization and efficient operation of government functions and the people.

The *Guanzi* also reiterates this message linking the ruler and the health of a state in an anecdote concerning Duke Huan of Qi and his minister, Guan Zhong. In "Conditions for Lord Protector," which likely dates to the early second century BCE, the author demonstrates that only after the duke "cut down the lines for hanging the bells and musical stones, relinquished the pleasure of singing and dancing, and emptied the palace of people 於是伐鍾磬之縣，併歌舞之樂。宮中虛無人," did his state begin to be revitalized and orderly.[29] While the story continues to narrate how the duke undertook many other governmental reforms as well, it intriguingly ends by returning to the issue of the bells and musical stones, which had since been repaired and reestablished in all their grandeur. Guan Zhong is given the last remark, saying "This is what I call real pleasure," which points to the pleasure of music specifically, relying on the double-entendre implied by the homograph *yue* 樂, which could be translated as "pleasure" or "music" depending on the context.[30] The implication of this statement is that only if the ruler embarked on the right policies would his music bring pleasure. "Correct" or "real" music in this example does not depend on the type or style of music performed; rather, it is wholly subservient to the capabilities and actions of the ruler. It is as though such instruments, along with the music to which they refer, symbolically encapsulated the general state of affairs in the duke's regime. When the state was run improperly, the instruments represented empty, morally pernicious pleasures. On the contrary, when the ruler correctly governed his state, all the instruments of his music chamber could rightfully take on meaning as objects of true pleasure: the pleasure derived from state order.

In third century BCE texts such as the *Xunzi* and *Lüshi chunqiu*, authors present a complicated relationship between music and the ruler's moral and physiological conditions, as well as between music and the state of the cosmos. Music begins to garner even more power not just as a vehicle for or indication of a ruler's capabilities or moral cultivation, but as an actual agent in and of itself for social change. Consider the following passage from Xunzi's "Discourse on Music" ("Yue lun" 樂 論):[31]

故樂行而志清,禮脩而行成,耳目聰明,血氣和平,移風易俗,天下皆寧,美善相樂

Therefore, when [proper] music is played, one's will becomes clear, and when rites are cultivated, one's conduct is brought to fruition. The ears and eyes are discerning and bright; material energy are harmonious and balanced. [It] changes customs and alters manners, [so that] all under heaven is tranquil, and the beautiful and good each in turn [give rise to] joy.[32]

Here, Xunzi speaks not only of aspects of a person's body; he also clearly shows how music will naturally regulate the customs of a state and bring peace to the world. This is different from the *Zuo* passage above, which depicts music as something that guides a ruler to virtue, who then goes on to order the world. Xunzi attributes a much larger power to music, which, he claims, is itself responsible for bringing peace and aesthetic/moral satisfaction to the people. Hence, the actual role of the ruler's virtue is diminished, and music gains the power to affect the masses directly instead of solely through the ruler's moral body, actions, and volition.

The author of the music chapters of the *Lüshi chunqiu* highlights the ruler-cosmos relationship in government. Unlike Xunzi, who speaks of music in terms of the socio-political world around him, this author goes further to link music to the larger sphere of a cosmic Dao:

成樂有具，必節嗜慾。嗜慾不辟，樂乃可務。務樂有術，必由平出。平出於
公，公出於道。

There are tools for completing Music: one must regulate one's appetites and desires. When appetites and desires are not debauched, music may then be worked at. Working at music has its methods: one must have it emerge from balance. Balance emerges from impartiality, and impartiality emerges from the Dao.[33]

Intriguingly, the Dao described by this author is conceived of as both the original source of proper music as well as harmony, equilibrium, and balance (*ping* 平) in the world: "When buds and sprouts were first stimulated, they coagulated into shapes; shapes and bodies had their places, and nothing was without sound. Sound emerged from harmony; harmony emerged from equilibrium 萌芽始震，凝堕以形。形體有處，莫不有聲。聲出於和，和出於適."[34] According to this vision, then, the ruler's psyche can be synchronized with the Dao by "working at music,"[35] which allows him to emulate the harmony, equilibrium, impartiality, and balance of the Dao. Ruler, music, and Dao thus come together into Nathan Sivin's "single manifold"—and harmony and equilibrium are the threads that hold them together.

Cosmic rulership such as that described in the *Lüshi chunqiu* chapters on music is leadership based in the harmonious patterns of the Dao, also referred to as the "One."[36] Such rulership can bring about results that not only "bring joy to ruler and minister and harmonizing those distant and near 樂君臣和遠近," but that also help bring order to the natural, cosmic world by "making cold and heat appropriate, and wind and rain timely 樂君臣，和遠近."[37] Thus, the type of leadership exerted by the cosmic ruler represents control over an expanded arena of things and processes including seasons and weather patterns, not to mention everyday administration and government of the people. It is leadership brought about through a ruler's realignment of himself with the underlying harmonies of the cosmos.

Such realignment with the Dao is not passive conformity with its ultimate laws and processes.[38] Rather, it is characterized by the ruler's embodiment of an agency of the Dao (harmony and balance) that allows him to insure that the "great transformations 大化" (of the Dao) might be secured in the human world.[39] So, while the author favors the notion that the cosmic ruler is a mediator of the Dao on Earth, he is careful to depict him as a mediator that harnesses control in the world through the effective embodiment of the Dao. Intriguingly, in the chapters on music under discussion here, the cosmic ruler uses "Great music" to embody the Dao, thereby realigning himself with the harmonies inherent in the cosmos.

In early China, just as music could bring about and signal the health and well-being of the state and, in somewhat later texts, the cosmos as well, it could also engender the opposite. In third to second century BCE texts, one of the main concerns about music was the degree to which it might elicit and promote a ruler's unchecked desires such as lust and a greed for luxury. Rulers who let their desires get the better of them were often associated with doomed or perished states (亡國). Rather than attribute doomed states to wasted state resources or bureaucratic mismanagement, authors increasingly discussed the phenomenon in terms of the health and morality embodied by the ruler alone. In such a way, authors adopted the trope of excessive music, which served to signify and symbolize the decline in a ruler's virtue and/or health, as well as the downfall of states at large.

A close relationship between the sounds of a doomed state and the moral depravity of its ruler clearly emerged as a prominent motif during the Warring States. Authors warned against the music or sounds of a doomed state by presuming upon the unspoken linkages between musical style, the moral degeneracy of a state's ruler, and his state's chaos and ultimate downfall. Since discussion of doomed states could serve a didactic function for profligate rulers and leaders alike, the number of passages in the extant record discussing excessive music and doomed states seems to far outweigh the number of passages describing the opposite, positive scenario of proper music and idealized states. This focus on bad or "excessive" types of music indicates that authors saw writing as a sort of prophylactic—a vehicle by which one might duly warn rulers of the dangerous consequences of their actions.

In the *Guo yu*, for example, excessive music causes personal depravity and political distress. In one case, Music Master Shi Kuang shows how the mere knowledge of someone's musical taste allows one to predict the downfall of an entire ruling lineage. Music here takes on a role as "cultural omen," forecasting doom and despair based on its perceived moral content: "Duke Ping of Jin took pleasure in 'new tunes.' Music Master Shi Kuang said, 'Alas! The ducal house will be debased! The ruler possesses a clear omen of downfall! 平公說新聲，師曠曰：「公室其將卑乎！君之明兆於衰矣.」"[40] This passage goes on to explain the linkage between music and a ruler's downfall in terms of the natural phenomenon of wind, which has the power to spread one's embodied virtue far and wide.[41] For just as the winds of a region might be analyzed as divinatory augurs or omens, the sounds of one's music might also relay such precious predictive information about the state of a ruler's personal virtue, and thus, the ultimate fate of his regime.

A couple of negative comments about music in the *Zuo zhuan* impart a clear sense of not just a symbolic link between the depravity of a ruler and the downfall of his state, but a causal one as well.[42] In a famous and quite phenomenal narrative that features the music of the Odes, Gongzi Jizha 公子季扎 of Wu travels with an embassy to Lu in 544 BCE, taking the opportunity to listen to and provide commentary on a variety of ancient Odes. Based on his perception of the music, Jizha predicts and measures the success of a state and the virtue of its rulers.[43] Most of Jizha's remarks are positive, giving praise to certain Odes that help balance powerful emotions and provide one with a model for temperance and moderation. However, it is the negative comments about the music of certain regions that reveal what is really at stake for rulers and their governments.

Of the "Airs of Zheng 鄭風," Jizha states: "Simply beautiful! Yet there are excessive elaborations, and the people will not be able to take it. Does this not [show that] it (i.e., the state of Zheng) will be the first to perish? 「美哉！其細已甚，民弗堪也。是其先亡乎！」"[44] It is worth noting that the "tunes of Zheng 鄭 and Wei 衛," referred to styles and types of music denounced by many writers, especially the Ru, by around the middle of the fourth century BCE. Intriguingly, there is no indication in this *Zuo* passage that the Airs of Wei are to be shunned, and there is only a mild criticism of the objectionable qualities of the Airs of Zheng. The very fact that Jizha primarily considers these Airs to be "simply beautiful" contrasts sharply with comments in other texts from early China that outright condemn the "tunes of Zheng" as depraved and dangerously enticing.[45] Though Jizha criticizes the Airs of Zheng and predicts the downfall of the state of Zheng because of them, he does not seem to think these tunes depraved as such—only overly detailed, and perhaps frivolous. I think this moderately critical stance towards the Airs of Zheng attests to the fact that certain condemnations of musical styles were far from universal in the early years of the fourth century BCE, and that the canonization of music was a loose and ever-evolving process.

Nonetheless, it is clear that Jizha does not think favorably of the Airs of Zheng. His statement: "the people will not be able to take it," suggests the causal connection between musical style—in this case, the predominance of an elaborate, ornate style—and state disorder and downfall. The Airs of Zheng will bring about the downfall of the state because they fail to balance weighty and serious sounds and rhythms with light, detailed ones. Such a combination of sounds adversely affects those listening to such an extent that they actually feel ill at ease. Ostensibly, the people's sense of disturbance from the Airs of Zheng will translate directly into disturbances in the kingdom in general.

Following upon his evaluation of the Airs of Zheng, Jizha refuses to comment on those Airs associated with other particular states: "They played the songs of the state of Chen for him, and he said, 'When a state does not have a ruler, is it able to last for long? From the Airs of Kuai on, he made no observations 為之歌《陳》，曰：「國無主，其能久乎！」自《鄶》以下無譏焉."[46] Most commentators believe the statement, "From the Airs of Kuai on," refers specifically to the only remaining Airs listed in the current Mao version, the Airs of Cao. It is possible, however, that there were more Airs representing small regions that did not make it into the Mao version of the text, and indeed, the phrasing, "From the Airs of Kuai on," would certainly seem to hint at more than just one set of Airs.[47]

Regardless of which specific Airs Jizha is referring to, we see that the music of a region was thought not only to demonstrate the status of a state's ruler and its fate—whether it would prosper or perish—but also the people's responses to it. Music that leads to a ruined state is music whose qualities place the people and its ruler off-balance, as in the above-mentioned example from Zheng. Similarly, music of a perished state is music that demonstrates the utter lack of a core, or a central leader, as in the example here from the state of Chen.[48] The value of music here lies precisely in its ability to affect people's inner sense of balance, which is correlated to an outer state of orderly behaviors and ultimately, an orderly state. The subtext of such a discussion, therefore, reveals Jizha's faith in the powers of the emotional and bodily balance of both ruler and people alike in creating state order.

Note that this interpretation differs from that of Li Wai-yee, who has claimed that "musical qualities and attitudes per se do not directly 'cause' the rise or decline of persons and states; rather, it is their presumed direct link to the essence of person and polity that turns them into readable signs laden with moral, political, and cosmic meaning."[49] In my reading of these passages, the relationship of music to the order in a state or person is not just a matter of the symbolic power of music as musical signs or symptoms that allow one to predict outcomes and give a diagnosis of state health.[50] Rather, there is a clear, causal relationship between musical style, content, form, and rhythm on the one hand, and bodily and state health on the other. This latter understanding of music underscores how early authors readily discussed the physiological effects of music on humans, societies, and states. According to this view, musical qualities as harmony and balance are taken as crucial components in the therapeutic powers of music to bring about order in the body and state polity as well. Harmonious music not only augurs harmonious body and state; it engenders it too.

Other examples of the role of music in state disorder and downfall abound in the *Zuo zhuan*. In 12.7.4, the sound of bells is reason for a leader's overwrought distraction in face of impending disaster, much to the chagrin of remonstrating officers.[51] Similarly, *Zuo zhuan* 3.20.1 features a certain Earl of Zheng who had the following to say about Wangzi Tui's reaction to music:

「哀樂失時，殃咎必至。今王子頹〔穨〕歌舞不倦，樂禍也夫。...臨禍忘憂，憂必及之。盍納王乎！

When sadness and happiness are inappropriately timed, then harmful calamity [to the state] is sure to come. Now, Wangzi Tui sings and dances as though he were never to tire of it—this is being happy in the face of disaster . . . When one faces disaster yet forgets to be sorrowful, then [true] sorrow is sure to arrive. Wouldn't it be better to restore the king?[52]

Note that this passage does not differentiate good music from bad: blame lies in a ruler's reactions to music, not in the music itself. Nonetheless, one can easily infer—given the widely understood power of music to influence emotional states—that unbalanced music would certainly not bring about a balanced emotional state in the ruler who listens to it. Here, an improper reaction to music is defined according to an imbalance in one's expression of the opposing sentiments of happiness and sadness. Thus, as in Jizha's critique of excessive music, a ruler's moral awareness is considered tantamount to his level of emotional balance, influenced by music. The well-being of the entire state lies, so to speak, "in the balance" of a ruler's emotional-moral state, which is deeply affected by music.

Another way in which music helps bring about an individual's—especially, a ruler's—moral turpitude and, consequently, a doomed state is by drawing rulers away from their government duties. In the "Ten Excesses" chapter of the *Han Feizi*, for example, we find a story in which Duke Ling of Wei (r. 534–493 BCE) commands his Music Master (named Jüan 涓) to learn some "new tunes (新聲)" he has heard being played on the banks of the Pu River. When the duke arrives in the state of Jin, he has it performed for Duke Ping, whereupon the latter's Music Master—the famous Shi Kuang—proclaims it to be unfit for anyone to hear. Shi Kuang states: "These are the tunes of a doomed state! You must not continue [with it] 此亡國之聲，不可遂也."[53] When asked further, the Music Master explains that the music was composed by Yan (延), Music Master to the evil King Zhou of the Shang. After King Wu's attack upon King Zhou, Music Master Yan fled east and threw himself into the Pu River. For this reason, "As for he who first hears these tunes, his state is sure to be destroyed 先聞此聲者，其國必削."[54] With rich associative logic, this story hints at the malicious influences of depraved music, which easily preys upon humans blind to virtue and open to excessive tones (notably, one of the "ten excesses" listed in this chapter of the *Han Feizi*). Such tunes and tones transcend time: their pernicious effects can be felt by former kings such as King Zhou of the Shang—who brought his dynasty to ruin—as well as by royalty of the contemporary age, such as Dukes Ping of Jin and Ling of Wei. They also encapsulate the greedy, lustful characteristics of those who choose to listen, so that anyone who chooses to listen to depraved music necessarily lacks virtue, just as anyone who lacks virtue would choose to listen to depraved music. Thus, a ruler's music and his personal lack of virtue are both at once symptoms and causes of the downfall of his state.

So far, most of the texts that we have examined speak of the specific, parallel relationship among the ruler, the type of music that he enjoys, and the fate of his state. Such texts have paid relatively little attention to the notion of cosmic rulership as described in the *Lüshi chunqiu* passages above. Let us now turn our attention back to *Lüshi chunqiu*, which more clearly aims to position the ruler within a larger, cosmic schema of patterns. To be sure, the connection of music to the cosmos is explicitly stated in the following passage: "As for music, it is the harmonizing of Heaven and Earth and the attunement of Yin and Yang to each other 凡樂，天地之和，陰陽之調也."[55] Given this significant status for music, how was it thought to affect the fate of states?

We begin with a simple description of "extravagant" music found in the *Lüshi chunqiu* chapters on music:

夏桀、殷紂作為侈樂，大鼓鐘磬管簫之音，以鉅為美，以眾為觀，俶詭殊瑰，耳所未嘗聞，目所未嘗見，務以相過，不用度量。宋之衰也，作為千鍾。齊之衰也，作為大呂。楚之衰也，作為巫音。

Jie of the Xia and Zhou Xin of the Yin created extravagant music. As for the sounds of large drums, bells, chimes, flutes and pipes, they considered the large to be beautiful and the many to be wonderful. They first created strange and exotic things that ears had never before heard and eyes never before seen. They set about the task of always outdoing [what came before], employing neither rule nor measure. When Song was in decline, the Thousand Bell set was cast; when Qi was in decline, the Great Regulator Bell was cast; when Chu was in decline, the Shaman Tones Bell was created.[56]

This critique of extravagant music is unique in that the author specifically targets both musical styles and the size of one's instruments. Not intent upon singling out the tunes of any particular state as singularly depraved in character, he inveighs against the extravagant and injurious music of decadent rulers such as Jie of the Xia and Zhou Xin of the Yin of the past. In more recent history, he criticizes the nefarious tones and overly grand instruments of the states of Song, Qi, and Chu. At the core of his criticism, however, is the notion that political downfall, corruption, and decay are linked with bad, extravagant music. Upon what is this notion based?

According to the text, extravagance lies in desiring too much, too many, and that which is too strange. Though vague, this way of discussing music and its instruments appears to be connected to the notion of balance and harmony described above as attributes of the cosmic Dao. Music must produce joy 樂 and reflect "the true nature of music 樂之情."[57] In other words, there is something inherent about proper music that brings not just balance in the sense of a balancing of conflicting emotions, as in the *Zuo* passage discussing the Odes above. Proper music brings about the ultimate sentiment of joy, which seems to transcend any particular emotion to express an overall sense of satisfaction. According to this line of reasoning, then, extravagant music is bad because it fails to allow its audience to feel fully synchronized with the harmonious Dao of the cosmos.

The *Lüshi chunqiu* author discusses bad music in terms of a general philosophy on sagely alignment (or realignment) with the Dao.[58] His formula for bad music includes any performance involving sound that has derived from improper sagely cultivation and disorderly conduct in the social sphere. This latter condition, he notes, is signaled by a lack of joy and contentment:

亡國戮民，非無樂也，〔不樂其樂〕〔其樂不樂〕。溺者非不笑也，罪人非不歌也，狂者非不武也，亂世之樂，有似於此。君臣失位，父子失處，夫婦失宜，民人呻吟，其以為樂也，若之何哉？

It is not that doomed states and disgraced peoples lack music, but rather that their music does not bring joy. It is not that "a drowning man does not laugh," "a condemned man does not sing," or "a crazy man does not dance." The music of a chaotic age is similar to these [situations]. When ruler and minister fail to keep their proper places, father and son fail in their proper duties, and husband and wife fail to maintain their proper relationship, the people groan and sigh—but how can this be considered to be music?[59]

Bad music should not even be considered to be music because it does not fulfill its basic purpose: to produce true feelings of joy and contentment in the people.[60] Such music reigns during periods of social chaos, when human relations lose their grounding in the normative patterns of the cosmos.

In these third century BCE chapters on music from the *Lüshi chunqiu*, we see an expanded scope for the influence of music in the world. States and their rulers are not the only entities at risk here; whole dynasties, eras, indeed, nothing less than human relationship to the cosmos is at stake. Chaotic music is associated with chaotic ages, just as it is associated with chaotic states. Clearly, though this writing is similar to earlier discussions of music in that it characterizes music in terms of its relationship to balance and the emotions, the status of music has been upgraded in a critical way. Not only does music now represent the harmonization of cosmic components in the world, it also acts as a crucial tool in facilitating relations between human and cosmos. In the coming chapters, as we examine more texts dating from the third century BCE on, we will see that this change is not anomalous; rather, it reflects an increasingly prevalent view of music and its role in human life.

CONCLUSION

As a key part of Zhou ritual, music was used by early Chinese states for commemorative, religious, and diplomatic purposes. The Odes, which were sung and performed, became a mainstay of expression not just for statesmen on diplomatic tour, but also for the elite within each state to communicate in a civilized way with each other. We first looked at the ways in which music was used according to the Zhou ritualistic tradition. Then, we turned our attention to texts that drew a specific link between a state's level of order or chaos and the particular styles and types of music that were being performed there. Through such a discussion, we outlined the ways in which music was thought to affect and represent state order.

As early as the fourth century BCE, discussions of music continued to be intertwined with the moral logic of personal and political order. Associations were drawn among music, a ruler's unchecked desires, and socio-political chaos on the one hand, and music, a ruler's regulated heart-mind, and socio-political order on the other. Such a manner of thinking about music became common in discussions about the rise and fall of states. To be sure, state order and health hinged upon the performance and maintenance of proper music, and the ruler's body served as a potential site of virtue and source or signal of such order.

By the third century BCE, when the state of Qin had already begun to entertain notions of creating a unified imperial sphere under centralized control, music emerged as a tool not just of ceremonial and government affairs, but as a tool of cosmic rulership according to newly developing, unified systems of resonances and harmonious interrelationships. The link between music and state order, which was prominent in texts such as the *Zuo zhuan* dating to the fourth century BCE, appears to have been expanded to include the cosmos and its orderly patterns. Music, now linked to ideal cosmic operations, could provide humans—especially rulers—a critical means of plugging oneself into the complicated yet balanced rhythms of the entire natural realm.

The connection that obtained between music and cosmos would serve to justify a state's particular use of music, as centralizing states and imperial leaders increasingly sought not just after full dominion of their lands but—at the very least—claims of supremacy over everything in the cosmos. Cosmic rulership implied not necessarily control *over* the cosmos and all of its natural patterns, but one's full control *from within* a vast web of cosmic forces. The cosmic ruler hoped to sit at the helm of cosmic-human interactions and navigate properly the tricky interface between the two realms, serving as a key agent of cosmic change as well.

In the next chapters, we will continue to explore the role of music, and even sound itself, as both an agent and indicator of moral, orderly, and cosmically balanced rule. We will examine the ways in which music was thought to lend legitimacy to state leaders, and we will try to determine the extent to which music could be used as a political tool for cosmic control: for unifying cultural mores and civilizing the "other," and for establishing one's authority as the guarantor and central agent of cosmic functionality.

CHAPTER TWO

A Civilizing Force for Imperial Rule

In this chapter we examine arguments that promote music as a tool for cultural unification, cultural imperialism, and as a civilizing force in general. Just as music was thought to help cause and forecast the health and demise of a state and, sometimes, the cosmos, it could also help a regime unify cultural mores and add a veneer of civilized rule to the aura of imperial rulers. As a civilizing tool, music could promote the unification of values that aimed to place one's culture in a superior position to others. And to the extent that certain types of music would come to be considered cosmic or spiritual in nature, the Son of Heaven or ruler who controlled such music could ultimately assume the role of exclusive arbiter of cultural forms that were thought to be in conformity with Heaven itself. Below, I turn our attention to the ways in which music served as a means of fostering cultural refinement and notions of civilization, especially in the service of a burgeoning centralized or imperial state. We pay special attention to the ways in which rulers expressed imperialistic goals through their relationships to music.

MUSIC AND UNIFYING CULTURAL MORES

The unification of cultural mores was clearly a goal in early Chinese discourses on music, especially those that outlined new methods for attaining cosmic rulership, or what we have described as the goal of ruling over the human realm while also fully tapping into and harmonizing the powers of the cosmos. As early as the time of Confucius, authors tried to distinguish different types of music from each other, justifying their divisions through a variety of means. Many texts dating from the late fourth century BCE through the third and second centuries BCE do so by speaking of the power of certain types of music to unify the attitudes, behaviors, and practices of a people according to a cultural standard for civilization. While different texts present different versions of what cultural unification might entail, they all clearly address the problem of how music of a certain type might bring together in harmony peoples from a vast array of backgrounds and mindsets.

This emphasis on music as an important vehicle for cultural unification points to an interest in the politics of centralization that was so critical for a state's survival from the late fourth century BCE to the rise of the Qin Empire in 221 BCE. It continued to be important during both the Qin and Han imperial regimes, which faced the enormous challenge of incorporating diverse polities and populations into their centralized regime. That the problems of centralization should be articulated in terms of music and its relationship to the grand, unifying force of the cosmos attests to the significant role music played in court politics and discourses on cosmic rulership at the time.

The notion that music might help unify a people has roots beyond the centralizing tendencies of Warring States kingdoms. In a section of the *Analects* that potentially dates to the earliest stratum of the text, the author mentions Confucius' use of the standard, or *ya* 雅, pronunciation for the Odes and *Documents*.[1] Etymologically, the term *ya* appears to be the same as the ethnonym, Xia 夏, referring to the people of the Central States who were related ethnically to the so-called lineage of Xia.[2] This means that through his pronunciation of the lyrics of the Odes, Confucius accords with and reinforces a cultural standard of unification and civilization. Since for him the Odes represent primarily a musical performance in a ritual setting, this comment about pronunciation would have been relevant for the Odes as music, and not exclusively as text.

The *Zuo zhuan* provides a few examples in which authors link music to the ideal of a single, civilized culture.[3] In *Zuo* 5.24.2, Duke Xi comments on the harmony of Five Sounds—among other products of culture—associated with the peoples of the superior Zhou states:

耳不聽五聲之和為聾，目不別五色之章為昧，心不則德義之經為頑，口不道忠信之言為囂。狄皆則之，四姦具矣

He whose ear does not hear the harmony of the Five Sounds is deaf; whose eye does not see the brilliance of the Five Colors is blind; whose heart-mind does not measure the arrangement of virtue and righteousness is pigheaded; whose mouth does not speak the language of loyalty and trustworthiness is superficial. The Di (an alien group of peoples) are all of these; they are provisioned with the four villainies.[4]

Equating one's perception of the harmony of the Five Sounds with civilization, Duke Xi denigrates those whose music does not conform to the harmonic standards of Zhou culture. Certainly, his criticism here is not limited to music or the aural realm, but the fact that he includes it as one of the four measures of culture is significant. Music, like visual arts and moral virtues, helps refine a people through set patterns and standards, shared by all in the culture. Civilized music was the property of the Zhou, not the Di. It is interesting to note that archaeological evidence concerning the high prevalence of the vertical flute in tombs from the Southwest (in present-day Sichuan) and not in northern or southeastern China seems a clear affirmation of the idea that certain non-Zhou regions enjoyed music that differed significantly from that of the Zhou sphere.[5]

The next excerpt from the *Zuo* does not concern musical harmony *per se* as a means of unifying wayward aliens. Rather, high-ranking members of society might bestow musical instruments as feudal gifts to reward officers for their imperial victories over unruly, uncivilized others.[6]

晉侯以樂之半賜魏絳，曰：「子教寡人和諸戎狄以正諸華，八年之中，九合諸侯，如樂之和，無所不諧，請與子樂之。」

The Marquis Dao of Jin took gave half of this musical gift to Wei Jiang, saying: "You taught me how to bring harmony to the various Rong and Di tribes so as to rectify our relations with the various Hua peoples [descendants of the Xia; i.e., people of the civilized, Central States]. Within eight years I assembled the marquises nine times. Just as the harmonies of music, there is none that does not accord. I beg to share and have you take pleasure [in these things]."[7]

In the context of this quote, musical instruments are effective as gifts because they symbolize the harmony of music and Zhou cultural dominance over unruly outside tribes.[8] The Duke explicitly compares the harmony of music to the instruction Wei Jiang gave the duke in harmonizing the Rong and Di through military and diplomatic means. He thereby shows how the metaphor of musical harmony might be applied to such imperialistic goals as taming wayward aliens. The gift of musical instruments here is explicitly linked to broader notion of harmony, both musical and political, in which disparate elements come together in agreement and compliance.

A novel account of the effects of music on state unification can be found in the work of the famous Ru thinker and statesman, Xunzi. Though Xunzi lived mostly during the period just preceding the birth of the Qin Empire, his writings reflect an acute awareness of the centralizing concerns of states, lending support for a strong government with much direct control over its population. In his "Discourse on Music," Xunzi formulates an interesting view on mass psychology that promotes music as an important means by which rulers might control, organize, and demand the conformism of their people—thereby unifying the state according to a single standard of behavior and cultural norms. In short, Xunzi's presentation of music speaks directly of the virtues of music as tool for gaining effective control over the people as a psychological unity and ultimately helping bring about large-scale social order in a state.

Like many musical apologetics of the day, the "Discourse on Music" argues for the inevitable influence of sounds and music over human emotions.[9] But Xunzi does not stop with individual psychology, or even the human body. To Xunzi, proper music and the rites produce a series of beneficial results: they induce desirable psychological and physiological reactions, bring about a state of environmental and social order, and go on to produce an ultimate state of psychological well-being—that of joy 樂—in all humans of a given society.[10] Xunzi's descriptions of the effects of music on psychology thus run full circle from music to individual to society, and then back around again to every individual psyche in society, but this time from within a unified whole. The joy to which he alludes is therefore not merely individual joy; it is a shared joy that corresponds to the psychological health of society at large.

Xunzi's "Discourse on Music" abounds with passages attesting to the socio-psychological and political roles of music. In the following section, we see how music links the general attitudes and behaviors of the masses with the security of a state:

樂姚冶以險，則民流僈鄙賤矣。流僈則亂；鄙賤則爭。亂爭，
則兵弱城犯，敵國危之.

When music is seductive and wild so as to be nefarious, the people will be indulgent and indolent, iniquitous and base. Dissipated and indolent, they will cause disorder; iniquitous and base, they will cause conflict. With disorder and conflict, the army will be weak, city-walls will be violated, and enemy states will bring peril.[11]

Here, music brings about attitudes and behaviors that translate directly into deeper and deeper levels of social disorder. Doomed states with weak military forces, filled with chaos and contention, are the direct consequences of bad music. Thus, one clear function of music is to maintain the well-being and security of the state—a function that implies controlling the people and bringing peace and order to them.

For Xunzi, music serves as "the consummate means of bringing order to the people 治人之盛者也" because it harnesses and directs mass psychology.[12] Because of its incredible socio-psychological impact, the content and styles of music are of utmost importance. Each stanza must uphold valuable cultural mores and music in general must demonstrate restraint; these values of meaning, morality, and restraint are desired qualities to be guarded and preserved through strict state supervision. Citing from what is possibly his own, previous writing, entitled the "Arrangement of Offices (*Xu Guan* 序官)," Xunzi notes the following description of the duties of the Music Master (*Taishi* 太師):[13]

其在序官曰:修憲命審,誅賞禁淫聲以時順修 · · · 太師之事也.

This is found in the "Arrangement of Offices," which states: "Developing frameworks and commands, examining the stanzas of the Odes, forbidding excessive sounds, and making improvements in a smooth and timely fashion . . . —these are the duties of the Grand Master (of Music).[14]

This citation provides insight into the importance of state control over the content and styles of music. Beautiful compositions of the past, embodied primarily in the Odes, should be maintained precisely because they are a powerful means of mass psychological regulation. Thus, by promulgating the right type of music, a state might guide its people away from moral descent into depravity and excess, while at the same time insuring the unity of their psychological well-being and sense of decorum.

As a means of controlling mass psychology, music for Xunzi serves to unify moral sensibilities and, ultimately, cultural mores. This is because the mass psychology of which Xunzi speaks does not merely entail simple, emotional feelings; it entails an elaborate affective reaction to music that includes overarching moral stances and attitudes. Note that when describing the large-scale social effects of good music on society, Xunzi does not stop at a depiction of happy, contented people. Rather, he goes on to include its effects on the moral and intellectual attitudes of the listeners. Thus, for Xunzi, music brings about a complicated learning process deeply involving, but certainly not limited to, the emotions themselves:

使其聲足以樂而不流, 使其文足以辨而不諰,使其曲直,繁省, 廉肉, 節
奏足以感動人之善心,使夫邪汙之氣無由得接焉

[The former kings] made their sounds sufficient to yield joy but not indulgence; made their lyrics sufficient to mark distinctions without

forcing thought, made their [music] winding or straight, intricate or
simple, pure or robust, and restrained or progressive sufficient to stir and
move the good in people's heart-minds, so that perverse and muddy *qi*
would have no means by which to attach itself therein.[15]

An important aspect of Xunzi's musical psychology is the fact that it
involves an overall moral stance, which is characterized by a "good heart-
mind (*shan xin* 善心)." Such a stance is effectively brought about by a physiological and emotional sense of balance within. Balance is achieved not
merely through adequate harmonization of the emotions, but through the
regulation of one's capacity of discernment as well. Such regulation of the
heart-mind is also directly linked to the purity of one's *qi*. Thus, music, by
activating the "good heart-minds" of its audience through regulated and
restrained sounds, lyrics, and music, ultimately helps bring about their
purified *qi*. The result is a morally uplifted audience.

Since music has the power to guide people in the same intellectual
and moral direction, it binds them together psychologically so that they
embrace and internalize the same cultural forms. We see in the following
statement how music induces people's conformity to shared norms, thereby
powerfully reinforcing a sense of cultural unity:

故樂者、出所以征誅也，入所以揖讓也。征誅、揖讓，其義一也。出所以征
誅，則莫不聽從；入所以揖讓，則莫不從服

Thus [the principles of musical performance] are that by which in going
out, one engages in punitive expeditions, and in entering, one practices
[the rituals of] bowing and yielding. Punitive expeditions and bowing
and yielding—their significance is the same. When one goes out using
[the principles of musical performance] in punitive expeditions, there
will be none who do not follow obediently; when one enters using [the
principles of musical performance] to bow and yield, there will be none
who do not follow and submit.[16]

From this passage, we learn that music is an important tool for both military and civil functions. Its usefulness stems from its ability to teach and
unify the people psychologically and behaviorally. Conformity and obe-
dience results from the people's unified, and hence, orderly, responses to
punitive expeditions and civil rituals.

To round out his argument that music unifies cultural mores, Xunzi
underscores the fact that music is ultimately a tool for sovereign control in
an ordered regime:

樂中平，則民和而不流；樂肅莊，則民齊而不亂。民和齊，則兵勁城固，敵
國不敢嬰也。如是，則百姓莫不安其處、樂其鄉，以至足其上矣.

When music is central and balanced, the people will be harmonious and
not indulgent; when music is solemn and dignified, the people will be
uniform and not disorderly. If the people are harmonious and uniform,
then the military will be strong and the city-walls secure, and enemy
states will not dare to attack. If things are thus, then there will not be one
among the hundred surnames who is not at ease in his dwelling, happy in
his village, and thus fully satisfied with his ruler.[17]

In this phenomenal passage, Xunzi seamlessly moves from the people's harmonious, unchaotic uniformity to issues of state defense, the general feeling
of security in the population, and the people's ultimate contentedness with
their ruler. By claiming that a ruler's choice of music can help bring about a
unified affective and even behavioral state in the people, Xunzi projects the
psychological effects of musical self-cultivation onto an entire population
and, indeed, onto the state and the military and political success of its ruler.
Xunzi's idea of music as a tool for influencing and harnessing mass psychology therefore translates into a formula for establishing a strong, successful
ruler who reigns over a culturally unified and orderly state.

Xunzi is not alone in recommending that music help unify cultural
mores. Many texts from the late Warring States and early imperial periods
also delineate how music might "unify the people's heart-minds (tong min
xin 同民心)" so as to facilitate centralized control over a diverse region of
peoples.[18] Some texts promote the notion of a single, unified moral culture
by speaking of a legitimate transmission of upright music from the ancient
past. In Shi ji, for example, the Tyrant Zhou, who was responsible for the
downfall of the Shang Dynasty, is depicted as having enjoyed "new, excessive tunes (xin yin sheng 新淫聲)" and dancing.[19] Such tales from the past
lend legitimacy to certain forms of music—in particular, the Elegantiae
and Lauds that were considered to be part of the Odes—which did not
derive from what were considered to be depraved sources and had with-
stood the test of time in the Shang and Zhou courts. Such comments on
Tyrant Zhou thus imply that certain forms of music contribute both to
state order and the continuity of culture throughout the ages.

We see a similar critique of excessive, depraved music as it is associated with morally bereft cultures and "doomed states" such as the state of
Zheng, the music of which, incidentally, served sometimes as a negative
model for unification. In the Bohu tong 白虎通, dating approximately to
79 CE, for example, the author describes the Elegantiae music as "upright"
(zheng 正). He then recommends that one distance oneself from Zheng

tunes, mentioning that such sounds encourage the chaotic mixing of sexes through their lascivious, alluring, and overly sexual sounds.[20] Such carving out of musical styles on these grounds reinforces a sense of unity around a systematized set of cultural forms. The regulation of sex often goes hand-in-hand with cultural forms, yet music locates its power here by clarifying sexual norms as well as serving the larger cultural and moral interests of the Han state and society (the inheritors of Zhou ritual society).

Like Zhou ritual practices, musical forms provided a socio-political and cultural backdrop upon which behavioral and attitudinal norms might be defined and reinforced. Just as the consolidation of positive examples was critical to the unification of mores, the disavowal of negative ones was also necessary for the same purpose. Thus, the critique of the tunes of Zheng and the labeling of such music as lascivious and taboo served as the negative foil to the morally desirable and culturally acceptable Zhou ritual practices.

The defining of a cultural tradition of moral value is strengthened by claims for historical constancy and proper musical lineage. Appeals to a specific Zhou lineage of musical practices take on many forms, but by the early imperial periods, there appears to be a pervasive acceptance of the Elegantiae and Lauds as the legitimate descendants of culturally proper music. Even the *Huainanzi*, which often reflects what some scholars would refer to as non-traditional "Daoist" leanings, recognizes the importance of cultural difference while still promoting a centralized core—epitomized in the Elegantiae and Lauds: "[The ancient kings] took their cues from [the fact that people] delighted in tones to rectify the sounds of the Elegantiae and Lauds, thus winds and customs are not indulgent 因其喜音而正雅頌之聲，故風俗不流．"[21]

While the *Huainanzi* recommends the coexistence of a wide variety of cultures, each with different "winds and customs," it nonetheless promotes a form of centralization that aims to unify all of these in some way.[22] The author appeals to his special idea of diverse unity by linking everything organically through the all-encompassing and unifying web of cosmic pattern. This is reflected in his comments on music and its power to unify through cosmic connection:

堯《大章》，舜《九韶》，禹《大夏》，湯《大（護）〔濩〕》，周《武象》，此樂之不同者也。。　此皆因時變而制禮樂者〔也〕。譬猶師曠之施瑟柱也，所推移上下者寸尺之度，而靡不中音。故通於禮樂之情者能作，（音）〔言〕有本主於中，而以知矩〔矱〕之所員者也。

Yao had the "Great Emblem" performed, Shun the "Nine Euphonia," Yu the "Great Xia," Tang the "Great Obtainment," Zhou the "Martial Elephant."[23] This is how music differed from each other . . . This is how they all followed along with the changes in time to regulate ritual and music. It is like when [Music Master] Shi Kuang strummed along the fingerboard of the large zither: wherever he pressed up or down—whether an inch or foot apart—he never missed hitting the right note. Therefore, those who penetrate the nature of ritual and music can create it. This says that there is a fundamental ruler in the center, and by means of it one might know the universality of the carpenter's square and regulations.[24]

The author speaks here of "penetrating" the nature of ritual and music, which appears to be the key to his notion of unification. Just as Music Master Shi Kuang could take command over his entire performance without missing a note, sages can create music that complies with the essential natures of every geographic region by focusing on the root of all things. As with the carpenter's square, which serves as the source for all correct squares, there is a standard, central source for all music that can be apprehended and tapped by astute sages. This notion of a unifying center at the heart of things, and hence, all music, reflects the author's vision of an idealized form of centralization. According to such a vision, diversity in cultural forms (such as ritual and music) must exist, but they must necessarily be unified at the center by a sagely ruler who is understands how each essentially fits into the whole.

Cultural imperialism can also be justified through an appeal to ancient sages who unified and subdued a people through moral suasion. The rhetoric of *De* (virtue) had been used in China since ancient times to legitimize a leader's rule on the basis of his moral superiority or claims to the Mandate of Heaven. In the *Analects* and even earlier textual passages such as those from the *Book of Songs*, virtue induces the people's submission and attraction to a particular ruler.[25] Intriguingly, in some later contexts authors, such as that of the *Guo yu*, add music to the rhetoric of virtue by positing that music can serve as a primary vehicle by which virtue might be spread far and wide:

夫樂以開山川之風也，以耀德於廣遠也。風德以廣之，風山川以遠之，風物以聽之，循詩以詠之，循禮以節之。夫德廣遠而有時節，是以遠服而邇不遷.

Music is that by which the winds of the mountains and rivers are opened; that by which one's dazzling virtue is spread far and wide. One gives wind to virtue so that it may scatter itself broadly . . . Now when [one's] virtue is broad and far-reaching, and one regulates [things] in their proper time, this is when those that are far away submit themselves and those that are near do not move far away.[26]

Here, Music Master Shi Kuang speaks to Duke Ping of Jin about the power of music and its relationship to virtue. Music penetrates the winds of the natural landscape to allow for the successful and unimpeded scattering of one's dazzling virtue. Though not identical to virtue, music nonetheless serves here as a vehicle for transmitting attributes of moral perfection to faraway peoples and places, so that a universally favorable response to virtue takes effect. Music thus can act as a powerful tool in cultural imperialism and political centralization around the moral ruler.

Evidence from the historical record shows how emperors used music to symbolize the unity of their reign over conquered borderland regions. For one thing, Emperor Gaozu of the Han had allegedly appreciated the music from his homeland, the former state of Chu, known as "sacrificial music for the Inner Chambers" (*fangzhong ciyue* 房中祠樂).[27] It is noteworthy that during the second year of his son, Huidi's, reign (193 BCE), the Director of the Music Bureau, Xiahou Kuan 夏侯寬, changed the name of such music to "Music that pacifies the times (*an shi yue* 安世樂)."[28] That a regional music should be adopted by the imperial regime to express its victory and dominance over other regions attests to the role music played as a tool for cultural imperialism, even in the nascent stages of Chinese empire.

Similarly, a passage from Sima Qian's *Historical Records* details the history of music in an important and symbolic imperial sacrifice to the Great Unity (Tai Yi 太一) and the Earth Lord (Hou Tu 后土). While the reasons for Emperor Wu's decisions to promote music are not stated, one can easily surmise from his policies and actions that he deemed it useful in helping send a message to the world of unity, cultural authority, and the glory of his reign.[29] The entire passage is worth quoting here:

其春，既滅南越，上有嬖臣李延年以好音見。上善之，下公卿議，曰：「民閒祠尚有鼓舞樂，今郊祀而無樂，豈稱乎？」公卿曰：「古者祠天地皆有樂，而神祇可得而禮。」或曰：「太帝使素女鼓五十弦瑟，悲，帝禁不止，故破其瑟為二十五弦。」於是塞南越，禱祠太一、后土，始用樂舞，益召歌兒，作二十五弦及空侯琴瑟自此起。

In the spring, after the kingdom of Southern Yue had been wiped out, Li Yannian, who became one of the emperor's favorite ministers, attracted the ruler's attention because of his knowledge of music. The emperor was much impressed with his views and ordered the high ministers to open discussions on the following question: "At the places of worship among the common people, musical instruments and dances are still in use, yet at the present, no such music is employed at the suburban sacrifice. How can this be right?"

"In ancient times," replied the ministers, "music was used at all the sacrifices to Heaven and Earth, and thus the deities of those two realms were treated with the highest degree of propriety." Others said, "The Great Emperor Fu Xi ordered the Plain Maiden to play upon a fifty-stringed zither. The music was exceedingly sad and the Great Emperor tried to stop her from playing, but she would not cease. Therefore he broke the zither in two, making an instrument of only twenty-five strings."

As a result of their deliberations, sacrifices and prayers of thanksgiving for the success of the expedition to Southern Yue were offered to the Great Unity and the Earth Lord, and at these music and dances were used for the first time. A number of boys were summoned to sing at the services and twenty-five stringed zithers and harps of the kind called *konghou* were made. It was at this time that zithers and harps first came into use for religious ceremonies.[30]

We learn a lot from this passage about the role of music in early Han imperialism. First, like his ancestor before him, Emperor Wudi found it fitting to appropriate regional music (here: the music of the common people) for imperial purposes. By elevating this type of music, Wudi could effectively use what was originally "local" and "of the people" as a symbol for his newly acquired control over them. Second, the fact that music was introduced into what were known as the "suburban sacrifices" (郊祀) at this particular time—namely, in the wake of the successful campaign against Southern Yue in 111 BCE—demonstrates both the celebratory and symbolic value music held. Celebratory because it helped bring out the grandiose powers of the victorious emperor vis-à-vis an unruly frontier kingdom, and symbolic because it served as a link between Wudi and Zhou cultural traditions of the past (such as the suburban sacrifice), thereby underscoring his legitimacy as supreme leader. Both this and the previous example give us insight not only into how music was conceived as a tool for imperialism, but how music was actually used by emperors of the early period in congruence with the discourses on it.

It is worth noting that the use of music as a tool for cultural imperialism was not lost on Han contemporaries or those living in the wake of Emperor Wudi's reign. Certain late Western Han condemnations of Wudi's imperialistic behaviors were expressed poignantly through critiques of his musical excesses and the ultimate abolition of the Bureau of Music in 7 BCE. In what Martin Kern suspects is a fragment from a court memorial found in the "Record on Ritual and Music (*Li yue zhi* 禮樂志)," of the *Han shu*, a now anonymous statesman rails against "poems and songs of the suburban altars and ancestral temple 今漢郊廟詩歌" that are "not devoted to the matters of the progenitors 未有祖宗之事," as well as palace music performed by "talents from the women's quarters 掖庭 材人," and outside music from the "Bureau of Music of the imperial hunting park 上林樂府."[31] Presumably written before the mandated closing of the Bureau of Music, this statement shows how music was thought to be an issue that linked directly to a ruler's quality and style of governance. Whereas Emperor Wudi—under the guidance of the then Bureau of Music director, Li Yannian—embraced "new 新" and "changing 變" tunes that incorporated diverse, regional elements from newly conquered frontier zones and territories, later critics, who were no doubt critics of Wudi's overarching imperialistic policies, viewed such innovations as in defiance of classical ritual forms dedicated to the honor of one's ancestors.[32]

Also relevant to imperialistic ideologies and practices are the myths of the ancient sage emperors and their relationships to music. A common theme in many of the myths about the creation of music or musical tones is the theme of sonic standardization by a single, creative sage.[33] Standardization of weights and measures, among other things such as laws and bureaucratic units, was the hallmark of early Chinese centralization policies, especially those of the First Emperor of Qin.[34] The act of standardizing reflects the goal of unification by mandating the use of equal measures and practices across diverse regions, irrespective of cultural habits and norms. Thus, that the mythology of the late Warring States period—the period verging on the unification of China by Qin Shihuang—should strongly endorse standardization in a variety of areas, including music, should come as no surprise.

Of no surprise should be the fact that the rhetorical trope, the "music of antiquity 古樂," seems to have developed alongside sagely genealogies that attempted to define a singular cultural heritage and line of musical development for the past. Part of the process of unifying disparate civilizations in early China involved establishing myths of identity that help shape a culture's self-perception and connect its disparate elements into a seamless whole. Martin Kern observes that the "music of antiquity" as a trope seems to have begun around the mid-third century BCE with the writing of the *Lüshi chunqiu*.[35] I have found its occurrence as well in the "Xing Zi Ming Chu," which appears to date to a slightly earlier period than the *Lüshi chunqiu*.[36] Regardless, only later, in late Western Han and Eastern Han texts, was such a trope elaborated into a "fully fledged history of ancient music, where each title is assigned to a sage from the past, beginning with the Yellow Emperor and ending with Zhou Gong."[37] Such a finding corresponds with the notion that music was considered to be directly relevant to empire-making and ethnogenesis, insofar as the establishment of a musical lineage and discussions of whether a given ruler conformed or deviated from such a lineage offered rulers a way to legitimize their rule while at the same time offering statesmen and thinkers a means of criticizing certain imperial approaches to governance.

When we examine the mythology related to the creation of music at the dawn of the imperial age, we see that the Yellow Emperor often represents the single, imperial leader who creates music. This is not only the case in the *Lüshi chunqiu*, but in the "Yue ji" of the *Book of Rites* and *Han shu* as well, among other late Warring States and early imperial texts. In the following citation from the *Han Feizi*, for example, the Yellow Emperor creates music only after performing an elaborate ritual that details the various levels of imperial and bureaucratic power at his court:

昔者黃帝合鬼神於泰山之上，駕象車而六蛟龍，畢方並轄，蚩尤居前，風伯進掃，雨師洒道，虎狼在前，鬼神在後，騰蛇伏地，鳳皇覆上，大合鬼神，作為清角。

In ancient times, the Yellow Emperor called spirits together on the top of the Mount Tai. Riding in an ivory carriage by six dragons, the god Bifang keeping pace with the linchpin, the god Chiyou stationed before him, the Wind Earl to sweep the way, the Rain Master to sprinkle the road, tigers and wolves in the vanguard, ghosts and spirits behind, writhing serpents on the ground below, phoenixes soaring above him, he called the spirits to a great assembly and created the music of the pure *jiao* mode.[38]

Here, the ritual line-up and assemblage of deities from every direction and sphere of the cosmos reflects designs for state order and control over cultural forms. Orderly music derives from an ordered social body. Only from an orderly social body can the music that emerges be pure and representative of beginnings, as is characteristic of music in the "pure *jiao* mode 清角."[39]

So far we have seen how various texts and practices underscore music as a key to the cultural unification of a state and the pacification of wayward groups of people. While some texts focus much more on music as a means of tapping into the authority or unifying force of the cosmos, others such as the *Xunzi* emphasize music as a means of harnessing mass psychology that might be used effectively for centralized control. Either way, this interest in music as an important vehicle for cultural unification and state control points to changes in the socio-political climate starting from the fourth century BCE and continuing on into the early imperial period. In particular, it seems to be related to the Central States' rampant adoption of centralizing theories and measures, culminating in the rise of the first Empire of the Qin during the third century BCE.

"CHANGING CUSTOMS AND ALTERING MANNERS":
MUSIC AND CULTURAL IMPERIALISM

The Han Dynasty text *Canon of Filial Piety* quotes what becomes a rather common phrase about the powers of music and ritual in society: "In changing customs and altering manners, nothing surpasses music; in pacifying the powers above and ruling over the people, nothing surpasses ritual 移風易俗，莫善於樂。安上治民，莫善於禮."[40] Closely related to the notion of unifying cultural mores is the idea of changing regional customs in an effort to form a sleeker, more unified imperial state. In this section, I add to our discussion of the unification of cultural mores by focusing on the classical phrase, ("changing customs and altering manners," or literally, "moving winds and changing customs") a sort of touchstone that links discourses on music to early forms of cultural imperialism. Through a closer examination of just how authors proposed to streamline culture in the early imperial periods, we will gain even more insight into how aesthetic practices such as music became appropriated as civilizing tools that concur with fundamentally moral, imperial, and sometimes even ethnocentric agendas.

In Xunzi's "Discourse on Music," he repeatedly mentions the concept of "alien customs" in association with depraved music. Conversely, he shows that proper music has the power to bring about larger cultural and social order, which Xunzi refers to as "changing customs and altering manners (*yi feng yi su* 移風易俗)."[41] Xunzi recommends cleaning up musical practices "so that alien customs and depraved tones do not dare wreak havoc upon the Elegantiae 使夷俗邪音, 不敢亂雅."[42] Contrasting the Elegantiae with alien customs and depraved tones, Xunzi demonstrates that entire cultures, and not just individual desires and unbalanced, bodily *qi*, might produce unhealthy and socially detrimental sounds.[43]

This citation corresponds to the criticism of specific types of music (that of the state of Zheng) in *Analects* 17.18, and it is noteworthy that in both the *Analects* and *Xunzi* passages, the Elegantiae are hailed as the ultimate standard of proper, upright music. Standing opposite of alien customs and depraved tones, the Elegantiae represent the epitome of civilization and refinement. By asserting the superiority of the Elegantiae in bringing about unified states of psychological well-being not just in individual bodies but in whole societies, Xunzi creates a clear rationale for Ru musical practices from the perspective of more imperial forms of control. In this light, it is interesting to note Robert Eno's discussion of a possible etymology of the term Ru ("ritual specialist"), which links it to dance masters whose duty it is to tame and civilize.[44] This intriguing but speculative connection, if true, would certainly help explain the special Ru interest in music as a source for promoting social order and reinforcing feelings of Hua-Xia ("Chinese") identity.

The phrase "alien customs and depraved music" reveals an ethnocentric element that defines what is moral by carving out what is native and traditional. It reminds us of other types of derogatory comments about music from traditionally non-Zhou regions, especially as such music was associated with moral degeneracy and the downfall of states.[45] The ethnocentric element in Xunzi's writing is supported by the fact that he defines proper music in traditional, Zhou terms. The Elegantiae, after all, represent the achievements of a single lineage of cultural transmission through the dynastic house of Zhou. Thus, Xunzi's choice of proper music reveals not only his support for Ru musical practices; it reveals the Ru's great desire to define high culture and civilization in terms of the Zhou traditions that they uphold. It reveals a desire to define Zhou—and the Zhu-Xia 諸夏 or Hua-Xia 華夏 people who follow the Zhou—as the superior ethnic group—at the very least, in the sense of a people who share a similar cultural heritage.[46]

The Huainanzi takes a slightly different approach than the Xunzi in promoting music as a vehicle for cultural unification. In accordance with their emphasis on "diverse unification" as mentioned above, the authors of Huainanzi speak of sages who "change customs and alter manners" because of their rightful connection to the cosmos: "If by posting laws and setting up rewards one cannot change customs and alter manners, then he is not putting forth his sincere heart-mind 縣法設賞，而不能移風易俗者，其誠心弗施也."[47] Here, the act of "putting forth" one's sincere heart-mind is akin to reconnecting oneself to one's idealized nature, which, as we have noted above, is grounded in a sense of cosmic balance and harmony. Such attunement provides the sage with a means of changing customs according to a larger cosmic plan. Though it is unclear exactly what this larger plan entails, it seems certain that the sage is only to "change customs" to the extent that diverse practices harmonize with each other from within a larger, cosmic whole. Given the authors' depictions elsewhere in the text of the diverse yet unified workings of the cosmos, such a plan would effectively allow the sage to temper regional discrepancies so as to harmonize with a larger whole while still allowing for local diversity and a variety of musical styles. Significantly, the authors speak nothing of an imperialistic state that effectively eradicates or subdues the cultural diversity of its regional parts.

According to the above-mentioned perspective on cultural unification, it is important for the sage in the Huainanzi to be able to transform cultures and their various styles of music according to the inner logic of the cosmos, not some traditional cultural pattern deriving from the Zhou, Qin, or even

Han courts respectively. In order to tap into such cosmic knowledge of music, one must possess sagely powers of apprehension:

至精入人深矣！故曰：樂，聽其音則知其俗，見其俗則知其化。孔子學鼓琴於師襄，而論文王之志，見微以知明（矣）〔也〕。延陵季子聽魯樂而知殷、夏之風。

The quintessential enters people deeply indeed! Thus one says: "As for music, upon hearing its tones, one knows the customs [of a place], upon seeing its customs, then one knows how to transform it." Confucius studied the drums and small zither with Shi Rang and was [able to] discourse on King Wen's intent. This is because he could apprehend the subtle so as to gain [overall] clarity [about the practices in a state]. Yanlin Jizi listened to the music of Lu and knew about the customs of the Shang and Xia.[48]

Clearly, knowledge of the customs of diverse places is valued, but having the knowledge and wherewithal to alter such customs if necessary represents the utmost goal. The various sages of the past—ever attuned to the essential nature of the cosmos—were able to perceive of the subtleties of different customs while possessing the power to transform what was bad among them. In such a way, ancient sages could fine-tune the diverse elements of an empire so that they might conform more readily to the essential nature of the cosmic whole, which itself was comprised of diverse elements. Thus, though difference was valued, the only acceptable differences were those that correctly harmonized or fit into the larger realm of the cosmic ruler. In such a manner, the author of *Huainanzi* appeals to the ultimate authority of the cosmos in order to promote his own version of cultural (and musical) imperialism: an imperialism that respects difference, but only if it contributes harmoniously to the whole.

Regardless of one's specific definition of "unity," the theme of the sage who uses music to help unify a diverse realm had lasting power throughout the early imperial period. A passage from the *Shangshu dazhuan*, a second century BCE text, echoes the *Huainanzi* passages just mentioned by allotting the power of unification—here presented as the "tuning" of the Empire—to the musical sage: "Therefore the sage-king tours the twelve provinces, observes each of their customs and manners, and trains each of their natures and dispositions. He thereupon organizes the twelve manners and fixes them using the Six Pitch-standards, Five Tones, Eight Timbres, and Seven Beginnings 故聖王巡十有二州，觀其風俗，習其性情，因論十有二俗，定以六律、五聲、八音、七始。"[49] An explanation of the usage of numbers in this passage is in order. The number twelve in this citation is not insignificant, nor is it simply a coincidence of geography. It points to an overlay of musical theory (which also served as the system of tuning instruments and standardizing measures, as we will see in chapter three) onto the geographical categorizations of empire. Even more fundamentally, the number twelve represented the twelve "Earthly branches": sections of the celestial circle that were matched up with the ten "Heavenly stems" to measure and delineate days of the year and time. Thus, in this passage, the "twelve manners" likely match up with the twelve pitch-standards (musical notes), derived from the basic six mentioned in the quote and rooted in astronomical observations and knowledge of the cosmos. And the "five tones" were probably to be matched geographically to the four directions and the center (for a total of five directions). Finally, various early commentators have noted that the Seven Beginnings refer to seven specific pitch-standards which each were correlated with Heaven, Earth, humans, and the four seasons.[50] These, along with the Eight Timbres, would have needed to be factored into the act of topographical apportionment in some manner as well.

What imperial goals can we discern from such a statement? It is impossible to know the exact musico-cosmography that would result from such an exercise, but we can offer a preliminary, speculative interpretation. First, it may be that "fixing" the various customs according to the pitch-standards and tones refers to the act of providing assignations for five larger geographical regions of musical diversity and twelve smaller regions according to the five general directions. The sage might then match those with the twelve pitch-standards so as to characterize each according to a specific note or musical mode. In such a complicated act of cosmic matching, the sage would also need to tailor his divisions according to the prevalence in each region of materials represented by the instrumental sounds of the Eight Timbres, such as metal, stone, silk, bamboo, gourd, earthenware, animal hide, and wood. And he would need to make sure that the seven the pitch-standards that held special relationship to the cosmic "beginnings" were also accorded regions that upheld their dual associations with Heaven, Earth, humans, and the four seasons.

In other words, of the twelve smaller regions associated with the pitch-standards, seven of them would be regions that also held special relationship to one of the Seven Beginnings of the cosmos. While the author is too vague and our knowledge of ancient music practices too scant to know how to interpret this passage more precisely, it suffices that the reader get the gist of the passage, which is to impart the importance of matching up the correct geographic regions of the world with the correct musical styles, and making sure that everything corresponds to the intrinsic sonorities and patterns of the larger cosmos.

Regardless of how one interprets the sage's alleged numerological arrangements, it is clear that he is to serve as a centralizing agent who brings region, landscape, and customs into alignment with the natural sonic qualities of the empire. In such a manner, the sage allots a space for regional diversity according to the overarching standards of a centralized regime and harmonious cosmos. He wields musical theory and tones to round out the rough edges of difference into a unified and, indeed, "well-tempered" imperial system.

CONCLUSION

In addition to using music as a vehicle for cosmic rulership, imperial rulers sought to employ music for the purposes of cultural unification and imperialism. The textual record reflects these two related applications in a plethora of ways. At issue was an author's particular vision of how unity might be achieved: either at the expense of diversity through measures of standardization and equalization, or by keeping diversity in mind through the harmonization of diverse elements. While some texts spoke about music in terms of the creation of single set of standardized pitches and fundamental tones of the cosmos, others stressed cosmic diversity that could be harmonized through a strong center. In most cases, however, the authors we examined in this chapter shared the goal of using the patterns and operations of the cosmos as a template for orderly systematization of the empire. For many of these writers, who lived during the centuries characterized by the rise and consolidation of imperial, centralized rule in China, unification of the empire meant linking up specific parts of the realm with what were thought to be corresponding sonic components of the cosmos.

Differing views of how to deal with diversity and better unify the empire likely represented divergent types of interests at court. The emphasis on equalization and standardization, in keeping with practices common to the Qin state and empire, stressed the supreme dominance of the central regime over the outlying kingdoms and their traditions. The other approach, perhaps conveniently referred to as the "diversity within unity" approach, attempted to give some level of space and legitimate voice to the outlying kingdoms (and, especially, to their kings, such as Liu An, patron of the *Huainanzi*). The former model recommended a sleeker, more homogenous state, likely supported by certain centralizing rulers and those at court who sought to oust entrenched powers in the regional kingdoms. This model would have been based more upon that of the Qin state and empire rather than the Warring States or Han Empire before the ultimately centralizing thrust of Emperor Wudi (141–87 BCE). The other approach was likely supported by the aristocratic regional powers in the various Warring States kingdoms or feudatories of the Han. It is perhaps not surprising that both types of claims highlighted different aspects of music to make a case for the particular vision of cultural unity that served their interests best. Thus, through these discourses on music we gain insight into competing visions of cultural unification, political harmony, and imperial control in early China.

CHAPTER THREE

Regulating Sound and the Cosmos

We have until now been analyzing the various functions, concepts, and rhetoric surrounding music and musical ritual in official, state-related spheres. One of the salient changes in ideas relating to music seems to have occurred in conjunction with the rise of more centralized states and competing visions for a unified empire. Music, as I have argued so far, emerged as a distinct aspect of ritual practice with a life and significance of its own. Fused with concepts of harmony and tightly bound to the operations of the cosmos, music stood out from other traditional, cultural, and man-made practices. It took on meaning as that which was "natural" or "intrinsic" to the subtlest aspects of the cosmos. It thereby became something that rulers or anyone who sought authority and a privileged status or power vis-à-vis the cosmos held close to their hearts.

As witnessed above, the rhetoric of "music," *yue*, as a cosmic phenomenon in late Warring States and early imperial China can be found throughout a wide variety of texts of the period. But for us to really understand why music and the cosmos obtain a special relationship at this time, we need to explore yet another concept that is singled out in some texts as the most fundamental aspect of music: sound. The following analysis of views on sound and its special access to cosmic order helps clarify and explain why many early Chinese authors considered music to be an effective tool for socio-political order. Our discussion of sound should not be separated from the previous analysis of music, since the type of sound we examine here is usually implicitly (if not explicitly) understood as musical sound, given its connection to "pitch-pipes," or musical instruments that were also taken to be the standard for tuning purposes.

In this chapter, I demonstrate how some late Warring States and Han period texts (roughly fourth–second centuries BCE) began to present musical sound as possessing religious, cosmic functionality. I first present a case for the rather mundane status of sound in many Warring States writings on music in society and self-cultivation. I then highlight a specific Warring States context—that of military divination—which appears to have taken a different stance toward sound. Such a context, I contend, accorded sound a special place in cosmic order and operations, thereby providing a crucial chronological backdrop to later developments. Lastly, I analyze certain texts of the Han period, including select passages from musical and military treatises, to show how sound definitively emerged in certain circles as an important aspect of cosmic functionality.[1] In particular, I examine Sima Qian's "Treatise on the Pitch-standards, Lü shu 律書" and the "Treatise on the Pitch-standards and Calendar, Lü li zhi 律曆志" chapter of the *Han shu* to demonstrate how pitch-standards served as primary agents in the regulation of the cosmos.

Writings that link sound to the cosmos became prominent in Warring States and early imperial times, as scholars began to elaborate on systems of intricate, resonant connections among objects in the cosmos.[2] According to the systems of spontaneous resonance that they proposed, innate linkages among objects or phenomena not only existed, but they exerted causal effects in the world.[3] Objects were categorized according to a system of correlations assigned on the basis of such properties as colors, tastes, bureaucratic office, virtues, numbers, directions (center, north, south, east, and west), sounds, and more.[4] As one of the many categories of spontaneous resonance, sound assumed an important ontological, and indeed, religious role. It served as a primary indicator of cosmic conditions, helping divine and designate how things will interact with each other. Sound also served as a cosmic agent, helping bring about and enhance order in the political sphere and natural world.

A NOTE ON TERMINOLOGY

There are two main terms that designate musical sound in ancient Chinese texts: *sheng* 聲 and *yin* 音. Most frequently, the term *sheng* has been translated as "sound"[5] and "melodies,"[6] while *yin* has been translated as "tone," "voice," and "sound."[7] The two were on occasion interchangeable, depending on the context, author, and date of the text under examination. This is apparent in the phrasing of the "Five Tones" as both *wu yin* 五音 in the Warring States and *wu sheng* 五聲 in some Han texts.[8] In Warring States usage, both terms *sheng* and *yin* point to a broad range of meanings beyond that of musical tunes, sometimes even describing the sounds of humans when they cry, wail, and laugh (*sheng*), as well as animal noises typical to each species (*yin*).[9] For this reason, I will translate both terms as "sound" or "tone," depending on the context. In general, however, I use "sound" to refer to aural phenomena that one hears, while "tone" refers to sound that has a musical pitch.

We shall also examine sound in terms of the pitch implied by the *lü* 律, pitch-pipes or pitch-standards.[10] In one sense, *lü* designates six of the twelve main pipes in Chinese music, blown vertically—each of a specified length. More generally, *lü* points to the entire phenomenon of the pitch-pipes, including the pitches of each of what became the standard twelve pitch-pipe instruments.[11] *Lü* therefore came to represent a crucial term for a standard pitch or tone ("pitch-standard"). Thus, depending on the context in which the term appears, it can be translated as either "pitch-pipes" themselves or the "pitch-standards" that derive from blowing on the pipes of varying, set lengths.[12]

In a different but related context, *lü* refers to legal statutes, or regulations. The association of *lü* with regulations is significant, for the usage of the term in musical and acoustic contexts underscores how music was associated with regulation, system, or pattern. The pitch-standards, taken as a whole, reflect set musical intervals that by early imperial times came to be systematically correlated with the numerical dimensions of instruments.[13] Historians paired *lü* 律 with *li* 曆, the term denoting the system of computational astronomy, further demonstrating how sound was associated with cosmic regulations and natural patterns. Given such implications involving cosmic regularity, it makes sense that *lü* refers both to legal and musical patterns and regulations.

One might question the rationale for discussing *lü* in relationship to music. Because the pitch-standards came to represent the foundation of tuning and understanding musical theory in early China, I contend that the study of the pitch-standards is more than the study of disparate tones issued forth by pitch-bearing instruments. Rather, the *lü*—as the basis of all music theory—naturally implicates the study of early Chinese beliefs on music and should be understood holistically in terms of its role in music at large.

The concept of *ming* 名, or names, words, and terms, also implicates sounds. Though this concept arguably refers primarily to the linguistic component that identifies objects in the world, it does point as well to the aural and phonetic qualities of words, terms, or names as they are pronounced in speech rather than written in script. In the works of the Mohists, for example, the word for sound, *sheng*, was sometimes interchanged with the word for name, *ming*, when referring to the notion of reputation.[14] In addition, the "Mohist Canon" explicitly links names to sounds in the phrase,

"The sounds which issue from the mouth all have a name 聲出口，俱有名."[15] The term also bears a close relationship to *ming* 命 (to decree), a term that similarly connotes sound, especially if Heaven is anthropomorphized so as to vocalize such a command or decree.[16] Though usually unrelated to music and musical contexts, this latter term can point to sound as the voice of one who commands—especially Heaven; or it can point to the command itself. Thus, the issue of sound in early China might be considered relevant—though not tightly linked—to discussions of names and, perhaps to a lesser extent, decree.

Despite the probable relevance of sound to the concept of names, many Warring States discourses on the topic do not generally focus on the aural aspect of names. In the Ru discourse of "rectifying names" (*zheng ming* 正名), for example, names are important because of the need to act in accordance with their normative meanings—fathers should be what "father" implies normatively, and so on.[17] Similarly, the later Mohists view names primarily in terms of their use as signifiers that help label, identify, organize, and normalize one's understanding of reality, not in terms of their aural qualities.[18] Other thinkers associated with the Warring States discussion of names, such as those who were later categorized as belonging to the Mingjia 名家, or "School of Names," seem also to have focused on names as a means by which to better analyze the organizing and signifying aspects of language, not its aural aspects.[19] Intriguingly, an excavated text included in the Shanghai Museum bamboo strip collection, "Heng Xian 恆先," speaks of names in terms of the cosmic development of language and names. It includes a graph which could be understood as either *yin* 音 (sounds) or *yi* 意 (mental image/meaning).[20] If indeed names were closely linked to sounds in early China, which remains to be seen, this would significantly affect our understanding of early Chinese views on the psychological relationship between musical sound and language development. For now, however, we will concentrate on the aural and musical meanings surrounding the terms *sheng*, *yin*, and *lü*, and consign a brief discussion of the relevance of names (*ming*) to sound to another chapter.

WARRING STATES BACKGROUNDS FOR COSMIC SOUND

In most texts of the early to middle Warring States (fifth–fourth centuries BCE), authors presented sounds and tones as neither cosmic agents nor agencies. For the most part, sound was to be either cherished or disdained for its effect on humans and its ability to communicate emotions, desires, and intents in the human and spirit world. Though such authors may have considered sound to be intrinsically linked to the cosmos through *qi*, at the very least, it seems significant that they did not discuss sound in terms of *qi*, let alone in terms of cosmic operations and functionality. They chose instead to emphasize musical sound as a product of culture.

A few examples from key Warring States texts clarify these points. In the *Laozi*, sounds and tones are what the ears hear. They are produced by external, mundane objects and are of negligible value in the process of self-cultivation. Consider the following example: "The Five Tones deafen human ears 五音令人耳聾."[21] This statement proclaims that objects of desire, such as the "Five Colors," "Five Tones," and "Five Flavors," actually obstruct one's ability to apprehend the Dao. There is no evidence that the Five Tones derive from the cosmos, only that they interfere with one's innate ability to apperceive of it.

In a different vein, the *Guanzi* presents sounds as a valuable end in bodily cultivation, even though they possess no direct cosmological significance.[22] In the "Techniques of the Heart" chapter of this text, the fulfillment of one's desires impedes in the process whereby one might actually hear sounds (*sheng*):

心之在體，君之位也；九竅之有職，官之分也。心處其道，九竅循理；嗜欲充益，目不見色，耳不聞聲。

In the body the heart-mind assumes the position of ruler. The functions of the nine apertures correspond to the divisions of office. When the heart takes its abode in the Dao, the nine apertures comply with pattern. When one's desires fill and overflow, however, the eyes do not see colors, and the ears do not hear sounds.[23]

Standing opposite the Laozian claim above, abiding in the Dao here allows our senses to become truly perspicacious and open to sounds. Sounds in themselves do not impede one from attaining the Dao; rather, the Dao helps one fully apprehend sounds. One will note that while I reference "sounds" here, the term is actually *yin* in the *Laozi* and *sheng* in the *Guanzi* passage. Despite this difference in the two passages, neither sound nor tones possess cosmic agency or cosmic significance in these texts. They represent, simply, objects of human aural perception. This is supported by the use of both *sheng* and *yin* in the "Inner Work" ("Nei Ye") chapter of the *Guanzi*: "For this reason, such *qi* cannot be summoned by sounds but can be invited by tones 是故此氣也 . . . 不可呼以聲，而可迎以音."[24] Here, mundane sounds (*sheng*) are distinct from elevated tones (*yin*). The latter has the power to invite what is spiritual into the body to reside within; the former does not. Even so, both *sheng* and *yin* themselves are nothing more than objects of perception.

Similarly, while authors of Ru texts from the Warring States consider musical sounds to be extremely important in shaping humans into ethical beings, they do not generally view them to be cosmically powerful in any way. The power of sounds lies more narrowly in their expressive and evocative potential. For example, in the discussions of music in the "Xing zi ming chu" (~fourth century BCE), and the *Xunzi* (third century BCE), authors start from the assumption that music functions primarily at the level of the emotions. In the *Xunzi*, musical sounds (*sheng yin*) emanate from joyful people: "Joy is invariably expressed through musical sounds, and takes form in movement and stillness 樂則必發於聲音，形於動靜."[25] Just as musical sound emanates from human feeling, it affects humans on an emotional level. For this reason, "depraved sounds [*sheng*] excite humans and are met in response by rebellious *qi* . . . upright sounds excite people and are met in response by compliant *qi* 凡姦聲感人而逆氣應之 . . . 正聲感人而順氣應之 . . ."[26] Similarly, the XZMC impresses upon the reader that the connection between sound and emotions is primary and direct.[27] In both texts, sounds are, like colors or textures, aspects of the world that human perception picks up and responds to. Sounds in particular provide access to human emotions.[28]

Because of the special relationship between sound and the various aspects of human sentiment, early Chinese thinkers sometimes referred to sound as the channel by which one might come to understand another human being beyond mere appearances. The Later Mohists provide the following commentary on the term *shi*, "substance," or "reality": "Substance: when the *qi* of one's intent manifests itself. In making others know one's self, nothing is better than the 'sounds of bronze and the accompaniment of jade' 實：其志氣之見也。使人知己，不若金聲玉服."[29] The notion that sound provided the best means for communicating one's most heartfelt, inner reality—as opposed to misleading surface appearances—seems to have persisted well into the early imperial period. It is indicated through a famous anecdote concerning a zither player, Bo Ya 伯牙, and his friend Zhong Ziqi 鍾子期, who had the rare ability to appreciate Bo Ya's playing in the deepest possible way. A phrase that derives from this story, as narrated by Ying Shao in the late Han Dynasty is "bosom buddies" (*yin zhe* 音者, or *zhi yin zhe* 知音者).[30]

Understood literally, the phrase refers to a "knower of tones," or "one who truly understands the intent behind one's musical tones."[31] In time, it came to symbolize true knowledge of any sort about another human being—and not necessarily knowledge that arises via sound. Nonetheless, the original usage of sound is intriguing. By providing special access to the inner workings of human psychology and the supposed true nature or intent of another being, sound functions in much the same manner as it does in the *Xunzi* and the "Xing zi ming chu"—both Warring States texts, which we will examine in more detail in chapters four and five. Consider the following from the *Zhuangzi*, in which sound is the inadvertent expression of a dying animal's true, unmediated suffering: "When animals face death, they do not care what cries they make; their breath comes in gasps and a wild fierceness is born in their hearts 獸死不擇音，氣息茀然，於是並生心厲."[32] Clearly, sound serves as a vital tool for detecting and evaluating the authenticity of an individual's (here, an animal's) current psychic reality.[33]

So far, we have seen that in some Warring States texts sound took on significance as an instrument of culture, society, and personal communication of one's inner reality. This seems to generally describe discussions of sound before the rise to prominence of cosmologies of spontaneous resonance, starting from around the fourth century BCE, but really taking hold from the third century BCE on. During this later period, notions of sound began to emerge as more important than ever. Authors increasingly discussed sound as representing the underlying harmonious "voice" of the cosmos, according it a vital role in cosmic operations. Used effectively as a tool to achieve harmony with the cosmos, sound became a critical factor in imperial rule and the religious cosmology that that served as its foundation.

In what follows, I examine a distinct religious context dating to the Warring States period that may have contributed to the above-mentioned transformation in the status of sound: military divination. I argue that the tantalizing but uncommon textual evidence we have of such a practice in the Warring States, if confirmed to be true, may have foreshadowed the central role sound played in later imperial beliefs about cosmic functioning. Such an analysis sheds light upon one of the possible origins for the practice of using sound, and especially, the fundamental pitch of the Yellow Bell, as a standard for representing, measuring, evaluating, and evoking cosmic order.

SOUND AND *QI*: COSMIC COMPONENTS IN MILITARY DIVINATION

Of our few early sources on military divination during the Warring States period, a couple of sources attest to an intriguing use of sound. In such contexts, sound is clearly a component of the cosmos, though it is unclear whether it possesses special cosmic efficacy, as it does in later, Han times. The following passage from Sima Qian's *Shi ji*, though admittedly written during the Western Han period, suggests that sound was traditionally used to forecast auspicious or inauspicious conditions for military operations:

其於兵械尤所重，故云「望敵知吉凶，聞聲效勝負」。

They [the six pitch-standards] are especially valued as an alert for troops. Therefore it is said, "By facing the enemy you can come to know what is auspicious or inauspicious; by listening to sounds you will find models for victory and loss."[34]

We might surmise that the practice Sima Qian describes above was historical to a certain extent, not simply because Sima Qian claims that it had been "the unchanging way for hundreds of [generations of] kings 百王 不易之道也,"[35] but because the use of sound in military divination is also described in the *Zuo zhuan*.[36] Sima attempts to support his claim that this practice has a long history by narrating the following story, which retells a practice allegedly dating to the early Zhou period:

武王伐紂，吹律聽聲，推孟春以至于季冬，殺氣相并，而音尚宮。同聲相 從，物之自然。

When King Wu of the Zhou attacked the Shang tyrant, Zhou, he made use of a practice of blowing the pitch-pipes and listening to their sounds. He played [each of the twelve pitch-pipes beginning with that which was correlated with] the first month of spring and ending with [that which was correlated with] the third month of winter.[37] A diminishing *qi* mutually resounded and the reverberating tones remained in the [key of the] tonic.[38] It is the natural course of things that sounds of the same kind mutually follow upon each other.[39]

While none of this proves the historicity of this practice, there is a chance that while Sima Qian was almost certainly not describing something that dates as far back as the early Zhou, such a practice may in fact have been in vogue a century or more before Sima's own time.[40] In other words, it is possible that the practice described here dates as far back as the Warring States period, if not earlier.

What does this passage tell us about sounds and the cosmos? King Wu was able to find out about his enemy because he was able to produce sounds on the pitch-pipes and then read and decipher a set of reverberating *qi* and tones [*yin*] which emerged from somewhere. One wonders the extent to which the tones mentioned here were seen as indicators of cosmic conditions, and possibly, those conditions in the enemy's encampment. From the passage alone, we cannot know for sure what the tones stood for: was it King Wu's cosmic destiny at large; some apprehensible quality stemming from the enemy encampment (such as its overall morale, strength, size, and organization); or the mere auspiciousness of the physical terrain upon which the enemy was encamped?

On the basis of a citation from the *Zuo zhuan*, which I discuss shortly, I would like to suggest that the tones reflected some apprehensible quality about the enemy encampment. On this interpretation, it appears that the *qi* and tones of reverberating sound could carry more than just musical meaning: they could relay vital information about certain unknown qualities of an enemy's circumstances. Indeed, the role of sound here is reminiscent of its role in the phrase "bosom buddies" described above—as that which provides a subtle manifestation of what is hidden from view.[41] The main difference is that, rather than providing a clue to another person's authentic emotional stance, sound—like a foolproof spy—reflects upon the hidden stance or *gestalt* of an enemy's troops.

The fact that *qi* is included in this discussion of divination is important. Since *qi* is often also associated with macrocosmic conditions such as the weather, climate, and seasons, one senses that the type of "hidden stance" that "*qi* and the tones" reveal could be related to the general "cosmic positioning" of enemy troops. But with the information given, we cannot verify that this is so. We can only go so far as to say that this particular practice recorded by Sima Qian implicates sound as a harbinger of cosmic orderliness or disorderliness.[42] More importantly, the close correlation between *sheng* (sounds) on the one hand and *yin* (tones) and *qi* on the other suggests a link between sound and the cosmic attributes of *qi*. This linkage is significant because it could help explain the emergence of a belief in sound as an inherent aspect of cosmic functionality.

To ascertain whether the practice of military divination reveals a certain, cosmic understanding of sound, let us analyze another passage of interest—this one from the *Zuo zhuan*—about three diviners. In it, sound appears as an indicator of the overall cosmic conditions surrounding enemy troops:

師曠曰不害。吾驟歌北風，又歌南風，南風不競，多死聲。楚必無功。董叔曰：天道多在西北。南師不時，必無功。叔向曰：在其君之德也。

Shi Kuang said, "There is no harm. I have repeatedly [listened to] the singing of the Northern Winds as well as the Southern Winds.[43] The Southern Winds are not strong and are filled with dying sounds. The state of Chu will certainly not have success." Dong Shu said: "The Dao of Heaven is predominantly in the Northwest. Since the Southern Troops are not on time, they will necessarily not be successful." Shu Xiang said: "[All of this] stems from the ruler's virtue."[44]

The passage depicts two predictions of the downfall of the Chu army based on what appear to be different, but possibly related, methods of determination. The first method associates sounds (as "Winds," *Feng* 風) with military success, the other speaks of the Dao of Heaven without ostensibly mentioning its relationship to sound. At the end, the author presents

Shu Xiang's interpretation that such manifestly ominous signs are causally linked to the virtue of the ruler. Clearly, the author of this passage believes that the particular musical styles (sounds, winds) in a given region generally reflect the state of a ruler's virtue.[45]

The description of "sound (wind)-reading" in this passage is intriguing. It suggests that tunes carry messages about the state of affairs in the location from which they emerge. Instead of drawing an explicit connection between sound and *qi*, as in the passage from the *Shi ji* above, the author connects sound and another cosmic phenomenon—the wind. To be sure, such a linkage seems to have been ancient, as regional tunes were often referred to as "Winds" in the musical poems now found in the *Book of Odes*.[46] Elsewhere in the *Zuo zhuan* as well, there is clear evidence of a linkage between sounds and winds.[47]

But to what extent does this passage link sound to cosmic functionality? Is sound merely transported by wind, or is it an actual quality of wind or the atmosphere that implicates the way the cosmos works? Though Dong Shu the diviner mentions the strength of the "Dao of Heaven" in the Northwest, we cannot be sure whether his prediction feeds off of the previous one by Shi Kuang, and is therefore related to the types of sounds described by him, or whether it constitutes an entirely independent prediction based on either direct observation of the skies or some other externally manifest phenomena, not including sound.

The interpretation I endorse considers both Shi Kuang's and Dong Shu's statements together, as statements that build on each other and culminate in Shu Xiang's commentary on a ruler's virtue at the end. On this reading, Dong Shu's remarks about the Dao of Heaven interpret Shi Kuang's information about the musical styles of the South. The dying sounds (*si sheng* 死聲) coming from the South correspond to weak *qi* emanating from Chu troops. Combining this with the fact that the Dao of Heaven prevails in the Northwest, one may conclude that the cosmic positioning and state of Chu is not good, and so it will lose on the battlefield. Hence, we might conclude that sounds relay vital information about cosmic workings—namely, the state of the Dao of Heaven—that mirror a ruler's state of virtue.

If this interpretation were correct, then this passage, perhaps the only passage referring to sound in military divination that we can more reliably date to the pre-Han period, links sound to the functionality and order of the cosmos.[48] This would suggest that there were some Warring States contexts—namely, that of military divination—in which sound served to indicate certain cosmic conditions. Taken together, the statements from Sima Qian and the *Zuo zhuan* give us reason to believe that the cosmological significance that sound held during the early imperial period might trace its origins in part to the practice of military divination in earlier times. A more modest claim would be that the practice of military divination, which seems to date at the very latest to the Warring States period, reflects certain beliefs about sound and its connection to the cosmos (via wind or *qi*) that became pronounced in later religious beliefs and practices.[49]

SOUND AS COSMIC INDICATOR AND AGENT

During the late Warring States and early imperial period of the Qin and Han, musical sound, and certain relationships between pitches in particular, began to represent a primary element in cosmic functioning and order. This conceptual development is significant because it marked the beginning of a new orientation towards the role of musical sound in the social, natural, and religious order. Musical sound no longer merely represented what the ears heard or what humans produced to convey emotions and messages of import to each other and to spirits. While such commonplace roles for musical sound did not disappear entirely during the early imperial periods, a newer view of sound in relationship to the cosmos came to occupy center stage, especially in texts that dealt with imperial rites and control. In this section, I outline the most central developments concerning the relationship between sound and the cosmos. In particular, I highlight two views that underscore the importance of sound in cosmic terms: the belief in sound as an indicator of cosmic conditions, and the belief in sound as an agent of cosmic processes.

Already during the late Warring States, some texts give evidence of change in the status of sound. As we saw above, the late Warring States author, Xunzi, generally did not view sound as anything but a mundane, human creation. Yet even his writing hints at a burgeoning connection between music and cosmic operations. In his "Discourse on Music," Xunzi asserts that proper music—and hence, proper sounds—typify an ideal state of cosmic functioning. While musical sounds do not actually invoke cosmic operations or possess cosmic efficacy, they resemble them:

舞意天道兼, 鼓其樂之君邪, 故鼓似天, 鐘似地, 磬似水, 竽笙(簫和)筦籥似星辰日月. 桃枕拊鞷椌楬似萬物.

... and the meaning of the dance is as universal as Heaven's Dao.[50] The drum—is it not the ruler of music? Thus, the drums resemble Heaven; the bells resemble Earth; the chime stones resemble water; the *yu* and *sheng* mouth-organs, the flutes, and the pipes resemble the stars, the planets, the sun, and the moon;[51] and the swivel-drums, woodblocks, shakers, and mallets resemble the myriad things.[52]

Here, Xunzi idealizes music by affirming its likeness to basic elements of the cosmos itself. In other words, though the various components of music are man-made creations that influence humans in mundane ways, the underlying "meaning" (*yi* 意) of a musical performance resembles the universal meaning of the cosmic Dao itself.

By the early imperial period, we find evidence of a belief in sound as an indicator of cosmic conditions, and not merely as something that holds metaphorical likeness with it. In military contexts dating to the early imperial period, we clearly see how musical sound reflected current cosmic states. Such beliefs are most likely extensions of Warring States practices of military divination discussed above, although the cosmic connections are much more obvious in later texts. For example, in *Taigong's Six Secret Teachings*, a military classic that probably dates to the Han Dynasty, sound is fully related to the cosmos and its divine workings.[53] An entire chapter of this text is dedicated to the importance of the Five Tones (*Wu yin* 五音) in foretelling impending military victory or defeat.[54] In particular, the author focuses on correlations between the Five Tones and the Five Phases (*Wu xing* 五行), outlining the specific category of cosmic resonance that is relevant for each.[55] He then goes on to assert that these tonal signs of the Five Phases relay vital information about current cosmic configurations facing the military leader, which in turn foretell military success or failure. And lastly, the author associates specific timbres of sound and certain visual cues with the Five Tones, and thus, the Five Phases, thereby providing the reader with even more information about how seemingly mundane aural and visual data associated with battle might be harbingers of what is to come.[56]

This Han period explanation of sound in military divination suggests that sound is viewed as one possible medium that provides insight into cosmic functioning, correlation, and ultimately, the favorability of circumstance. Moreover, it demonstrates that by later times, sound had become clearly linked to the cosmos, standing in as a reflection of cosmic conditions in a particular place and time.

In the next chapter of *Taigong's Six Secret Teachings*, certain types of sounds reveal whether or not one has received spiritual assistance of some sort:

三軍齊整 . . . 金鐸之聲揚以清，鼙鼓之聲宛以鳴。此得神明之助，大勝之徵也。行陳不固 . . . 金鐸之聲下以濁，鼙鼓之聲濕如沐。此大敗之徵也。

When the three armies are well ordered . . . the sound of the gongs and bells rises up and is clear; and the sound of the small and large drums clearly rises—these are portents of having obtained spiritual, enlightened assistance, foretelling a great victory . . . When their formations are not solid . . . the sound of their gongs and bells sinks down and is murky; the sound of their drums is wet as rice-cooking liquid—these are portents of a great defeat.[57]

Here again, sound is not the only clue that provides information about cosmic systems or spiritual favor. Visual data such as colors and the direction of a city's *qi* also impart vital information of such sort.[58] Nonetheless, the use of sound as one important indicator of spiritual assistance or cosmic patterns is important, and reveals the powerful role that sound takes on in connecting human beings with either the higher powers of the cosmos or those of local deities in the region (the text is not clear on what type of spiritual assistance is indicated).

Other early imperial texts, possibly containing material that dates to the late Warring States, go further than military texts to view sound not just as an indicator of cosmic conditions but as a cosmic agent, or actor that helps fulfill the operations and creative potentials of the cosmos. The "Yue ji," or "Record of Music," found in the *Book of Rites*, develops the linkage between music and the cosmos by positing a cause-and-effect relationship between the two.[59] It proclaims music to be a cosmic agent that conforms with the "harmony of Heaven and Earth 與天地同和."[60] Similarly, music is capable of perfecting and completing the cosmos by penetrating its fundamental harmonies (perhaps by synchronizing or resonating with them) and rendering its operations even more effective.[61] Admittedly, though music is different from sound, insofar as it incorporates dancing and visual performance, as well as musical sounds, it is possible that the author's focus on the concept of harmony in these passages refers most directly to its aural aspects.

The "music chapters" of the *Lüshi chunqiu* also make extensive connections between sound and the cosmos. Like the author of the "Yue ji," the author of these chapters claims that music is inherent in the processes of the cosmos. He goes further, however, to demonstrate that sound in particular (*sheng*) is intrinsic to the very shapes and forms of everything in the cosmos 形體有處，莫不有聲.[62] The author goes on to claim that the music of the Former Kings (sages) is ultimately natural, since its principles of harmony and suitability arise from the sounds inherent in the cosmos:

聲出於和，和出於適。和適先王定樂，由此而生

Sound emerges from harmony; harmony emerges from what is fitting. When the Former Kings fixed their music, [they let it] emerge from these principles of harmony and the fitting."[63]

The sage, in organizing musical patterns inherent in the cosmos, is able to use sound in such a way so as to realize the natural fit between music and cosmos.

The fact that music derives from the cosmos sets limitations on its production by humans. If humans are to produce music, an essentially natural and spiritual entity, then they need to abide by certain rules of the cosmos that will allow them to re-create, or uncover, that which is already inherent in the cosmos itself. The use of the term *"sheng 生"* (to produce; to emerge from) in the following statement reveals the idea that music is brought about through nature, not through human means. Since life and the giving of life are key aspects of this organic process of creation, sages "produce" music much as farmers grow millet. This is because the basic harmonic patterns of the cosmos are already inherent in the sounds and raw materials of music, just as the fundaments of life are inherent in the seeds of millet.

The notion that sages produce music from the inherently harmonic processes of the cosmos continues to develop even further during the Han.[64] The ideal of sagely attunement with the cosmos is further expressed through Han Dynasty proclamations of the deep, ontological connection between sound (*sheng 聲*) and the sage (*sheng 聖*)—two homonyms in ancient Chinese—epitomized in the following statement in Ying Shao's *Fengsu tongyi*:[65]

聖者聲也通也，言其聞聲知情，通于天地條暢萬物。

The sage "sounds." [He] penetrates. This is to say that his ability to hear sounds and thereby understand the nature [of things] penetrates all of Heaven and Earth while arranging and letting flourish the myriad things.[66]

Interestingly, unlike the claims in the XZMC, which puts forth the simple idea of using music to penetrate or fathom another person's authentic emotions or psychological state of being, the sagely ideal in this passage is to penetrate the entire cosmos, with everything in it. Whereas the scope of the gentlemanly ideal outlined by the XZMC lies well within the realm of the social and human, the scope of the sagely ideal outlined by the *Fengsu tongyi* is clearly cosmic and all-encompassing. Sound—closely affiliated with the sage—represents the medium by which the sage comes to know not just others, but the entire realm of the cosmos as well.

The elevation of sound from cultural to cosmic tool is not unique to discourses on sagely and imperial ideals of the Han. Another very different context—that of the arts of the bedchamber—demonstrates how self-cultivation practices also adopted the notion that sound was primary point of access to the cosmic Dao. In Han Dynasty texts from Mawangdui concerning the arts of the bedroom chamber, there are intriguing references to the five sounds (*wu sheng*) and five tones (*wu yin*). Such sounds represent one of a series of cosmic goals for both men and women during sexual intercourse.[67] Though it is unlikely that these references to the five sounds and five tones refer to the actual singing of musical tones during the act—referring instead to breathing and sounds made by the mouth—it is clear from the context that the vocalization of sound is integral to one's harmonization with the cosmic Dao itself.[68] This interpretation makes sense only if one understands the five sounds and five tones to be constituent to the operations of the Dao. As such, sound in and of itself (and not just musical sound) is capable of giving humans efficacious access to and communion with the idealized workings of the cosmos.

COSMIC REGULATION AND THE SOUNDS
OF PITCH-STANDARDS

Having just demonstrated the development of a close relationship between sound (*sheng* 聲 or *yin* 音) and the cosmos, we may now turn our attention to the concomitant emergence of particular pitch-standards (*lü* 律)—and especially that of the Yellow Bell (*huangzhong* 黃鐘)—as foundations for cosmic order. Writers based the legitimacy of the state on claims that it was divine and harmonized with the natural order. They depicted the latter as a sacrosanct but nonetheless intelligible system of resonances and attempted to systematize such resonances by categorizing and delineating intricate—and often, highly mathematical—correlations among objects in the world.[69]

A primary way in which the imperial state claimed this control was by organizing and granting the seasonal calendar. In the imperial periods and even earlier, a ruler might properly delineate the seasons by connecting the sound of the pitch-standards [*lü*] with the harmonies inherent in the cosmos.[70] Pitch-standard sound not only provided the Han emperor with a means of tapping into knowledge about the natural cycles and states of affairs in the world. Its mystical capacity to resonate with cosmic *qi* and thereby complete natural cycles also rendered sound an effective tool which he might use to regulate the natural order and thus himself serve as the spiritual arbiter of cosmic prosperity in the social microcosm.

In his "Treatise on the Pitch-standards," Sima Qian discusses the link between the pitch-standards and cosmic regularity.[71] By way of correlative and mathematical interrelationships, he systematically relates the tones (*yin*) of the Five Tones and the sounds (*sheng*) of the pitch-standards to such natural phenomena as the seasons, times of the day, various winds, the patterns of cosmic *qi*, and, ultimately, the movements of the heavenly bodies.[72] Pitch-standard sounds thus come to represent data that might be linked, through number, to cosmic phenomena and time, thereby linking the spheres of musical harmony with mathematical astronomy.[73] To demonstrate the cosmic importance of the pitch-standards, Sima states:

律曆，天所以通五行八正之氣，天所以成孰萬物也。

The pitch-standards and the calendar constitute the cycle by which Heaven progresses through the five phases and the *qi* of the eight rectitudes, and by which it matures and completes the myriad things of the world.[74]

In other words, the pitch-standards and calendar bring about and fulfill the cosmic cycle.

This explicit and important connection between pitch-standards and the cosmos demonstrates that pitch-pipe sound is more than just an indicator or representation of a natural cycle. It shows that there exists a special, resonant affinity between pitch-pipe sounds—produced as wind is blown through these simple instruments—and cosmic patterns, expressed on Earth via the meteorological phenomena of moving *qi* and winds. This resonant affinity causes things to happen; it is not just a static correlation but an active one in which the seeds of cosmic causation are rooted. Sound is therefore more than an indicator in cosmic change; it is a critical agent for it.

In such a context it becomes easier for us to understand statements such as the following, also from Sima Qian's "Treatise on the Pitch-standards," which assert the importance of the six pitch-standards in helping bring about state order:

王者制事立法，物度軌則壹稟於六律，六律為萬事根本焉。

When kings govern affairs and establish laws, things attain their measure through rules and regulations and are uniformly endowed by the six pitch-standards. The six pitch-standards are the roots of the myriad affairs of the world.[75]

What does it mean for things to be "uniformly endowed by the six pitch-standards"?[76] If the sounds of the pitch-standards represent the varied patterns of a resonant cosmos, that phrase is true because their sounds are inextricably tied in with the natural, cosmic destinies of things. Thus, these pitch-pipe sounds not only mark patterns of the cosmos, they actually effect the operations of such patterns in the world. Sima Qian does not exaggerate when he states that the particular sounds of the pitch-standards serve as the foundation of all things.

Having found a source for understanding audible, acoustic sound in relationship to the cosmos in Sima Qian's "Treatise on the Pitch-standards," we can now turn to the "Treatise on the Pitch-standards and Calendar" of the *Han shu* to ascertain the extent to which this relationship became a primary one—at least in relation to the imperial court—during Han times.

In that text, the author first establishes the natural origins of the twelve pitch-standards in the cosmos. This justifies their importance as elements of the cosmos:

黃帝使泠綸，自大夏之西，昆侖之陰，取竹之解谷生，其竅厚均者，斷兩節間而吹之，以為黃鐘之宮。制十二箭以聽鳳之鳴，其雄鳴為六，雌鳴亦六，比黃鐘之宮，而皆可以生之，是為律本。至治之世，天地之氣合以生風；天地之風氣正，十二律定。

The Yellow Emperor ordered Ling Lun to go from the shady side of Mount Kunlun, West of the Great Xia, to pick a piece of bamboo growing in Jie Valley that had an inner hollow of even thickness throughout. The [Yellow Emperor] cut off the part between two nodes and blew through it to produce the *gong* sound of the Yellow Bell. [He then] bored twelve holes based on the singing of the phoenix. There were six male birdcalls and also six female birdcalls. All the pitch-standards can be produced in relationship to the Yellow Bell, as this latter is the foundation of the pitch-standards. In eras of social order, the *qi* of Heaven and Earth joins together to produce wind. When the wind of Heaven and Earth is regular, the twelve pitch-standards are established.[77]

Here we find a two-part myth of origin for the twelve pitch-standards. The proximate origin for the Yellow Emperor's discovery is in the calls of the male and female phoenixes. But the ultimate origin of both the calls of the phoenix and human pitch-standards lies in the regulated *qi* of the cosmos (specifically, "Heaven and Earth")—in the form of "winds" (*feng* 風). One need only mention the *Book of Odes* sections referred to as the "Winds of the States" (*guo feng* 國風) to understand how the author has linked up the musical meaning of the term "*feng*" to its more literal meaning as a natural function of the cosmos.[78] Since the pitch-standards arise from the winds of cosmic order by way of the calls of the phoenix, their sounds echo the patterns of interaction between Heaven and Earth.

The sound of the Yellow Bell especially emerges as the root of all pitch-standards, which constitute the key elements of cosmic regularity. We see how this is so in the opening section of the "Treatise on the Pitch-standards and Calendar," which proclaims the importance of perfecting numbers, harmonizing sounds, and standardizing weights, measures, and volumes in bringing order to the world. Not surprisingly, in all of these efforts, the Yellow Bell serves as the ultimate standard of reference. For example, when perfecting numbers, an ambiguous phrase that seems to refer to the calculation of numbers of cosmic importance, the root of all such mathematical computation "arises from the number of the Yellow Bell," which is set at nine.[79] The proper length of a bamboo flute tuned to the Yellow Bell mode is nine *cun* (寸), which can be ascertained by measuring out ninety average grains of black, sticky rice.[80] The length of the Yellow Bell divided by ninety equals a standardized length of grain, or one *fen* (分). Ten *fen* equals a *cun*, and hence, nine *cun* equals ninety *fen*.[81] Thus, the standard tuning for the Yellow Bell mode derives from the length of its pitch-pipe—at nine *cun*—determined by the measuring out of ninety average-sized grains of black rice. This length provides a reference point for standardizing units of length according to ninety equal allotments of *fen*, from which *cun* can be derived (a factor of ten times one *fen*). Intriguingly, the same logic concerning the primacy of the Yellow Bell pitch-pipe as a reference point for lengths applies to procedures for standardizing volumes and weights as well.[82]

As mentioned in the passage above, the Yellow Bell—the "sweet spot" of the cosmos—engenders other pitch-standards useful in bringing harmony to the world. Consider the following passage on what I label "calendrical harmonics," which explains each pitch-standard not only according to a set of linguistic associations but also according to its role in cosmic development and seasonal cycles:

大呂：呂，旅也，言陰大，旅助黃鐘（宮）〔宣〕氣而牙物也。位於丑，在十二月。太族：族，奏也，言陽氣大，奏地而達物也。位於寅，在正月。夾鐘，言陰夾助太族宣四方之氣而出種物也。位於卯，在二月。

The *"lü* 呂*"* of the "Dalü" refers to travel [*lü* 旅].[83] It states that when the [phase of] Yin is great, it travels to assist the Yellow Bell, and emanates *qi* to stimulate the [growth of] things.[84] Its position is *chou* 丑 (the second of twelve Earthly Branches), at the [location on the horizon corresponding to] the twelfth month.[85] The *"cou* 族*"* of "Taicou" refers to strumming [*zou* 奏].[86] This states that when the phase of Yang *qi* is great, it strums the earth and makes things develop. Its position is *yin* 寅 (the third of twelve Earthly Branches), at the [location on the horizon corresponding to] the first month. The "Jiazhong" states that the Yin enfolds [*jia* 夾] the Taicou to assist in emanating the *qi* of the Four Directions. And so it reaches the diverse kinds of things. Its position is *mao* 卯 (the fourth of twelve Earthly Branches), at the [location on the horizon corresponding to] the second month.[87]

Here, various pitch-standards assist the Yellow Bell or otherwise act upon its fundamental *qi* so as to nourish and help develop the diverse things in the cosmos. By assuming in turn their ascendant position during the annual cycle and fulfilling their functions by manipulating *qi* in some way (by "strumming," "clasping," etc.), these pitch-standards each help further the development of life.[88] Yet they do so according to a set hierarchy of importance, and the Yellow Bell takes precedence over them all as the beginning of the sequence and "pitch-standard of original *qi* 元氣律者."[89] Moreover, since the sounds of the pitch-standards act as key agents in fulfilling life cycles and helping develop the seasons, the sage ruler who possesses the proper knowledge of how to use these sounds is able to exert enlightened, priestly control over the patterns of the cosmos.[90]

Such passages provide a solid testament to the power of pitch-standards in affecting the order of the cosmos. As intrinsic elements of cosmic harmony, the sounds of the pitch-standards were considered to be integral to the fulfillment of idealized, cosmic functions associated with the natural cycle of the seasons. Played at the proper times and overseen by the emperor himself or his religious surrogates, these sacrosanct sounds could serve a critical role in political and religious control. They offered emperors a means of keeping the entire natural and human worlds in alignment with each other, not of sanctifying and legitimizing the imperial Han state.

In both the "Treatise on Pitch-standards" and the "Treatise on the Pitch-standards and Calendar," musical sound—understood in terms of pitch-standards—takes on a key role in cosmic functionality. Another context in which pitch-standards serve a crucial function in relationship to cosmic order can be found in the ancient practice of "watching the ethers."[91] In an article discussing this practice, based on a later essay in the *Later Han Shu* "Treatise on Pitch-standards," Derk Bodde shows how the pitch-pipes were cut and used not just to establish the basis for the twelve-tone pitch-standards, but also to give people a basis for observing the ethers of the cosmos (*hou qi* 侯氣).[92] The practice involved constructing a roofed chamber of three walls in which the twelve pitch-pipes were buried directly into the earth in an arrangement that accorded with their months and compass directions. The open ends of each pitch-pipe were filled with fine reed ashes. Each month, as the *yin* or *yang qi* rose through the relevant pipe, the ritualists could see ashes floating from that pipe only.[93]

From this practice and its many variations described by Bodde, we can see how sound was fundamentally connected to cosmic processes. Han cosmologists used the pitch-pipes to detect the inaudible sounds of Heaven and Earth. As Bodde notes, "Though the pipes are never said to emit any sound when this happens, the idea of the ethers 'blowing' into them and thereby expelling their ashes is no doubt based on the analogy of the human breath (also known as *ch'i*) that passes through them when they are musically sounded."[94] Though the idea that *qi* produces sound was probably age-old, the notion that regulated *qi* of the cosmos could make itself manifest through the inaudible "sounds" they produced in the pitch-pipes, and that such sounds represented the fundamental harmonies or disharmonies of the cosmos, was not.[95] The practice of "watching the ethers," therefore, gives us another indication that by Han times, people were thinking of the *qi* of sound in terms of cosmic processes.

In the example of "watching the ethers," sound does not seem to act as an agent in cosmic processes in the same way as it did in the examples from *Shi ji* and *Han shu*. Rather, mediated only by the sacred, natural pitch-pipes, it reveals what is happening in the cosmos. This appears to be more in keeping with the divinatory role of sound found in military divination practices, likely dating at the latest to Warring States times.[96] The ritual specialists who watched for the ash to move might be compared to physicians whose charge was to diagnose not the *qi* of the somatic microcosm but that of the macrocosm.[97] Since the Han court sponsored such practices, it is clear that rulers used this method as a diagnostic for their rule and to harmonize their actions with cosmic patterns and designs.

The case of watching the ethers also provides an intriguing description of cosmic sound—one that we have not hitherto encountered. Cosmic sound is considered to be inaudible yet visible. Unlike the "soundless sound" of the Dao to be described in chapter five, this type of cosmic sound takes on a specific form: that of soundless *qi*. This is perhaps because the breath of Earth itself, not human breath, produces it, and it arises from *qi*, not a formless Dao.

In the case of watching the ethers, Han emperors and ritual specialists understood sound in material terms and embraced a cosmological perspective delineating a science of *qi*. Watching the ethers was an imperial practice in which soundless but visible sound was taken to represent a ruler's cosmic "report card." It validated policy and foretold outcomes. Sound manifested itself materially as *qi* that indicated how well the ruler harmonized with the natural patterns of the cosmos. Thus, it was a ritual means to an end, not a spiritual ideal in its own right. Clearly, Han imperial practitioners were thinking about religious power in terms of their success at creating standardized procedures for accumulating, measuring, and reading material data from their natural environment. Thus, their religiosity was perceived in quite material ways, as the cosmos was thought to function not so much as an inscrutable entity as a system of intelligible patterns.[98]

CONCLUSION

Before imperial times, sound was not a power in the cosmos. Indeed, an analysis of the values assigned to sound suggests that, though it was indeed important in communicating with cosmic spirits and ancestors, and though it may have been linked to cosmic *qi* from early on, it did not affect the operations of the cosmos itself. By the late Warring States and

Han periods, however, authors placed a much greater emphasis on the link (already existing in certain circles) between sound and the workings of the cosmos. They built on a known link between sound and cosmic *qi* to speak of the former in terms of a newfound power over or efficacy in cosmic operations. This development is important because it points to a fundamental religious transformation that culminated in the third and second centuries BCE. We apprehend such a vital transformation through the writings of intellectuals who increasingly described the cosmos as a natural, regulated system of causal resonances. For them, sound represented an integral part of cosmic functioning precisely because of its close relationship to *qi*.[99]

We might at this point ask ourselves the following questions: Why in certain situations was sound, of all possible things, man's primary point of access to the cosmos? Why, especially in the discussions targeted at the early imperial court, did sound become one of the most fundamental indicators of and agents in cosmic operations? And why did the Yellow Bell come to hold a special power over and above the rest? These are not easy questions, and there is not much in the record that will answer them explicitly for us. A few musings, however, provide some insight.

First, let us consider the issue of why sound became such an important means to cosmic insights. Sound had long been related to winds and *qi*. Perhaps this is because *qi*—as wind, breath, or ethers—was thought to create acoustical harmonies. Although today we understand that wind or air can carry sound waves, it is perhaps not too far-fetched to think that the early Chinese thought of sound as just another manifestation of the movements of wind, air, and breath. Indeed, to the early Chinese, *qi* and sound may have been considered one and the same entity, or at least genetically linked in some way. This interpretation suggests that the link between sound and cosmos would have been as ancient as the concept of *qi*.

During the period under scrutiny, *qi* became a key component and catalyst for all cosmic transformations and operations. It especially rose to prominence during the late Warring States period as cosmologies of resonant correspondences and a more systematic understanding of the cosmos dominated court and intellectual circles. Since *qi* emerged clearly in early China as an underlying aspect of cosmic operations, it was but a short, logical step to include sound, as related to *qi*, in one's picture of the cosmos and its patterns.

The concept of *qi* as the breath of the cosmos also lends itself well to a metaphorical or transcendent understanding of sound as the voice of nature, congruent with references found in the *Taiyi sheng shui*, *Zhuangzi*, and *Laozi*, which we examine in greater detail in chapter five.[100] In all of these texts, the sonic, "cosmic *qi*" of the Dao is not audible or aural— indeed, it had no form, let alone that of *qi*. Yet *qi* and sound are surely implied through the image of something that blows through the pipe hollows of the world, lending spiritual vitality to it. Similarly, the practice of "watching the ethers" makes use of the metaphor of sound as the breath of the cosmos. Ritual specialists proceeded with their interpretations of the movements of such *qi*—traceable through visible means—using pitchpipes and ashes.

This brings us to the relationship between sound and wind. Mark Lewis remarks on this relationship by linking the phoenix to both wind and music: "The written character for its name was originally identical with that for 'wind,' and it was in fact an embodiment of the wind, dwelling in the wind-caves and following the cycle of the wind.[101] Moreover, the tones of the pitch-pipes were copied from the song of the phoenix, and several musical instruments were supposedly replicas of its body or wings. So this embodiment of wind was also the prototype of music."[102] While the idea that the tones of the pitch-pipes derived from the songs of the phoenix appears to be a later development that has more to do with myth than reality, Lewis is right to point out the ideological linkages of both music and the phoenix to wind, especially as it was related to *qi*.[103] Since in the later Warring States period concepts of *qi* and cosmological theories of yin and yang began to take precedence over more ancient ways of viewing the cosmos, it makes sense that thinkers should try to explain the existence of sound—and hence, music—in terms of wind and *qi*.[104]

Another explanation for why sound became so crucial to the cosmology of the early imperial period lies in the association between sound and an individual's authentic emotion or inner reality. The notion that sound could convey authentic human emotions or dispositions—a notion we will explore in more detail in chapter four—might have easily been transposed onto the cosmic realm to imply the authenticity of cosmic dispositions, or the true quality of its operations. Also, the very science of cosmic resonance that came to dominate later Warring States and early imperial texts is reminiscent of musical contexts. The fundamentally acoustic metaphor of cosmic resonance points naturally to sound as a mechanism for cosmic functionality. Sound was considered a primary component of the cosmos quite possibly because people perceived it to lie at the root of all resonant interactions among objects.

It is very difficult to say why the Yellow Bell in particular emerged as the hinge between the cosmos and the proper standards and cycles for human flourishing. Without much more research and data on the adoption of musical theory to the principles of cosmological correlation that developed in the late Warring States and Han, one might assume that it gained importance simply because of its position as the fundament of the eleven other pitch-standards—something analogous to middle C.[105] The name, "Yellow Bell," which incorporates the standard color of the Earth and center in Five Phases resonant cosmology, might also provide insight into why it became primary, although one suspects that a linguistic explanation might point merely to a convenient, *ex post facto* justification for a name that had already been established earlier in musical contexts, without regard to its special cosmological status in early imperial times.

PART TWO

Music and the Individual

CHAPTER FOUR

Music and the Emergence of a Psychology of the Emotions

While music developed in relationship to a growing sense of the private sphere in later periods in Chinese history, discourses on music predating 200 BCE still largely regarded music in terms of public performances and larger spheres of reception. This is not to say that the early Chinese did not appreciate the value of a small, private performance or a singularly personal (solo) use of music.[1] Confucius and his disciples, after all, were well known for their abilities to pick up certain types of instruments and incorporate music ad hoc into their everyday routines and practices. The fact that most extant texts from the period more openly discuss the value of public performances does not diminish an author's interest in private as well as public forms of music. Nonetheless, regardless of the scale and purpose of any given musical performance, many authors of early China still showed interest in discussing the effects of music on the private, individual sphere. They spoke of music not just in association with rulers and states, but in relationship to individuals hoping to achieve a higher aesthetic, moral, social, and even spiritual status. In this and the chapters to follow, we change our focus from music and the state to the ways in which music—still largely discussed in terms of pubic, courtly performances—was thought to impact discrete individuals and the development of themselves and their bodies in society and the cosmos.

Of the manifold comments on music and the individual present in texts from 400–200 BCE, one type of claim, embedded in the very term for music itself, became quite fundamental in the history of Chinese aesthetics. It is the claim that music (yue; Old Chinese: *ngrawk 樂) is equivalent to joy, or happiness (le; OC: *rawk 樂).[2] As homographs that shared a phonetic root, the Old Chinese terms for music and joy had always been

89

closely linked.³ This close linguistic association no doubt influenced the way people understood the relationship between music and human emotion throughout early Chinese history. But it was not until around the early third century BCE that authors began to exaggerate this linguistic connection by asserting the equivalence of the two terms, music and joy. In so doing, authors thus exploited an implicit linguistic connection so as to highlight and enhance the relationship between music and a primary human emotion.⁴

This chapter examines how authors began to lay out a psychology of the emotions as a means of justifying their claims concerning music in emotional development, moral education, and aesthetic refinement. Their elaborations on human nature, the emotions, and *qi* shed light upon various views concerning the role of music in effecting individual moral attainment. We direct our attention primarily to discourses stemming from Ru circles, analyzing in detail how discourses on music began to embody a moral psychology and even incorporate beliefs about the body into a fledgling science of the heart-mind. We focus on Ru authors because they tend to take the most interest in the moral effects of music on the individual.

In this chapter, the term "psyche" is a hermeneutical tool, which points to a set of general phenomena involving the *xin* (心), "heart-mind." In using the term "psyche" rather than "mind," I steer us away from thinking of early Chinese views of the body according to a Cartesian duality between mind and body. This corresponds with the term's broader etymological meaning in ancient Greek times as breath, life, soul, and spirit. Yet even in Platonic times men distinguished between *psyche* and *soma* (corporeal body).⁵

In addition to referring to the physiological aspects of the *xin*, all references to the "psyche" include the emotional, motivational, and cognitive forces of the body that help constitute basic, mental activity. Chinese terms of relevance therefore include the emotions (*qing* 情), *qi* (material forces 氣), intent (*yi* 意 or *zhi* 志), and human nature (*xing* 性). One should note that the emotions are not exclusively associated with *xin* in many of the texts of this period. Therefore, when I refer to such terms as "psyche," or "psychology," I am interested in highlighting a discourse that does not always focus exclusively on *xin*.

THE RELATIONSHIP OF DE (VIRTUE) TO MUSIC

Many ancient authors explore the relationship between music and an individual's cultivation of morality. Such a relationship is epitomized in the early link between the virtue of *De* (德, often translated as "virtue," "power," or "charisma") and musical sounds, tones, and the wind. It is as though *De*, like these latter phenomena, possessed a quality that might spread freely through empty space. In the following discussion, *De* is talked about in musical terms, especially as it relates to the notion of harmony. It is also conceived of as something, like music, that has enormous transformative power over individuals, so that sages or people who possess *De* might serve as "musical instruments" of virtue in society and the cosmos at large.

Donald Munro has addressed the visual roots of *De* in Western Zhou times,[6] but only a handful of scholars have mentioned its connections with music. Jane Geaney clarifies: "The accumulation of *de* fills out the visual, and especially aural, forms."[7] Geaney cites various passages from the *Mencius* and the *Zhuangzi* in which an individual's *De* demonstrates harmony in himself and, in the case of the ruler, throughout the state.[8] That *De* is related to harmony is clear in the following passages from the *Zhuangzi* as well: *De* is cultivation that completes harmony 德者，成和之脩也，[9] and "They let their heart-minds wander amid the harmony of *De* 而遊心乎德之和."[10] Indeed, *De* here appears to be some visceral power or force that might bring all cacophonous things subtly into balance with each other, in keeping with the general use of the term "harmony" in early Chinese texts.

De is sometimes mentioned as something with physical properties in our early sources. The *Zuo zhuan* cites the *Book of Documents*, where *De* is described as fragrant and capable of bringing about the harmony of the people.[11] Even in the following passage from the *Guo yu*, *De* takes on perceptible form:

夫樂以開山川之風也，以耀德於廣遠也 . . . 夫德廣遠而有時節，是以遠服而邇不遷。」

Music is that by which the airs of the mountains and rivers are laid open and that by which *De* is made to shine far and wide . . . When *De* is spread far and wide and has timeliness and form, the distant will submit and the nearby will not waver.[12]

The author, using visual metaphors of something "shiny" to describe *De*, depicts *De* as a physical entity traveling through space and time. Thus, David Schaberg states that "song and ritual are a necessary part of the message of virtue (*De*) that the airwaves will carry."[13] From this particular example, it would appear that *De* travels through the medium of music to garner a positive response in the people of a vast kingdom.

The relationship between *De* and "airwaves" seems to correspond with other uses of *De* in the early literature. This is especially born out in the way wind might also carry moral virtue akin to *De* from one place to the next: "Therefore, of those who hear the wind of Bo Yi, the obstinate become right-minded, the weak become resolute 故聞伯夷之風者，頑

夫廉，懦夫有立志."[14] *De*, as something that can travel physically through the wind, is intricately linked to music since its tones and sounds travel as well through such a means. The phrase, "tones of *De* (*De yin* 德音)," sometimes translated separately as "virtue and tones," thus gains meaning as someone's outwardly spreading aura of moral virtue.[15] Whether that aura spreads through the medium of music or the winds, or indeed by virtue of the powers of *De* itself, depends on the context.

Another explanation of the causal influence of both *De* and music on individuals emerges with the rise of cosmologies of resonance. Such an explanation relies not so much on the physical travel of virtue or tones through the air as much as on the remote influence of correlative objects on each other through resonance. As Mark Csikszentmihalyi explains, the transformative effect of a sage's virtue on others is understood in some texts in terms of resonance, as expressed through the musical images of a vibrating jade stone that agitates the sounding of the metal bell.[16] This image of remote, correlative influence focuses on the musical notion of resonance as a mechanism for causality and a driver behind change, and does not necessarily imply direct transmission through the air. Either way, *De* is depicted similarly to music by effecting transformation upon the individuals it reaches.

Not only is the concept of *De* linked to music in terms of the manner in which it influences people; *De*, above all other moral virtues, seems to represent the virtue most often achieved through musical cultivation. In the *Book of Changes*, for example, we find the claim that the ancient kings created music in order to celebrate *De*.[17] As a result, *De* is reflected in the type of music to which a virtuous ruler listens. Here, music serves as the proper means of expressing *De*, perhaps because, as we have seen above, both music and *De* were thought to contain similar powers of influence on people's emotional and moral attitudes. This general linking of music and *De* is confirmed in the *Book of Rites*, in an anecdote in which Music Master Yi (師乙) tells disciple Zigong that the point of singing is to correct one's own self and then marshal one's *De* 夫歌者，直己而陳德也.[18] Clearly, music provides the means not just to simple moral cultivation as in the attainment of moral acts, but to the obtainment of the highest power to transform others in virtue: the obtainment of *De*.

THE EXPRESSIVE POTENTIAL OF MUSIC: MUSIC AND THE EMOTIONS IN THE *ODES*

It would not be possible to analyze music and individual emotional expression in early China without reference to the Odes, or the ritualized musical performances that both infused public occasions with a sense of refined culture and inspired Ru and others alike to plumb their lyrics for moral meaning. Most scholars agree that the Odes in early China represent a complex matrix of music and poetry in a ritualized, performative context, and not the textual canon of poems that developed later, during the Han period.[19] I distinguish the musical Odes from the *Odes* as a canonical text by referring to the former in non-italicized form and the latter as the *Odes* (italicized) or *Shi jing*, meaning *Canon of Odes*. As a musical genre itself, it would seem superfluous for the Odes to extol music and its benefits to the individual. Yet every now and then we find an Ode that self-references itself and the reason for its existence as part of a musical form. It is during these moments of authorial self-consciousness that we find interesting clues to how its authors/lyricists thought of the relationship between music and the emotions, or more precisely, between the Odes and individual expression.

Since so little is verifiably known about the composition and purposes of the Odes in their original contexts, it is not advisable to take the explicit purpose of an Ode at face value as a testament to some elusive, "authentic" reason behind its existence. However, the fact that these lyrics would have been received by a public that understood their values makes the lyrics worth consideration—at the very least as a testament to a "culture of expression" embraced by the Odes.[20] As Martin Kern puts it, the Odes at times "describe their own ritual contexts, often in meticulous detail."[21] They do this not only through their form, style, and linguistic aspects, but also through narratorial self-proclamations about their composition. We might therefore examine the stated purposes of particular Odes so as to gain a sense of what some early Chinese thought were worth singing aloud and making public—if not to the world at large, then at least to an elite group of cultured men at court.

While the notion of self-cultivation is more implicit in a text like the *Odes* than in a pedagogical handbook like the *Analects*, the medium of lyric poetry lends itself perhaps better than moralistic prose to vivid descriptions of the moral gentleman. In the lyrics of the Odes, the relationship between music and the gentleman appears to be quite simple: the gentleman sometimes expresses his innermost emotions through song. Yet this simple relationship masks the necessary relationship often posited in the text between the emotions and music, as well as the implicit importance of expressing one's emotions publicly as a means of vindicating the self. Pressed by a feeling of necessity and at risk of being misunderstood by those in his immediate environment, the gentleman in the Odes cannot but use music to express his innermost feelings to the world. This feeling of necessity is underscored in Mao 109 and 204, in which the gentleman narrator proclaims his sorrow or sadness as the immediate prompting for the creation of the song: "It is my heart's sadness that makes me chant and sing 心之憂矣，我歌且謠,"[22] and, "A gentleman made this song; that his sorrows might be known 君子作歌，維以告哀."[23]

In these self-referencing moments, the narrator insists upon the necessary, causal, and immediate connection between his emotions and his outward lyrical expression of them in song. He stresses the subject of expression or revelation, even public proclamation of his sadness, as though suppressing or hiding such an emotion would betray himself and others. Indeed, it is as though outward expression of one's sadness is supposed to somehow vindicate the sadness itself. The public proclamation of one's sorrows, in addition, suggests the fulfillment of one's duty to share the truth of one's innermost feelings. Thus, the relationship between music and the gentleman's emotions is necessary both in a causal sense ("my heart's sadness" makes me do this) and moral sense (I do this so that my "sorrows might be known").

Musical expression not only fulfills a duty to one's emotional core; it also displays and confirms one's sense of inner morality. In another *Shi jing* passage that self-references the narrator's composition of the song, we find the following sentiment: "That is why I made this song; To tell how I long to feed my mother 是用作歌，將母來諗."[24] Here, the subject of the song verbalizes his recognition that song really speaks to people, and that his moral feeling of filial devotion might be expressed through it. By formulating his intentions in terms of the rhetoric of emotional necessity mentioned above, the narrator finds an acceptable means of manifesting his righteousness and displaying his own personal cultivation. This is because filial devotion is understood and presented as a type of emotional feeling. Hence, since music relays one's inner, emotional feelings, and since one's morality might be authenticated or legitimized to others as an emotional feeling, one's morality might be adequately measured through musical expression.

The Odes of the *Shi jing* reflect a conception of music as an expression of one's innermost emotions and moral attitudes. Of special interest is the fact that narrators who self-consciously address their relationship to the composition of any given Ode view music in terms of moral necessity and public communion. More specifically, they suggest a necessary, causal relationship between their innermost personal emotions and the creation of the Ode that expresses such emotion outwardly to the world. Sometimes a physiological necessity, sometimes as a moral necessity, music (and in particular, song) is presented as the critical voice of a hidden and authentic emotional core that needs representation within the social world.

MUSICAL EXPRESSION AND
MORAL PERFECTION IN THE *ANALECTS*

In the *Analects* not only is music an important means of self-expression; it takes on the distinct pedagogical role of helping teach and train a person to be refined and gentlemanly. Music is therefore viewed as something that helps complete an individual's moral training, or self-cultivation. In this section, we examine many of the passages in the *Analects* that feature either direct comments about music or a description of music being performed or enjoyed. Our aim is to determine the specific ways in which Confucius and his disciples conceived of the role of music in moral development, as well as the ways in which the expression of emotion—and that of joy in particular—was linked to both music and morality.

The text speaks frequently about ritual music such as the Odes (in particular, the Elegantiae and Lauds) performed during sacrifices to the royal ancestors in the states of Zhou, Lu, and Song. In addition, it also features passages in which Confucius and/or his disciples sing or perform music more casually in conjunction with their daily, moral training and routines.[25] While it is unclear what the precise boundaries of the term for music, *yue*, might be in the *Analects* (i.e., whether or not it includes the more informal performances just mentioned, or whether it is restricted to official, formal ritual music sanctioned by each ducal state and the Zhou royal court), *yue* functions indisputably as a means by which one unifies and integrates one's moral knowledge. For example, in *Analects* 8.8, music surpasses both ritual and the Odes in serving as that which ultimately perfects an individual, much as icing to the cake or the last, signature flourishes added to a valuable painting.

Reinforcing this notion of music as the perfection of one's moral education is the idea, suggested in *Analects* 11.15, that the very style of one's music making indicates one's mastery of the subtleties of becoming a *junzi*, or gentleman. In this passage, Confucius expresses dismay that disciple Zilu plays his grand zither (*se* 瑟) on the premises of his school.[26] He asks: "Why is Zilu playing his grand zither (in such a manner?) in my school 由 之瑟奚為於丘之門?"[27] While there are many possible interpretations for Confucius' question, most commentators seem to agree that Zilu's performance style indicates a lack of moral cultivation. Ingrid Furniss has recently considered the issue of the importance of the *se* in Eastern Zhou and Han times, concluding that the predominance of *se* as compared to *qin* 琴 in Eastern Zhou tombs (and especially those in the Southeast) suggests that it was the string instrument of choice for many elite men and women.[28] Perhaps Zilu had breached a ritual protocol by performing such a grand instrument in the wrong place and for the wrong occasion? Regardless, the passage continues with the statement that Zilu loses the respect of the other disciples.[29] Confucius then saves Zilu from this disrespect by qualifying his judgment in the following way: "Though Zilu has ascended the Hall, he has not yet entered into the Inner Chambers 由也升堂矣，未入於室也."[30] It is possible that this spatial metaphor invoked by Confucius specifically refers to the layout of musical orchestras at an important ritual service, such as the ancestral sacrifice. According to such a metaphor, Zilu's style was perhaps good enough to satisfy the *hoi polloi* and basic imperatives of a specific ritual event, but not good enough to satisfy the more spiritual needs of the gods and inner circle, where the performance of the *se* would be more appropriate. Regardless of how one interprets the metaphor, the fact that Confucius equates either one's performance style or one's knowledge of the role of music in ritual with moral achievement is evident and marks the value placed on the musical arts as a part of ritual and in self-cultivation.

The relatively lengthy vignette in 11.26 describing Confucius' querying of four disciples on the use of their talents makes a nod to music and self-cultivation in an interesting way. It is perhaps not coincidental that the disciple Dian 點 (also known as Zengxi 曾皙), who emerges as the most morally elevated of the four, should respond to Confucius only after having completed his casual strumming of the grand zither. Aside from giving us a sense of the way music was used in more informal settings—during a casual master-disciple interaction, no less—this passage strategically implies that the one who seems to care most about simple, personal, musical expression is also the one who best understands morality and how to fulfill a moral goal. Zengxi is the most modest in his choice of goals, so that the fulfillment of it seems easy, natural, and beautiful—much like the fading out of the sound from his musical performance described in the passage. By emphasizing fulfillment and aesthetic pleasure, the passage reminds us of Confucius' remark in 8.8 about the role of music in completing or perfecting one's moral training. Zengxi's literal completion of his musical strumming symbolizes the perfection of his moral character, which is then explicitly confirmed by Confucius himself. Music clearly does not play a peripheral role in this passage; it points to the easy, natural, and aesthetically appealing perfection of one's moral person that Confucius himself held in high esteem.

Related to this connection between aesthetics and morality in the *Analects* is the notion that the proper expression of one's emotions reflects moral achievement. Indeed, one might go so far as to claim that a *junzi*'s moral discernment regarding the appropriate context for any given emotion is in part defined by his aesthetic sensibilities. To support this claim, let us examine the emotional implications of the previous passage, 11.26.

In it, Zengxi not only seeks after the joy and pleasure associated with his chosen activity of bathing and enjoying the breeze with friends and peers, but he also clearly manifests moral discernment in understanding that such emotions are appropriate for the given occasion. He further reveals moral understanding by showing how well he grasps the emotions of himself and others, insofar as he does not propose to stretch himself or others beyond what they are capable of appreciating. And lastly, Zengxi's choice of activities—to bring joy and a sense of ease to himself and a small, intimate group of others—in itself reflects an aesthetic appreciation for the fullness of emotion that such modest activities might bring. For all these reasons, Zengxi's display of emotional attunement translates into a very high level of moral awareness.[31]

In 11.26 we also find a theme common to many passages of the *Analects*: that taking joy in certain modest endeavors or activities constitutes a moral goal, reveals moral understanding, and is reflective of the moral life. Joy (*le* 樂), an emotion that Chinese writers often associated with music, is thus linked to a *junzi's* primary state of being. Indeed, the very first passage of the *Analects* speaks of a *junzi's* sentiments in response to situations that deserve to be cherished, and joy is among them.[32] And throughout the text, one finds depictions of *junzi* in a state of joyful fulfillment when engaging in certain activities—especially in music and learning—which warrant such an emotional response.[33] Such depictions lend credence to Confucius' statement: "To know it is not as good as to be fond of it, and to be fond of it is not as good as to find joy in it 知之者不如好之者，好之者不如樂之者," which not only links moral attainment and joy, but presents joy as the utmost kind of feeling one might have for an object or activity.[34] That joy is valued as an emotion appropriate for the *junzi* is further expressed in Confucius' response to the elevated music of Shun: "When the Master was in the state of Qi and heard the *shao* (music of the legendary Emperor Shun), he did not notice the taste of meat for three months. He said, 'I never imagined that music could bring one to such a state' 子在齊聞《韶》，三月不知肉味，曰：「不圖為樂之至於斯也!"[35] This statement renders clear the implicit connection between joy, moral attainment, and music in the text.

Of course, the *junzi* is not to be joyful in every situation. One sign of self-cultivation is the lack of joy in situations that demand other types of emotional response. So while joy is appropriate when a *junzi* engages in certain activities befitting him, such as learning, music-making, and enjoying the company of friends or like-minded individuals, some contexts demand another type of expression: "If on a particular day the Master had wept, then he did not sing 子於是日哭，則不歌."[36] Similarly, *Analects* 17.21 states: "The gentleman in mourning does not delight in fatty foods, does not feel joy when listening to music, and does not feel comfortable at his own home

夫君子之居喪，食旨不甘，聞樂不樂，居處不安."[37] Aside from the fact that music and music-making are linked to the emotion of joy in both of these example, we also see that the morally attained man knows how to properly feel, express, and give rise to emotions such as joy. He can evaluate each situation separately to ascertain the proper emotional response. Of utmost importance is that he can lend true feeling to his expressions, not diluting or cheapening them with other, conflicting expressions. In such a manner, he conveys sincerity and depth of emotion, which ultimately adds moral value to his character. Perhaps not surprisingly, this emphasis on sincerity and depth of emotion resonates with certain ideals for music making, explicitly described in later Ru texts.

In contrast to the *junzi*, whose aesthetic sensibilities seem to coincide with what is morally appropriate, the non-*junzi* displays a lack of both moral and aesthetic sensibility. This is evident in the use of music by various powerful families of Confucius' day. In *Analects* 3.2, for example, Confucius recites an Ode, the musical performance of which had allegedly been commissioned at a certain ritual occasion by the three aristocratic families of the state of Lu.[38] He laments that the meaning of the lyrics, which describe an august, dignified ruler, do not at all apply to the three families in question.[39] Though in this example the ostensible topic of discussion is the inappropriate usurpation of ritual prerogatives by contemporary aristocratic families, the fact that the three families failed to appreciate the basic meaning of the Ode that had been performed also signals a lack of aesthetic and moral cultivation on their parts. Their use of music, therefore, has the effect of being not only gauche and unrefined, but completely inappropriate for the circumstances. Indeed, because the *junzi*'s sense of aesthetics is in line with morality, music for him is not merely a show of empty forms, as it is for the moral pedant. This is what is meant by the following statement: "Surely when one says 'The rites, the rites,' it is not enough merely to mean presents of jade and silk. Surely when one says 'Music, music,' it is not enough merely to mean bells and drums 禮云禮云，玉帛云乎哉？樂云樂云，鍾鼓云乎哉.'"[40]

At the same time that Confucius extols music as a means or sign of higher levels of moral cultivation, he stresses the primacy of one's moral character over and above the music itself. In 3.3, the Master said, "If in being a person one is not humane (*ren*), then of what use are the rites? If in being a person one is not humane, then of what use is music人而不仁，如禮何？人而不仁，如樂何?"[41] Clearly, both music and the rites are subordinate to the actual moral fiber of a person. This does not make them negligible, but it does explicitly show that Confucius viewed such things as educational implements, taking pains not to confuse them with the actual object of cultivation: one's self and moral sense. Indeed, the point of the passage is not to diminish the value of the rites and music, which for Confucius constitute the basis for much of what is beautiful and refined (*wen* 文) about Zhou courtly heritage. Rather, it is to exploit the known value of the rites and music so as to elevate the virtue of humanity to the highest possible level. This stance is noteworthy because it makes a distinction between music as a tool for self-cultivation and one's actual level of self-cultivation. In later texts, as we will see below, the value and role of music begins to fluctuate, so that one cannot take it for granted that in a text like the *Analects* personal attainment is to be distinguished from and valued over the music itself.

MUSIC AND "BEAUTIFYING THE EMOTIONS" IN *XING ZI MING CHU*

In the *Shi jing* music is often a cultural form that gives expression to one's emotions and level of moral development. The *Analects*, we have seen, begins to move the discussion away from emotional expression towards the role of music on individual moral and psychic development. In many Warring States texts, we see this latter emphasis take off, as authors focus more exclusively on music not just as a means of expressing one's inner reality, but as a vehicle by which one might shape that reality. Indeed, authors of this era seem to have gained interest in delineating the psychology underlying "musical development"—or, self-cultivation through music—and, therefore, they began exploring the ways in which music might serve as a specific mode of education.

There are several mid-late Warring States texts that devote whole sections or chapters to the topic of music and its beneficial effects on humans. This is new to the writings of the Warring States and suggests that advocates of music felt the need to justify their existence in a manner that they had not needed to until then. It is likely that this development was a consequence of the influence of early Mohist attacks on the use of ritual music at court, which perhaps reflected a growing, general sentiment against music among officials in an increasingly competitive and centralized court environment. In any case, the specialized, musical apologetics that developed during the Warring States are exceptional sources to examine for insight into the relationship between music and the individual. To be sure, it is precisely from these writings on music that we might gain a sense of an emerging moral psychology and psychology of the emotions.

Discussions of music in certain Ru texts of the fourth through third centuries BCE helped develop moral psychologies that implicate the emotions. The psychologies that were developed in Warring States writings provide a cogent rationale for the belief that music has a moral effect on humans and lay the groundwork for many later claims that connect music and the heart-mind to the larger cosmos. A text—most likely of a Ru lineage and given the modern label, "Xing zi ming chu 性自命出" ("Human Nature Emerges from Heaven's Command"; hereafter XZMC)—provides one of the earliest phenomenological accounts of how one's emotions (qing 情) relate to human nature (xing 性) and external stimuli such as sound and music. Because this text is rather new to the textual corpus of early China, it is worth first explaining a few of the details concerning the text before launching into an analysis of is stance on music in self-cultivation.

The XZMC was discovered in 1993 at Guodian and made available to international audiences in 1998. It appears either to predate or be contemporaneous with the *Mencius*, and derives from a lineage that clearly propounded Ru ideals. In particular, the XZMC not only provides justification for and explanation of the effects of music and ritual on moral self-cultivation, it also mentions the ancient sages in relationship to their creation of the *Odes*, *Documents*, rites, and music—traditions which were later to form the bulwark of the Ru Canon.

Though the text does not have any extant, transmitted counterpart, what appears to be another version of it has been found among the ancient bamboo strips purchased recently by the Shanghai Museum.[42] This other version, called "Xing Qing Lun 性情論" (XQL, "Discourse on Human Nature and the Emotions"), is much the same as the XZMC in its words and textual order, though it deviates slightly in terms of the graphical forms and expressions it uses. The XQL and XZMC each have a few unique sentence chains. Though such differences could in some cases point to the existence of missing strips in both versions, some of the divergent sentence chains occur in the middle of a section that is otherwise completely the same in both versions, and, significantly, they occur where there is no evidence of textual rupture.

The *Shanghai bowuguan* also provides a slightly different textual arrangement than that given by the compilers of the Guodian strips. This divergence in textual arrangement could represent the mistakes of the original compilers and editors of the Guodian strips, who faced enormous challenges in their initial ordering of the strips. Or it may simply attest to the way in which texts were compiled and transmitted in the Warring States—an era before the production of fixed texts and canons.

Apart from these few differences, the two texts are so similar that editors of *Shanghai bowuguan* felt justified in filling in entire swaths of text that was missing from the XQL with what they believed were the same parts from the XZMC. Indeed, it appears that missing portions of the XZMC can be replaced with text from XQL with a high degree of confidence. For example, the phrase, "The sounds of bronze and stone . . . (five missing blanks) 金石之有聲" in XZMC can be supplemented with text from the same section in XQL to read, "As for the sounds of bronze and stone, [they] will not ring if not struck 金石之有聲也弗扣不鳴."[43] Such interchangeability strongly suggests that we really are talking about the same text, and that we should regard these writings as two versions of the same text, just as we refer to the Mawangdui, Heshanggong, or Guodian versions of the *Laozi*.[44]

One of the most striking aspects of the XZMC is its commentary on human nature. Unlike Mencius, who grants human nature a special role in helping to determine the growth of our moral selves, the author of XZMC gives great power to external things and forces in shaping and, ultimately, giving direction to our unfixed wills (*zhi* 志) and natural endowments: "Although all humans possess human nature, the heart-mind does not possess a fixed (regulated) will 凡人雖有性心定（正）志."[45] This provocative first sentence concedes to a shared, universal nature among humans, but it immediately qualifies the power of such a nature to determine the courses of our lives. Such a quick qualification of human nature shares an affinity with the only direct claim concerning human nature provided in the *Analects*; namely, that we are all similar in nature but different through practice (*xi* 習).[46] However, the fact that the XZMC explains human difference not immediately in terms of practice, as in the *Analects*, but in terms of the fundamental indeterminacy of the heart-mind and its related function, the will (*zhi* 志), suggests that XZMC is much more psychological in its orientation. Indeed, in the XZMC, unlike anywhere in the *Analects* or even any extant, reputedly pre-Mencian text besides the "Nei Ye," we find an intricate discussion of the workings of the psyche and its relationships to the external world—in particular, to music.[47]

In the opening statements of the text, the author of XZMC shows that the direction of our wills is contingent upon "external things," "pleasures," and "practices." Moreover, the natural emotions 情 (which "stem from human nature") are not expressed without "external things grabbing hold of them 物取之."[48] Certainly, this author paints a very passive picture of human nature, one that suggests a blank slate.[49] However, while he stresses the significance of environment, he also takes pains to acknowledge and address the basic characteristics of human nature as well as the particular ways the environment may interact with and draw out these aspects. This suggests not a blank slate but an apparatus that is endowed with fixed but changeable characteristics that regulate how the environment may act with and upon it.

Due to its potential for defined change, human nature can be guided according to what the author refers to as the human Dao (*ren dao* 人道).

This Dao is not merely a goal of attainment; it is a path and medium that guides our personal endowments toward attainment. Thinking of Dao in this way, the author underscores the natural connections of Dao to the human emotions:

性自命出，命自天降，道始於情，情生於性，始者近情，終者近義.

Human nature emerges from Decree; Decree is sent down from Heaven. The Dao begins with emotions; emotions are born of human nature. He who is beginning (on the Dao) is near to the emotions; he who is ending (on the Dao) is near to rightness.[50]

This passage establishes an undeniable connection between Dao and emotions, which stem from human nature and, ultimately, Heaven.[51] According to this translation, Dao is not a natural product of emotions, and it does not appear to be an innate part of the human endowment, or human nature. It is the path whereby one moves from a state in which human nature and the emotions manifest themselves according to their original characteristics to a state in which they manifest themselves according to the tenets of rightness. In other words, the Dao transforms the raw endowments of a person into a developed capacity for moral judgment and behavior.

The author's phrasing of the progress of Dao from the emotions (i.e., that which is endowed in human nature) to rightness is critical. It shows that the process of the Dao is continuous—that there is a seamless line between human nature and rightness. This suggests wholesome, organic change that does not violate human nature, as Mencius would say.[52] The text confirms that the emotions are connected to the Dao in a seamless fashion by intimating that compliance with the Dao consists not in ridding oneself of emotions but in expressing them properly: "If you [act] by using emotions, then though you transgress, there is no dislike. If you do not [act] by using emotions, then though something is difficult, it will not be valued. If you possess your emotions, then even though you have not yet acted, the people present will believe you. 苟以其情，雖過不惡，不以其情，雖難不貴，苟有其情，雖未之為，斯人信之矣."[53] Clearly, the author does not intend for the emotions to disappear or lose their fundamental characteristics when one complies with Dao. The Dao thus does not seem to alter one's human nature radically; it works to extend and enhance what already exists within. As it guides human nature in the proper, moral direction, it accepts what is already there, changing it with each progressive step.

For the author of XZMC, the "human Dao" is the most important means to self-cultivation. This particular Dao functions through teachings (jiao 教), of which music plays an integral part:[54]

而學或使之也，凡物亡不異也者，剛之桓，剛取之也，柔之約，柔取之也，
四海之內，其性一也，其用心各異，教使然也.

[Y]et learning is that which drives it. Of the many things [of the world],
there is none that is not different. A bowl has the quality of being hard
because hardness grabs hold of it. A rope has the quality of being soft
because softness grabs hold of it.[55] Within the four seas, nature is the
same. That each uses its heart-mind differently is because upbringing
makes it so.[56]

This last statement suggests that *jiao*, in its broadest sense, encompasses
the various influences and even qualities of the external world that grab
hold of one's nature and shape it accordingly. This is because *jiao* is responsible not just for the development of a moral sense but for causing differentiation in the very application of our flexible, indeterminate heart-minds.
This broad definition of *jiao* as "upbringing" or "environmental influence"
is also strongly suggested in a linguistic analysis by the Han lexicographer,
Xu Shen, and later commentators to his dictionary.[57]

It is precisely in this more general context that the author of XZMC
draws a relationship between human emotions, the heart-mind, and sounds.
He develops a psychology of the emotions, which posits that sounds are
powerful forms of *jiao*, or environmental influences, on our emotional and
intellectual constitution:

凡聲其出於情也，信，然後其入拔人心也，厚，聞笑生則鮮如也，斯喜，聞
歌謠則舀如也，斯奮，聽琴瑟之聲則悸如也，斯嘆.

It is generally the case that sounds, when they exit sincerely via the emotions, they enter and take profound hold of one's heart-mind. When you
hear sounds of laughter, you will feel freshness. This is happiness. When
you hear singing and chanting, you will feel jovial. This is excitement.[58]
When you listen to the sounds of the lute and zither, you will feel stirred.
This is distress.[59]

Here, sounds that carry certain evocative potential seize upon innate elements of the human psyche—both the heart-mind and the emotions deriving from human nature—so as to elicit certain affective responses. One
possible interpretation of this process is that emotional states are physically
transmitted in the sound itself, and are not merely responses to it.[60]

The scenario above demonstrates that sound is transmitted from one
human to the next so as to grab hold of the recipient's heart-mind, subsequently triggering the expression of a certain emotion from within.[61]

Clearly, the author of XZMC believes that certain emotions are characteristically present in one's human nature. This means that the process described in XZMC cannot simply be one in which external forces directly deposit content and agency into a blank slate. For the author of XZMC, the human body necessarily possesses characteristic responses to external forces. The process of sound transmission therefore involves a simple mechanics of outside influence and inside emotional response.

As just seen, the author of XZMC connects sound to emotions by outlining a mechanics of sound transmission and emotional response. But how does he explain the relationship between the emotions and music? The implicit distinction between *jiao* as environmental influences and *jiao* as the moral teachings of the sages provides critical clues to this relationship. In his discussion of the latter type of *jiao*, the author of XZMC specifies that there is only one kind of Dao that humans can follow.[62] This Dao appears to be grounded in the teachings (*jiao*) of the sages, which is characterized by a specific menu of tradition, that of 1) the Odes (Poetry/ Songs), 2) the *History* (*Documents*), 3) ritual, and 4) music.[63] Interestingly, the author clarifies that "when they [these aspects of teachings and tradition] first emerged, they were all produced (given birth) by humans 其始 出皆生於人."[64] The music of the sages, then, unlike other sounds of the universe, is man-made. As a man-made creation, it possesses its roots in the cosmically endowed resources of humans—in particular, the sage's heart-mind.[65] Such a stance on music is different from some later Warring States and early imperial stances, previously discussed, which take music to be an inherent creation of the cosmos, with roots in the very operations of the cosmos.[66]

The XZMC also shows how music, as a product of sagely heart-minds, helps individuals express their emotions properly: "He who knows emotions is able to express them; he who knows morality is able to internalize it 知情者能出之，知義者能入之"[67] One will recall that the path of Dao starts with the individual in the raw and proceeds to transform those raw characteristics and potentials into moral characteristics with emotional value. Music thus serves a means of guiding these raw characteristics and potentials effectively along the human Way:

笑喜之薄澤也，樂喜之深澤也，觀賚武則齊如也，斯作，觀韶夏則勉如也，
斯儉，養思而動心蔑如也.

Laughter is the spreading of happiness; joy is the deepening of happiness (XZMC: Laughter is the X of the rites; music is the deepening of the rites)[68] . . . When you watch the Lai and Wu dances, you will feel confrontational.[69] This is being incited. When you watch the Shao and

Xia dances you will feel focused. This is frugality (?). [Music] nourishes one's thinking and moves the heart-mind so that you feel dignified (?).[70]

Music, which in the text encompasses both aural and visual aspects of performance, makes use of an individual's endowed processes by eliciting certain important affective responses. The experience of these responses in the correct measure helps one arrive at moral goals or, the Dao that is "near to rightness."[71]

In this passage, the author also shows that various types of music, such as the ancient *Lai, Wu, Shao,* and *Xia* dance performances, help one become aware of morality because such music is expressive of moral qualities.[72] But what does this mean? The author continues to state that this particular music "resides at length in restraint;[73] carefully reverts back to goodness and repeats itself from the beginning; and is smoothly expressed and internalized. These are its virtues 其居次舊，其反善復始也，慎，其出入也，順，司其德也."[74] Taken metaphorically, such statements liken music to a cultivated gentleman. A more literal, phenomenological reading of this passage, however, suggests that this music possesses qualities that the psyche perceives to be moral.[75]

In summary, how does music transmit moral knowledge? Let us consider the following made-up example of what the text essentially states (and we have just analyzed) in more detail: such musical performances as the *Shao* and *Xia* convey the "heart-mind" (intentions, aims, attitudes) lying behind the acts of the sage leaders, Shun and Yü, as they ruled in antiquity. This heart-mind seizes upon the listener, who can—via this music—perceive most directly of the austerity of such leadership. A feeling of austerity arises in the listener and interacts with his or her natural emotions, giving him or her a sense of how this emotion, among other related emotions, might properly be expressed. It also provides the listener with a means of judging, understanding, and internalizing the good heart-mind of the sages. In other words, music grabs hold of an individual's psyche (emotions and heart-mind), while the psyche serves as a passive, yet characteristic receptor of its expressive and informative content.

The author of XZMC does not merely recommend music as a viable means to moral cultivation. Music, he claims, holds paramount importance over other forms of teachings, for it is the quickest means of "seeking one's heart-mind 求其心."[76] This particular psychological goal, which appears in the *Mencius* as well, suggests that individuals uncover true aspects of the heart-mind (intentions, motivations, and aims) that underlie the surface actions and dispositions of others or themselves.[77] It can be compared with Confucius' distinction in the *Analects* between the simple ritual action, devoid of the proper attitude or feeling, and ritual action performed with full sincerity or reverence.[78] Similarly, it is reminiscent of a later musical expression that reveals the authentic emotional connection between two people: *zhi yin zhe* 知音者 , or "bosom buddy," "knower of [one's] tones"), mentioned in chapter three.

By discussing music in terms of its unadulterated impact on human emotions and morality, the author of XZMC establishes the primacy of music as a vehicle for self-cultivation. He outlines a psychology of influence that explains why music is both effective and efficient in moral transformation of the human body. Though the author does not equate proper music with the workings of the natural cosmos, his explanations of its origins in the heart-mind of the sage and his belief in the close affinity between music and the emotions suggest that music interacts naturally and organically with the human psyche. The author's attempt to link music and the cosmic, or Heavenly endowed aspects of our psyche constitutes an initial step in the direction of viewing music as an integral component of the cosmos.

The idea that knowledge, ideas, and intents of a variety of sorts might be transmitted emotionally through musical performance continues well into later times. An anecdote written after the fall of the Han elucidates not the transmission of moral knowledge, but knowledge of an entire event through music. In this example, the great scholar Cai Yong heard the sound of the *qin* being played by a musician behind a screen in the home of his host. In the music, Cai traced the notion of killing and immediately felt uneasy and wished to leave. When his host interrogated the musician, the latter explained that just as he was performing, a mantis devoured a cicada as its prey. Thus, the *qin* player had unwittingly transferred knowledge of this event through his music.[79]

In this example, though Cai Yong ostensibly hears musical notes, his sagacity allows him to detect all the elements enveloped through such sound, including even the unintentional, emotional reaction of a *qin* player to the cicada's death, along with knowledge of the entire tragic event. Though this might seem like a form of prognostication, it is far from it. Such an act represents the power of music to impart knowledge—and not just sentiments—of all sorts, as well as the acute attunement of the sage to the full expressive potential of music.

XUNZI ON MUSIC AND EMBODIED EMOTIONAL DEVELOPMENT

We have examined Xunzi's "Discourse on Music" in chapter two in relationship to its advocacy of a form of cultural unification and imperialism. But we have not yet examined certain aspects of that text that relate more exclusively to the individual's emotional and psychological response to music.

Like many musical apologetics of the day, Xunzi's "Discourse" also argues for the inevitable influence of sounds and music over human emotions. And like the author of XZMC, Xunzi is able to articulate his claims about music in terms of a rather detailed psychology of influence. But he differs from the author of XZMC in an important way. Below, we briefly consider two citations that shed light upon Xunzi's psychological or—perhaps a more apt description—his psycho-physiological rationale underlying his claim that music plays an important role in the development of the moral body.

Like the author of XZMC, Xunzi agrees that the effect of music on human beings is both profound and quick. One sees this clearly in the following renowned phrase: "Musical sounds enter into people deeply and transform people quickly 夫聲樂之入人也深，其化人也速."[80] The relationship between music and the emotions is also necessary: "Thus Music is the great evening of all under Heaven; it is the ordering of centrality and harmony; and it is that which human emotions simply cannot avoid 故樂者天下之大齊也，中和之紀也，人情之所必不免也."[81]

In this passage emotions "simply cannot avoid" music because they lie in a necessarily causal relationship to it, as well as to the centrality and harmony that it produces. Does this mean that, like the narratorial voices in the Odes, human emotions are necessarily expressed through music, or that an individual's emotions are inevitably elicited, shaped, and transformed upon their encounters with proper music? While the causal order is not clearly specified in this passage, judging from the text as a whole, one might say that Xunzi's focus is not so much on the fact of one's emotional expression as it is on the reality of one's emotional response in the cultivation of individual morality. Xunzi thus shares the same core concerns as the author of XZMC in speaking about the benefits of music on emotional development, and not strictly about the benefits of music as a means of emotional release.

For Xunzi, music works its wonders on individuals because the human body has a naturally strong reaction to sound. While for him sounds might be divided into many sorts, there are but two predominant, human responses to any given sound: those that lead to order and those that lead to chaos. In either case, sounds naturally induce a powerful reaction from individuals, as seen in the following step-by-step account of his psychology of musical influence:

凡姦聲感人而逆氣應之，逆氣成象而亂生焉；正聲感人而順氣應之，順氣成象而治生焉。唱和有應，善惡相象，故君子慎其所去就也.

In general, when licentious sounds stimulate a person, a contrary material energy [from within] responds to them. When this contrary material energy takes outward form, disorder is produced therein. When proper sounds stimulate a person, an agreeable material energy [from within] responds to them. When this agreeable material energy takes outward form, order is produced therein. Shouts and harmonies each have their own responses, and good and bad are each in turn given outward forms— thus the nobleman is cautious in what he approaches or leaves behind.[82]

Unlike in the XZMC, where the author sees sound as something that takes hold of the heart-mind so as to effect certain emotions, Xunzi does not explicitly refer to "heart-mind" in his explanation, choosing instead to focus more directly on material energy (qi), a notion of physiological as well as psychological relevance. His discussion of the psychology of influence intriguingly refers to the technical phrase "stimulus-response" (gan ying 感應), which later becomes a dominant concept for explaining the mechanics of influence that occurs between the human body and events in the cosmos.[83] By focusing on the movement of material energy, Xunzi's description of the interaction between sound and sentiment is even more explicitly embodied than that found in XZMC.[84]

In the passage above, emotional responses to music can be expressed, via material energy, through physical cues that help bring about a certain degree of social order. By stressing the physical accommodations of the body to sound, this type of formulation appears to heighten the sense of immediacy and inevitability with which the transaction between sound and body takes place. Music is no longer just the most effective tool for attaining a certain state of heart-mind: it is a powerfully influential, manipulative, and fool-proof device for eliciting certain uncontrolled responses from the entire body, including the heart-mind. Social order is the result of proper music because the latter necessarily elicits an individual's appropriate physical responses, such as a reverent attitude and moral behavior, to his or her environment.

CONCLUSION

The relationship between music and an individual's emotional and moral core is outlined in a variety of ways in texts dating before 200 BCE. In this chapter, we first discussed the close relationship between the paramount moral virtue, De, and music, especially in terms of how each is described as having the ability to spread physically outward to "infect" or influence all individuals with whom it has contact. We then examined four texts on the topic of music and self-cultivation: the Shi jing, Analects, XZMC, and Xunzi's "Discourse on Music." In every one of these texts, authors connected music to the emotions, often speaking of such a connection in terms of necessity and a causal relationship. Some texts went further than others to explicitly link certain forms of emotional feeling with moral feeling, so that cultivating one's emotions became part and parcel of the process of moral cultivation and gentlemanly refinement. It is from this context of musical discourse *cum* discourse on moral self-cultivation that a psychology of the emotions emerged in Chinese discursive thought. Such a psychology outlined the specific manner in which music affects an individual's emotional, moral, and physiological constitution.

With the *Shi jing* we encountered a pre-Warring States world in which music was primarily an expressive medium that served many ritualistic, communal, and individual functions. With respect to individual expression, we saw that some narrators self-consciously addressed their own relationship to song by couching such a relationship in terms of the power of their emotional or moral feeling. They believed that such feeling necessitated expression in the musical form of an Ode, and thus spoke of their relationship to music in terms of an inevitable, emotional (and, at times, moral) response. Through this emphasis on the emotional necessity of music, such narrators stressed the importance of music as a form of human release, expression, and communication. As such, they concerned themselves less with the notion that music could in turn benefit and refine one's emotional core, as became normative discourse for later, Warring States authors, and more with the importance of music in providing a natural yet regulated form of emotional expression.

In the *Analects* music is not only an exquisite expression and indicator of one's emotional and moral feeling; it also serves as an important medium or tool for self-cultivation. Though the authors of the passages in the *Analects* remain terse with respect to the process of moral cultivation through music, they nonetheless stress the idea that both music and the rites form a dyadic pair that is integral to one's proper cultivation of moral attitudes and virtues. Intriguingly, music seems to take on a special position above even the rites, insofar as it is deemed necessary for the perfection or fulfillment of one's character and moral development. It seems clear that the idea music stood at the pinnacle of the moral arts was beginning to be pervasive in some Ru circles.

Certain Warring States treatises that expound the merits of music in relationship to moral psychology demonstrate the triumphant position of music in self-cultivation. The XZMC and Xunzi's "Discourse on Music" each put forth a psychology of musical influence that carefully delineates how music impresses itself upon an individual's emotional and physiological constitution. The detail with which the XZMC correlates certain types of sounds with emotional responses is remarkable and seems to mark an emergent science of psychological discourse at the time. Xunzi's

"Discourse" also appears to share many values and perspectives on musical influence with the XZMC, so that the two texts appear to represent an unfolding intellectual lineage of discourse on moral psychology and musical self-cultivation.

All of the texts and comments on music analyzed in this chapter share a similar core belief: that music and the emotions are inextricably linked, and that music might provide an individual with a powerful way of tapping into the core of his or her emotional or psychological being. However, they also differ in certain ways. The concern of the XZMC and "Discourse on Music" with the explicit ways in which music affects one's morality is notably different from the more exuberant emphasis on music as a form of individual expression formulated in certain Odes of the *Shi jing* and in parts of the *Analects*. One might account for this difference in many ways. For one thing, the genres in which these formulations occur differ radically from each other, and the gap in time is potentially as much as several centuries. For another, the likely authors of these texts would have had very different reasons for talking about music. And lastly, the narrative of music as moral tool and the concomitant moral psychology that emerged alongside it developed along a clear trajectory of Ru inquiry into methods of individual cultivation. It should therefore come as no surprise that the Ru built their theories by focusing primarily on the merits of music on self-cultivation, rather than on a celebratory pronouncement about the expressive potential it carries. After all, if we accept the idea that the early Mohist attack on music had had a noticeable or lasting impact on political practice, then the very survival of music as an important court ritual depended in part on the ability of the Ru to persuade others of the moral value of music.

The merging of the emotions with moral attitudes and goals formed the basis of many Ru discussions on music. As such, morality and the emotions were not perceived to be in isolation of each other but as intertwined elements in the making of an aesthetically sensitive and morally perspicacious individual. Music was not only helpful in shaping the emotions and supporting a particular ethical stance; it was also critical to the aesthetic expression of a variety of possibly conflicting emotions. Thus, music was much more than a tool for cultivation of one's raw emotions; it was an expression itself of individual moral cultivation and grace. As we will discuss in the next chapter, this expression of individual moral cultivation becomes, in later texts, a mark of one's connection with the larger cosmos.

CHAPTER FIVE

Sagely Attunement to the Cosmos

Around the third century BCE, with the emergence of beliefs in cosmologies of resonance, another idea about music and the individual rose to prominence. It was the notion that the sage—often, the sage-ruler—might use music to attune himself to the natural rhythms and cycles in his environment. At such a time, correspondences among music, cosmos, and the psyche began to develop according to a triangular relationship, and a notion of cosmic attunement emerged as a distinct goal of sagely self-cultivation.[1] Such a goal identified music with the harmony of the cosmos, encouraging the sage's psychic, spiritual communion with it.

At the same time that authors became increasingly vocal about the harmonious attributes of the cosmos, they also began to elaborate on the various connections between the cosmos and the human psyche. The connection between music and one's psychological well-being was, as we have seen so far, firmly rooted in the intellectual discourse of the age. Now, in an era of new cosmological perspectives, the idea that both music and the human body might—in their ideal forms—represent and reflect the harmony of the cosmos rose to prominence. In such a context, music had the power to help an individual identify with the sacred cosmos itself, or, in a manner of speaking, "near oneself to God." Aside from such spiritual uses, achieving the cosmic attunement of a sage would no doubt also have helped advance one's social status, though such latter uses of music will not be the focus of this chapter.[2]

Below, I explore the triangular relationship among music, cosmos, and psyche as it developed and was expressed in a handful of fourth to second century BCE texts. In particular, I define the new goal of cosmic attunement, which, unlike moral and aesthetic cultivation, emphasized the sage's psychic, spiritual union with the patterns and functions of the entire cosmos. Unlike our analysis of music in chapter four, many of the authors who speak about music and an individual's cosmic psychology cannot be linked exclusively to any single intellectual lineage of the day, such as the Ru.[3] Also, some of the texts we examine, ranging from standard histories to imperial compendia and even the "Outer Chapters" of the *Zhuangzi*, limit the goal of cosmic attunement to the ruler himself. Even so, while the ostensible goal of such texts is to help rulers achieve and maintain cosmic rulership in their state—a goal outlined in chapter one—the explicit focus is not on the state itself but the ruler's individual body. For this reason, it makes sense to analyze such passages in light of what they propose as individual, bodily forms of achievement.

THE COSMIC REPERCUSSIONS
OF MUSIC IN THE "YUE JI"

Scholars have consistently linked Xunzi's "Yue lun" ("Discourse on Music") to somewhat later accounts of music found in the "Yue shu" ("The Book on Music") of Sima Qian's *Shi ji* and the "Yue ji" ("Account on Music") of the Confucian classic *Li ji*. Scott Cook clarifies that while much of the "Yue lun" appears verbatim in the "Yue ji," it is the latter that is borrowing from Xunzi's former, not the other way around. In terms of the dating of the "Yue ji," I agree with Cook, who dates the compilation to the Western Han, but adds that much of its content would have stemmed from Warring States materials.[4]

The two texts, "Yue shu," and "Yue ji," contain many passages that are virtually identical, and they are similar in general. Chinese scholarship since Tang times has reached a general consensus that the "Yue shu" was not written by Sima Qian.[5] According to Martin Kern, almost ninety percent of the "Yue shu" "is virtually identical with the complete *Li-chi* chapter 'Records of Music,' differing only in some textual variants and an alternative arrangement of a few paragraphs."[6] Kern convincingly outlines how Sima Qian was unlikely to have composed the received version of "Yue shu."[7] However, it should be noted that when Kern suggests a late Western/early Eastern Han dating for the "Yue shu" and "Yue ji," he refers exclusively to the creation of these as specific texts, not to the dating of much of their content. Because the "Yue shu" is likely a copied version of the "Yue ji" that was not written by Sima Qian, I will refer more simply to the "Yue ji" when referencing these texts.

Even though Xunzi's "Yue lun" influenced the "Yue ji" account substantially—indeed, much of Xunzi's work appears verbatim in this latter text—there are additional passages in the "Yue ji" that draw connections between music and both cosmos and psyche in a more explicit manner. In particular, the "Yue ji," while reflecting largely traditional concerns about the role of music in self-cultivation and broader education, incorporates a belief that music can help complete, rather than merely represent or duplicate, the cosmos. This claim is significant because it points to the new role of music as fully part of and functional in the workings of the cosmos, not as something that merely suggests or points to it. That we should notice this difference in two such similar texts supports the argument that later textual compilations, such as the "Yue ji," reflect an expanded awareness of music in terms of its role in the patterns and operations of the cosmos.

The "Yue ji" speaks of music in terms of its cosmic significance and affinity with natural principles.[8] It claims: "Great music conforms with the harmony of Heaven and Earth 大樂與天地同和."[9] In a similar vein, it states: "Music is that which penetrates [natural] principle and pattern 樂者通倫理者也."[10] The fact that "great music," or music that achieves a certain ideal of perfection, both conforms with cosmic harmony and penetrates principles and patterns intrinsic to the cosmos, clarifies the larger role for music and its new links to astrological knowledge. Music does more than just represent or allude to cosmic harmony. It synchronizes itself with the natural rhythms of Heaven and Earth so as to contribute to the overall harmonious functioning of the cosmos.

This view of music as an agent of cosmic harmony is further strengthened through the author's assertions that great music, along with its counterpart, ritual, enhance cosmic operations:

及夫禮樂之極乎天而蟠乎地，行乎陰陽而通乎鬼神；窮高極遠而測深厚。樂著大始，而禮居成物。著不息者天也，著不動者地也。一動一靜者天地之間也。故聖人曰「禮云樂云」。

As for ritual and music perfecting Heaven and relying on Earth, moving along with *yin-yang* and penetrating [the realms of] ghosts and spirits; they exhaust what is high and reach the limits of the distant, plumbing all depths. Music illuminates the Great Beginning while ritual abides in the completion of things. That which illuminates without rest is Heaven; that which illuminates without movement is Earth. One moving, the other tranquil, this is the interaction between Heaven and Earth.[11] Thus the sage [i.e., Confucius] says, "Ah, the rites; ah, music!"[12]

In this passage the author underscores how ritual and music possess the power to aid in cosmic operations. Music and ritual are capable of "perfecting Heaven and relying on Earth," of exhausting "what is high" and "plumbing all depths," and of illuminating "the Great Beginning" and abiding "in the completion of things." In short, both of these aspects of human culture participate in and enhance the basic operations of the cosmos.

In addition to accentuating, aiding, and participating in cosmic processes, great music also gives critical efficacy to cosmic operations. Music necessarily completes the cosmos:

> 樂者敦和，率神而從天，禮者別宜，居鬼而從地。故聖人作樂以應天，制禮以配地。禮樂明備，天地官矣.

> Music is lovely and harmonious; it directs spirits and follows along with Heaven. Ritual is discriminating and fitting; it secures ghosts and follows along with Earth. Therefore the sage creates music to respond [appropriately] to Heaven; creates ritual to be congruent with Earth. When ritual and music are clarified and perfected, Heaven and Earth [can fulfill] their functions.[13]

Here, the author describes music and ritual as human responses to the cosmic realm—responses that interact with Heaven and Earth in a harmonious and appropriate manner. In addition, as made clear in the statements about directing the spirits, securing ghosts, and helping Heaven and Earth fulfill their various functions, the actual efficacy of cosmic operations depends on the perfection and clarification of human music and ritual. Because of the intrinsic connection between music and cosmic operations, one can look to music as an indicator of how successfully the cosmos is functioning. Similarly, one can control music so that cosmic processes might be fulfilled effectively. As part of the fabric of the cosmos, music provides humans with a means of tapping into its powers so as to insure the smoothness and functionality of its operations.

How did this view of music and cosmic operations affect the way authors spoke about the sage's psyche and self-cultivation? Again, the "Yue ji" deviates just enough from the *Xunzi* to make it interesting as a text that builds on earlier beliefs yet changes with the times. One significant difference from Xunzi's "Yue lun" is the greater emphasis the author of "Yue ji" places on music as a means of cosmic control rather than just state control or self-cultivation. Another important difference is that the author of "Yue ji" discusses how the sage's psyche might confirm the authenticity of great music. Unlike the XZMC and *Xunzi*, which speak almost exclusively about how music affects humans and society, the "Yue ji" pays special attention to the issue of how certain humans can come to know about and authenticate music by attuning their own heart-minds to the cosmos. Such a focus attests to a new effort to exhort rulers to know music (or sponsor sages who do), so that they might employ the right type of music in state control.[14] It completes the triadic relationship between music, cosmos, and psyche that develops especially after the third century BCE.

In the "Yue ji," Great Music is true, authentic, and good because it conforms to cosmic principles and harmonies. As cosmic music, it has the power to help bring about social and natural order. This places music squarely within a cosmic schema of control that easily lends itself to the interests of the state. Certain types of music can serve both as a fundamental tool to help effect social and cosmic order as well as a rhetorical tool to justify a ruler's claims to cosmic power. For these reasons, it is in the interests of those who control music to be able to judge music on the basis of its cosmic efficacy—or whether or not it truly is great, or cosmic, music.

The author of the "Yue ji" exerts a considerable amount of effort in delineating who is capable of knowing and making decisions about music: "Therefore, he who knows the nature of ritual and music is able to initiate, and he who understands the patterns of ritual and music is able to complete. He who initiates is referred to as 'sagely,' he who completes is referred to as 'clear' 故知禮樂之情者能作，識禮樂之文者能述。作者之謂聖，述者之謂明."[15] Here, knowledge about ritual and music is an enabling factor that legitimizes one's sagely qualities. Music is not just something that helps one learn and become moral; it is something in and of itself that a sage, or sage-ruler, might master and come to understand.

Significantly, the "Yue ji" attempts to explain why sages are capable of knowing and making decisions about great music by linking the human heart-mind with a Heavenly nature that is inherent from birth: "That humans at birth are tranquil is because of their Heavenly nature. That they are stimulated by external things and are moved by them is because of the expression of this nature 人生而靜，天之性也；感於物而動，性之欲也."[16] Moreover, this author claims, humans are endowed with an innate framework, called "Heaven's pattern 天理," and this framework is congruent with the harmony of great music.[17] We know that this framework is good because the loss of it leads to utmost disorder in one's actions and heart-mind. For example, when one is influenced by external things without being able to reflect upon the self, and when one does not have any sense of measure in one's likes and dislikes, "Heaven's pattern is destroyed 天理滅也."[18] Furthermore, when Heaven's pattern is destroyed, "one will possess an intractable and conniving heart-mind 有悖逆詐偽之心," which will give rise to disorderly affairs.[19] In such a manner, the author establishes an intrinsic correspondence between the cosmos and the human constitution. But if such a pattern is intrinsic to all, then what makes the sage special?

Since great music stems from the cosmic processes of Heaven and Earth, it stands to reason that only he who can preserve the original imprint of Heaven's pattern on his heart-mind will be able to understand such music, and vice versa. The text shows us that the sages originally created music.[20] It also claims that only the gentleman is capable of understanding music.[21] Underlying these claims is the implication that only these types of people are able to keep their "Heaven's pattern" intact. Such an implication is new and not found in the XZMC or *Xunzi*.[22] Notably, neither of these latter texts defines human achievement or the creation of music in terms of the simple preservation of what was inherent in the psyche from the beginning. In "Yue ji," however, not only does the human psyche derive from the natural world; it is endowed with an imprint of Heaven's pattern that it can use to create, understand, and even legitimize great music in the world. Great music exists not only because the sages worked hard to create it, but because they and other gentlemen were able to preserve the Heavenly pattern endowed in them from birth, and to identify it in great music.

Our analysis of the "Yue ji" demonstrates how authors began to think of the achieved human psyche as a functional blueprint for idealized cosmic operations. As such, sages possessed the potential to create cosmic music, and both sages and gentlemen could apprehend and evaluate music that engaged and embodied the harmonies inherent in the cosmos. Rather than merely demonstrate the power of music to help cultivate the individual, the author of the "Yue ji" asserts the fundamental power of the attained psyche to authenticate music by virtue of its own intrinsic connection to the cosmos. Such a perspective invokes the powers of the cosmic psyche to insure the promulgation of great music, which in turn helps bring about cosmic order.

COSMIC ATTUNEMENT IN THE LÜSHI CHUNQIU AND ZHUANGZI

We find striking examples of the goal of what I will call "cosmic attunement"—an individual's act of attaining spiritual attunement with the cosmos—in texts dating from the late Warring States period that do not maintain an ostensibly Ru agenda. The discussion of music in the "music chapters" of the *Lüshi chunqiu*, for example, revolves not only around the creation, production, apprehension, and thorough understanding of cosmic music. To a greater extent than in "Yue ji," the author of the "music chapters" of *Lüshi chunqiu* discusses how one should appreciate music by attuning oneself to or communing with the cosmos.

The author first provides an account of the cosmic nature of both music and human nature. In the chapter "Great Music," he outlines the genesis of music, in which he explains that 1) music is inherent in the processes and principles of cosmos, 2) sound is intrinsic to the very shapes and forms of everything in the cosmos, and 3) the music of the Former Kings (sages) is based on principles of creating harmony out of the sounds inherent in the cosmos.[23] Indeed, there is a true cosmic nature (*qing* 情) to great music, just as there is a true nature to humankind (*xing* 性).[24] It is the job of the sage to insure that an idealized, triangular relationship among music, cosmos, and psyche remains complete.

According to the text, because only a sage can produce music of cosmic efficacy, knowledge of how to become a sage is of primary importance. Similar to the discussion in the "Yue ji," the sage must ready his heart-mind so as to understand music and allow it to "come to fruition 成."[25] The key to this lies in attaining a state of "equilibrium" 平, which appears to be a state in which the psyche regains the cosmic balance that is original to it: "There is a method for working on music. It must necessarily emerge from equilibrium. Equilibrium emerges from impartiality, impartiality from the Dao. Thus, only a man who has attained the Dao can discourse on music 務樂有術 , 必由平出 。平出於公 ，公出於道 。故惟得道之人， 其可與言樂乎！"[26] The equilibrium of the human heart-mind according to the Dao constitutes the psychological prerequisite for one's correct involvement with music. Thus, proper self-cultivation involves preparing one's psyche to be in balance with the cosmic Dao before one can understand, let alone produce and reap the benefits from, great music.

How does one bring the psyche into balance, or what I am calling "attunement," with the cosmos? Just as in the "Yue ji" above, this process involves recovering the original patterns of the cosmos within. Consider the following, lengthy passage on what balance means in both bodily and musical terms:

樂之有情，譬之若肌膚形體之有情性也，有情性則必有性養矣。寒溫勞逸饑飽，此六者非適也。凡養也者，瞻非適而以之適者也。能以久處其適，則生長矣。生也者，其身固靜，或而後知，或使之也。遂而不返，制乎嗜欲，制乎嗜欲（無窮）則必失其天矣。且夫嗜欲無窮，則必有貪鄙（浮）〔悖〕亂之心，淫佚姦詐之事矣。故（疆）〔彊〕者劫弱，眾者暴寡，勇者凌怯，壯者幫幼，從此生矣.

Music possesses a nature just like muscle, skin, form, and the body each possess essential traits and a nature. As long as there are essential traits and a nature, then there must also be nurturing of nature. Cold and heat, work and rest, hunger and satiation—these six are not [always] in balance. In general, nurturing involves observing what is out of balance and putting it in balance. If one is able to remain in balance for a long while, then his life will be long.

When born, one's body is inherently tranquil. When one is stimulated and then becomes aware, this is because the act of stimulating made it so. If one follows [along the path of stimulus-response] and does not reverse [this process], then one will be controlled by one's cravings and desires. If one is controlled by one's cravings and desires, then he will certainly lose what is natural within [i.e., that which derives from Heaven]. Furthermore, if there is no end to one's cravings and desires, then he will certainly have a heart-mind characterized by avarice, baseness, rebelliousness, and disorder and will undertake actions characterized by excessiveness, idleness, debauchery, and deceit. Therefore, the strong will rob the weak, the many will oppress the few, the bold will bully the timid, and the strong will lord over the meek. All of these originate from this."[27]

In this intriguing passage we see how human nature derives from Heaven, or the cosmos, and possesses its own balance through tranquility. An excess of craving and desire upsets this balance by pushing an individual to be out of tune with his inherent, cosmic balance and causing all sorts of evil behaviors. The process of "nurturing nature" is therefore essentially a musical process of re-tuning oneself to the original cosmic balance of one's body.

The "Heaven Chapters" of *Zhuangzi* also speak of individuals attaining an idealized state of cosmic attunement to the harmonies of the cosmos. Although the type of music the authors refer to does not involve tangible sound and is therefore not the same music that other texts have been discussing, it is nonetheless music by another definition:

夫明白於天地之德者，此之謂大本大宗，與天和者也；所以均調天下，與人和者也。與人和者，謂之人樂；與天和，謂之天樂.

He who has a clear understanding of the Virtue of Heaven and Earth may be called the Great Source, the Great Ancestor. He harmonizes with Heaven; and by doing so he brings equitable accord to the world and harmonizes with men as well. To harmonize with men is called [making] human music; to harmonize with Heaven is called [making] Heavenly Music . . . This is what is called Heavenly Music.[28]

Here, the author underscores self-cultivation in terms of the harmony achieved between an individual sage and the cosmos. While "Heavenly Music" can also be translated as "Heavenly Joy," I believe that because of the direct reference to harmony and making "human music," along with previous allusions to the "piping of Heaven" in the "Inner Chapters," it makes sense to interpret this passage as referring more directly to music than to joy.

While it can be argued that, in this passage, music is merely a metaphor for the attainment of the Way, one nevertheless cannot overlook the fact that it invokes music to beautify, praise, and/or give cosmic legitimacy to what is primarily a mental achievement. In this sense, this passage resonates well with the claim in the "Yue ji" and *Lüshi chunqiu* that cultivating the heart-mind is tantamount to achieving a sense of cosmic harmony. The process of spiritual cultivation is, thus, an inherently musical process.

The *Zhuangzi* also adopts the idea that cosmic (i.e., "Heavenly") music is the sage's vehicle for achieving social order. In the passage above, the author asserts: "Heavenly Music is the heart-mind of the sage which is used to rear all under Heaven 天樂者，聖人之心，以畜天下也."[29] Here, it becomes clear that through the sage's heart-mind—a heart-mind that is in tune with the music of the cosmos—the benefits of the Way can be reaped on earth. The particular harmony that the sage achieves with the cosmos allows for the nourishment and continued vitality of everything in the world. In keeping with the imperial focus of the previous texts examined, "Heavenly Music" is more than just a metaphor for individual cultivation and achievement of the Way. It is a psychological state achieved by the sage to bring spiritual order and harmony not only to one's body, but to the entire natural and social worlds.[30]

The ideal of sagely attunement or music-making with the cosmos is further elaborated through Han Dynasty proclamations of the deep, ontological connection between sound (*sheng*) and the sage (*sheng* 聖)—two homonyms in ancient Chinese. The *Bohu tong* (79 CE) is perhaps one of the first texts to explicitly link the *sheng* of sounds with the *sheng* of the sage.[31] Such a connection is epitomized in the following statement, associated with Ying Shao's *Fengsu tongyi*: "The sage 'sounds.' [He] penetrates. This is to say that his ability to hear sounds and thereby understand the nature [of things] penetrates all of Heaven and Earth while arranging and letting flourish the myriad things 聖者聲也通也，言其聞聲知情，通于天地條暢萬物."[32] Interestingly, unlike the claims in the XZMC, which puts forth the simple idea of using music to penetrate or fathom another person's authentic emotions or psychological state of being, the sagely ideal in this passage is to penetrate the entire cosmos, everything included. Whereas the scope of the gentlemanly ideal outlined by the XZMC lies well within the realm of the social and human, the scope of the sagely ideal outlined by this excerpt is clearly cosmic and all-encompassing. Sound in this passage—closely affiliated with the sage—represents the medium by which the sage comes to know not just others, but the entire realm of the cosmos as well.

This leads us to a related discussion of the role of sound in sagely attunement with the cosmos. While we have already discussed sound as a powerful vehicle for cosmic rule in chapter three, we have not yet explored the discursive arenas in which sound serves as the primary vehicle for an individual's attunement and spiritual communion with the cosmos. The following section helps us see how such an idea likely had Warring States origins, and how it might have stemmed from contexts in which the cosmic Dao was conceived of in terms of a formless, mysterious entity.

ACHIEVING COMMUNION WITH THE
SOUNDLESS SOUND OF THE DAO

Another type of formulation concerning sagely communion with the cosmos involves a conception of the Dao in acoustical terms: as a soundless entity. One will recall from chapter three that with the rise of cosmologies of resonance during the Warring States and early imperial periods, sound emerged as a sacred aspect of the cosmos. But to the authors of some texts, what was most sacred in the cosmos—the Dao—intrinsically possessed no form. So if sound or music were to be associated with the ineffable and formless Dao of the cosmos—and clearly, our sources suggest that it was becoming commonplace for some people to link the two—then such sound would necessarily have to be soundless and without form. In this section, I examine a few Warring States texts in which the notion of "soundless sound" appears to represent the functionality of the cosmic Dao.[33] Though in many ways the goal of attuning oneself to "soundless sound" is very similar to the goal of attuning oneself to cosmic harmony, the two types of beliefs are grounded in significantly different perspectives on the way the cosmos works. As we will see, "soundless sound" implicates music in the same way that certain discussions of sound as pitch-pipes and tones implicate music: by referencing the aural building blocks and theoretical frameworks upon which music was built.

Though the discourse on names (ming 名) in Warring States China is generally not directly related to developments in the concept of sound, there is at least one reference during that period that gives us reason to ponder its aural relationship to cosmic operations.[34] The Taiyi sheng shui 太一生水 (Taiyi Gives Birth to Water), a short, recently excavated text appended to various assemblages of phrases from the Daodejing, quite possibly uses the term ming with reference to sound and cosmic functionality.[35] If my interpretation of the following passage is correct, such a usage demonstrates the existence of a Warring States interest in sound as a key function of cosmic operations that shares much in common with the notion of "soundless sound."[36]

The following passage from Taiyi sheng shui speaks of both an appellation [zi 字] and name [ming] for the Dao, which appears to implicate sound in some fashion:

下, 土也; 而謂之地. 上, 氣也; 而謂之天. 道亦其字也. 請問其名. 以道從事者必託其名. 故事成而身長. 聖人之從事也, 亦託其名.故功成而身不傷. 天地名字並立, 故過其方不思相.

Below, there is the ground. We call this "Earth." Above, there is *qi*. We call this "Heaven." "Dao" is also its appellation. I beg to ask its name! He who uses the Dao in abiding in affairs must necessarily rely on its name. In such a way affairs are completed and bodies develop (persons grow). Sages also abide in affairs by relying upon its name. In such a way they achieve merit and their bodies are not harmed. When the names and appellations of Heaven and Earth are both established, [then even if] either one were to exceed its boundaries, both [would] automatically compensate each other as appropriate.[37]

In this tantalizing yet elusive comment, the author distinguishes between the appellation and name of the Dao. One way to interpret this distinction is to say that the identifying label of the Dao is a vocalized appellation (*zi*) of a thing, but this is not the same as the reality of the Dao itself. The appellation is but a formal (linguistic, visual, and aural) representation of such a reality. The name (*ming*) of the Dao, on the other hand, appears not just to label but to *invoke* it at an ontological level—a level of function and being that allows the sage to fulfill his affairs and achieve merit.[38]

This begs the question, to what extent is sound implicated in the author's reference to "name"? And furthermore, what does it mean for a sage to "rely upon," or "entrust oneself to" (*tuo* 託) the name of the Dao? One interpretation might take "name" in the passage above to refer to the actual sound of the Dao. The idea behind this view is that, as is common in certain religions, the actual sound of a particular word mystically invokes the power, presence, and grace of the deity or ultimate realm of being in question.[39] But by reading the *Taiyi sheng shui* in this light, we encounter a significant problem; namely, that the author clearly and cunningly refuses to impart the name or sound of the Dao to the reader. We cannot ignore such an omission, since if the author had actually intended for aspirants of the Dao to invoke a particular sound to this end, he would presumably have identified such a sound for his audience. This leads us to believe that the author does not intend for the aural nature of sound to be the critical aspect in the name of the Dao, and that some other interpretation is in order.

To correctly interpret what the passage above means by "relying upon" or "entrusting oneself in" the name of the Dao, I believe we can follow cues given to us in what seems to have been the companion text to the *Taiyi sheng shui*, or the *Laozi* (*Daodejing*).[40] Unlike the *Taiyi sheng shui*, the Dao in the *Laozi* is nameless—"name" in this context referring to a conceptual label, just as the term "appellation" is used in *Taiyi sheng shui*. The main intent of proclaiming the Dao to be nameless is to negate any form or sets of boundaries that might be associated with the Dao of the cosmos. Assuming that the authors of the *Laozi* and the *Taiyi sheng shui* used different forms or ways of referring to the "constant Dao" of the cosmos, we might understand the "name" of the Dao in *Taiyi sheng shui* to refer not to the term "Dao," or to any simple label or conceptual category that uses sound and form to express it, but to the underlying meaning or operation of the Dao itself. In other words, we might assume that what the author of *Taiyi sheng shui* refers to as "its name" (*qi ming* 其名) corresponds to what the authors of *Laozi* refer to as the "nameless Dao."[41]

Since the author of *Taiyi sheng shui* refuses to provide the name for the Dao, one might conclude that its true "name" is ineffable, and, indeed, constitutes more than a simple label or tag. However, unlike the *Laozi*, which denies such a name any efficacy in the world, the "name" of the Dao in *Taiyi sheng shui* is said to hold meaning. It holds meaning, I believe, because the "name" in question is not so much a word but an approach to living that invokes the Dao's own being. Such an approach constitutes a profound act of religious communion, not dissimilar to that which is described by the notion of *wu-wei* in the *Laozi*.[42] Thus, while the mere appellation, or labeling, of the Dao provides a shorthand for learning about it, one only accesses and comes to know the Dao in all its fullness via the invocation of its true reality, or "name." One arrives at such an invocation not through a vocalized or linguistic means but through one's whole being.

On this latter reading, the *Taiyi sheng shui* provides an example in which religious or spiritual communion with the Dao occurs not through a simple act of defining, labeling, tagging, or even vocalizing what it is, for that would be to place limits and boundaries upon something that is essentially boundless. Rather, one must "call it into being" by invoking its "name" in the largest possible sense of what a name might be: its mysterious, boundless powers. In this context, an individual's highest spiritual ideal is to transcend the boundaries of any ordinary name, including its aural aspects. He or she must entrust oneself to a name that is devoid of any form at all, not to mention sound.

If in this passage sound itself is not a crucial element in the sage's communion with the Dao, then why should I highlight it as a source for understanding the role of sound in the cosmos? I do so because it provides an example in which the efficacious cosmos seems to be perceived in terms of one specific type of form, albeit, transcendent in nature: the name. By using the word "name" to describe the full efficacy of the cosmos, the author of *Taiyi sheng shui* invokes a specific form—which notably includes an acoustic aspect (especially since "name" is contrasted with "appellation")—to point subsequently to something formless. Such an act is reminiscent of later cultural contexts in which authors employ the phrase "soundless sound" to imply the formless Dao. As we will see shortly, later authors make use of this particular type of negation to highlight a single type of form— sound—as a touchstone for the ineffable Dao itself.

The *Laozi*, in contrast to the implication in *Taiyi sheng shui*, never singles out sound as a form whose negation might best describe the Dao. It does, however, provide the rhetorical pattern for implying the Dao through a negation of forms of all kinds. This can be seen in chapter forty-one, in which the author points to the Dao not only in terms of a "Great Tone" (*Da yin* 大音) that "has no sound" (*xi sheng* 希聲, i.e., a "soundless sound"), but also in terms of a "Great Square," a "Great Vessel," and a "Great Image."[43] Similarly, in chapter fourteen, the author of *Laozi* speaks of the Dao as that which cannot be seen, heard, or touched.[44] Indeed, the Dao is imperceptible precisely because it possesses no form of any kind—be it image, sound, or texture.

Even though the *Laozi* does not highlight "soundless sound" as a primary means of accessing or describing the cosmic Dao, other Warring States texts seem to join the *Taiyi sheng shui* in hinting that "soundless sound"—or some type of acoustic "non-form"—aptly represents the idealized flow of the cosmos. In the "Inner Chapters" of the *Zhuangzi*, one finds a discussion of the so-called piping of man, Earth, and Heaven. Just as musical sound is produced by blowing wind through a pan-pipe, the "piping of Heaven" produces a manifestation of the formless, and hence soundless Dao in the world at large. The very fact that Zhuangzi describes such cosmic workings in terms of a piping that produces a soundless sound suggests a broader meaning for the notion of sound. Sound could encompass not just audible sensations but the workings of the Dao that allow every object to be itself, and to have its own identity and manner of functioning.[45] Even if one interpreted this passage in terms of a metaphorical usage of "piping" and sound, one cannot but concede that sound is somehow a key conceptual ingredient in describing cosmic operations.

Similarly, in a later passage in the *Zhuangzi*, discussed earlier in the chapter, the author co-opts musical terminology to idealize the relationship between the sage and Heaven. The sage is sagely because of his ability to harmonize himself, indeed, his whole being, with "Heavenly Music," or the Dao of the cosmos.[46] While "Heavenly Music" can also be translated as "Heavenly Joy," I believe that because of the direct reference to harmony and the allusion to the "piping of Heaven" earlier in the "Inner Chapters," it makes sense to interpret this passage as referring more directly to music than to joy. Intriguingly, the phrase, "the pinnacle of joy is no joy 至樂

無樂," found in the "Zhi le 至樂" outer chapter of the *Zhuangzi*, might be understood as a *double-entendre* referring as well to the idea that "the pinnacle of music is no music." However, the direct meaning in this latter passage involves the emotions, so "joy" is perhaps better for this latter passage.

As discussed previously, the goal of the Zhuangzian sage is not musical in the more narrow sense of being musical (by performing humanly music), but musical in the sense of attaining spontaneous union with the spiritual and harmonious processes of the Dao. This is very similar to the *Taiyi sheng shui*'s exhortations for one to "entrust oneself to" or "rely on" the name of the Dao. By advocating that one transcend the narrow, delimited parameters of either mundane names or mundane music, both texts effectively recommend that the sage "make music with the cosmic Dao," so to speak, by finding himself within the realm of its "true name," or soundless sound.

We have seen how certain Warring States authors—those who conceive of the Dao as a formless, natural, but nonetheless spiritual process—lay a foundation for thinking about inaudible sound, and at times, music, in terms of the larger processes of the cosmos. Some of these authors describe their formless Dao using the language of aural form, musical performance, or harmonious change. In so doing, they broaden the meaning of sound to include the musical workings of the cosmos, above and beyond the realm of what can be heard. The sage's perception of such sound thus points to a spiritual ideal linking the attained individual to the implicit, harmonious workings of the cosmos.

The emergent belief in audible sound (especially pitch) as one of the foundations of cosmic order, which we analyzed in chapter three, bears a certain resemblance to the notion of "soundless sound." Indeed, one need but glance at the imperial state's uses for sound in Han times to realize that the act of linking cosmic functionality and patterns to material, acoustic sounds—which consist of *qi*—is actually quite similar to the act of linking the workings of the cosmic Dao to "soundless sound." Indeed, in both types of belief, the fact that sound and the cosmos are inextricably intertwined is one and the same. Each type of belief consistently elevated sound or music to be compatible with their particular conceptions of true cosmic nature and functioning.

The main difference between these beliefs in sound, music, and cosmos lies in their divergent understandings of the nature of the cosmic functioning: one view stresses its ultimate materiality while the other idealizes its immateriality. Han imperial practitioners who specialized in pitch-pipe ratios were clearly thinking about religious power in terms of their success at creating standardized procedures for accumulating, measuring, and reading material data from their natural environment. Thus, their religiosity was perceived in quite tangible ways, as the cosmos was thought to function not so much as an inscrutable entity as a system of intelligible patterns.[47] Authors of texts such as the *Taiyi sheng shui*, *Laozi*, and *Zhuangzi*, on the other hand, all recommend that individuals (often sages or superior men of some kind) apprehend and perceive of the cosmos not through calculations and correlations, but through mystical union with its manifold transformations.[48] For them, the practice of apprehending the soundless sound of the Dao represents an aesthetic and spiritual ideal of the individual. It constitutes a goal in itself and not a means to the ultimate imperial goal of cosmic rulership and control. This difference seems to attest to the fundamentally different epistemological orientations of cosmologies of spontaneous resonance supported by the Han imperial court and those more influenced by a belief in the mysterious workings of the Dao.

As the notion of "soundless sound" continued to enjoy popularity as an aesthetic ideal in later Chinese history, it also likely influenced alternative ways of thinking about sound in the cosmos. The notion of apprehending soundless sound in some circles came to represent the pinnacle of human unity with the Dao of the cosmos, above and beyond achievements that rely on other sensory media such as sight, touch, taste, and smell. Perhaps it is not a coincidence, for example, that the later Zen spiritual practice of viewing the *shakuhachi* as an "instrument of dharma" in the Japanese Fuke tradition was heavily influenced by a Daoist-inspired sutra—the *Surangama Sutra*—that speaks of enlightenment via a process of transcending sound and hearing.[49]

MUSIC AND THE SAGE'S RESONANT KNOWLEDGE

The idea of a sage achieving cosmic attunement through music is not merely described according to his direct connection and communion with the cosmos. Since the cosmos was thought to function according to resonant patterns, where like things resonated with like, the sage who resembled the cosmos would naturally assume such characteristics as well. In this section, we explore the ramifications of cosmic attunement in the everyday life of a sage, in particular, in the type of mind and knowledge that he should strive to acquire whenever possible. This discussion will help demonstrate the extent to which a musical understanding of the world came to be translated as a deep awareness and insight into cosmic patterns, regularities, and "truths," as defined through all that is authentic in life.

In the *Lüshi chunqiu*, cosmic resonance is described in the following manner: "Things of the same category naturally attract one another; things of the same *qi* naturally come together; tones [in reference to the Five Tones] that are similar answer each other 類固相召，氣同則合，聲比則應."[50] This logic of resonance helps explain the sage's likeness to the cosmos. For, just as things of the same category attract each other, the sage who achieves a mind that is resonant with the cosmos will be able to function like the cosmos. In other words, he will be able to respond and resonate with things of similar category, *qi*, tone, and so on. In the *Lüshi chunqiu*, therefore, the sage is said to be able to accord with the "Great Transformations (大化)" of the cosmos—that is, he can incorporate every new fluctuation and change according to the underlying resonant causality of "like attracts like."[51]

As a miniature cosmos, or agents that function much like the cosmos, sages often possessed an acute, music-related awareness. Even if they were not musical themselves, or acting within a musical context, they often exhibited a sensibility that could be characterized as musical in some way. As mentioned in chapter three, the entire notion of "bosom buddies," or "knower of [another's] tones" (*yin zhe* 音者, or *zhi yin zhe* 知音者), attributed to Ying Shao of the late Han Dynasty, suggests a type of deep, authentic knowledge of another.[52] The fact that *yin* 音, or tones, serve as the root meaning of the phrase is significant, especially since we have seen that tones were often thought of as reflecting and engendering cosmic functioning. Just as ancient astrologers and priests would have had a special duty or power to read omens or divination results in the past, those who could properly read the tones of the cosmos were considered to be mediums of the divine realm. Similarly, one who could "know [another's] tones" might be likened to such spiritual figures in society. Such a sage would be specially endowed to read the most genuine signs of the cosmos as reflected in another human being.

Another way of interpreting the phrase "knower of another's tones" would be to view it as reflecting an underlying resonant relationship as described by the *Lüshi chunqiu* citation above. Since like responds to like, he who is a true bosom buddy is one that understands and responds to another merely by existing in a relationship of cosmic resonance with the other. The emphasis here is on the unstated, nonverbal, mysterious, yet deeply genuine and satisfying relationship that exists between two people on account of their similar frequencies of cosmic resonance. Describing the highest possible type of sagely knowledge of another, such a connection implies more than what the common turn of phrase "on the same wavelength" implies in English; it implies all aspects of one's spiritual being in communion with another. Understanding the phrase in terms of the notion of "soundless sound" described above, it also implies a level of understanding that transcends the realm of forms to that of the formless, non-verbal, primal-sounding (or perhaps, non-sounding) cosmos itself.

Music and acoustical language are also often used to reflect sagacious knowledge that has the power to foretell the future. We saw earlier how sound was used in certain types of divination practices. The following description, appearing in the *Shi ji*, is reminiscent of such practices, where music not only serves as the means by which one comes to deeply know the authentic state of another, but as the means by which one can intuit events that might follow as a result of one's character. It features Confucius as a music pupil (learning the drums and *qin*-zither) of Music Master Xiang (師襄子).[53]

A note about the usage of the *qin* in this passage is in order, not least because it helps to explain a motif that develops regarding the male, gentlemanly scholar or sage, his special knowledge and abilities to access authentic forms of knowledge. Intriguingly, Confucius, as featured in the *Analects*, played the *se* and not the *qin*.[54] In this story, which was written down by Sima Qian in the Han, he is a pupil of the *qin*. According to Ingrid Furniss' study of the visual and archaeological record of wooden instruments, the *qin* appears to have become more tightly linked with gentlemanly moral self-cultivation and the sage in Han times and later.[55] That this linkage might have been gendered is suggested by the sparse record of women playing the *qin* in the entire early Chinese tradition.[56] This all supports the notion that the motif of the male, solo *qin* player was developing during Han times to bolster the connections authors wished to make between sagely insight (which seems to have been predominantly male) and musical perceptiveness.

In the *Shi ji* passage at hand, Confucius first makes slow progress, not being able to fully grasp the music's phrasing and melody, meter, or musical intent. With increased effort, however, he not only understands all of these, but he reads into the character of the composer as well:

曰：「丘得其為人，黯然而黑，幾然而長，眼如望羊，如王四國，非文其誰能為此也！」師襄子辟席再拜，曰：「師蓋云《文王操》也。

Confucius remarked: "I have grasped the character of its composer. He is darkly black and grandly tall and seems to have eyes on a far-reaching goal, as though he plans to become king over the states of the four quarters. It must be the work of King Wen, for who else could have done it!" Music Master Xiang rose from his mat and bowed twice, saying: "Music masters generally say that this piece is the work of King Wen."[57]

This episode of character-reading not only tells of Confucius' ability to understand music in all its fullness; it also describes his ability to achieve insight into another person's character and ambitions through music. While the role of the cosmos is not readily apparent in this example, one sees that Confucius' understanding of King Wen reaches that of the sage and might be interpreted in terms of a resonant relationship reminiscent of those described above.

As a "knower of another's tones," Confucius garners the respect of his teacher and reveals himself as a sage in resonance or attunement with King Wen himself. So intimately does he recognize the latter's physical traits and mental state of being that Confucius is able to infer what types of events might be apt to occur in the future. Sagely, cosmic, and resonant attunement with another human therefore has prognostic value as well. As in the examples of how music could reveal doomed and flourishing regimes, we see how music here indicates or verifies the truth of a situation, allowing humans to peel back superficial appearances and peer into an object's purest form. This epistemological function allows for an accurate reading not only of the situation at hand but also of potential, future occurrences as a result of this state of affairs.

CONCLUSION

In texts dating from the third century BCE and on into the early imperial periods, authors did not entirely abandon the view that music plays a key role in our psychological development as human beings. Alongside the emphasis on how music nourishes one's moral psychology, another perspective emerged that stressed music as a means to or reflection of cosmic identity. This perspective, which one might label a "psychology of cosmic attunement," pointed to the potential of the human psyche to apprehend, experience, and reflect the fundamental harmonies and patterns—or music—of the cosmos.

The perspective on a sage's cosmic attunement goes hand-in-hand with the belief that music might fulfill and enhance cosmic operations by tapping into or reverberating with the harmonies intrinsic to the cosmos. Given this belief, it becomes imperative that humans create and perform only those types of music that have the power to effect cosmic harmony and, essentially, large-scale natural order. But in order to create and perform such music, humans must first have a means of understanding the basic harmonies of the cosmos. Passages from the "Yue ji," of the Li ji, the "Music Chapters" of the Lüshi chunqiu, and the later chapters of the Zhuangzi all posit that the sage or sage-ruler successfully attunes himself to the harmonies of the cosmos so as to bring about social and cosmic order. By fine-tuning his psychology in such a manner, he is further able to apprehend the significance of either the music of the cosmos itself (in the case of the Zhuangzi) or human music that enhances cosmic functions (in the "Yue ji" and Lüshi chunqiu), depending on the specific claims of each text.

Sagely knowledge of other human beings and the future appears also to be related to beliefs in the sonic potentials of sages as listeners of cosmic truth and beneficiaries of cosmically resonant insights. The later formulation of sages as "knowers of [one's] sounds" might be interpreted as harking back to notions of cosmic resonance and the power of sound to reveal truths and realities not only associated with the cosmos and its patterns, but with another person's human body as well. Once again, we have evidence of the triadic relationship drawn among cosmos, music, and human body that served as an underlying template for spiritual achievement and knowledge in early Chinese history.

The new emphasis on one's psychic apprehension of cosmic music described in this chapter makes sense in the context of a belief that music and musical harmony inheres in the cosmos. But how might one explain the reasons for this new perspective on cosmic music and one's attunement to it? Clearly, one answer involves understanding these changes in terms of large-scale transformations in religious and cosmological outlooks associated with the onset of cosmologies of resonance in the fourth to third centuries BCE. It can also be explained according to political changes of the day. Since many of the writings we examined in this chapter were likely to have been compiled for the benefit and use of the centralized state and not just individual aspirants in the Ru tradition, it seems appropriate that such writings would demonstrate an interest in the authenticity of music. After all, if music were to be of any use in helping maintain a sense of unity and imperial power, as many of these texts clearly state that it should, then it would need to be the right kind of music. That is, music would need to help justify state power on a cosmic scale, in keeping with claims concerning state access to and control over the cosmos that were prevalent in early imperial times. Thus, we might conclude that in some contexts, sages were necessary in order to authenticate imperial music that was truly "cosmic" in nature.

In other contexts, the resonant or cosmically attuned mind of the sage appears to be a motif that affirms the superior skills and/or spiritual, moral attainment of idealized individuals—mostly male gentlemen or sages—throughout history. I have highlighted passages from early texts that reference such an ideal in the context of music and tonal resonance. I did so in order to show how the notion of resonance was applied broadly to encompass human psychic capacities and serve as a standard for true or genuine knowledge of the subtle workings of the cosmos, life, and fellow human beings.

CHAPTER SIX

Music and Medicine

So it is that when [proper] music is in place then logic is clear, the ears and eyes are perspicacious and acute, blood and material force (*qi*) attain harmony and equilibrium, cultural environments and customs change, and all under heaven is tranquil.

—"Yue ji" ("Record of Music") from the *Book of Rites*[1]

... for I am much inclined to think, that music is to the mind, what opium is to the body, a DIVINE MEDICINE, and as extensively applicable in the one, as this article of Materia Medica, emphatically stiled "Magnum Dei Donum," has been found to be in the other.

—Edwin Atlee, *An inaugural essay on the influence of music in the cure of diseases*[2]

The development of the self through music in ancient China was not just limited to the moral and cognitive realms. Music was thought to have a great effect on our bodies and general state of health as well. The link between music and medicine not only stemmed from more spiritual, cosmic conceptualizations of a harmonious and balanced body; music in itself was hailed as a tool for therapy and improving psychological and physiological health. As a practical aid to healing and a method of achieving longevity, it could be used effectively in mantic rituals to help contact the spirits for medical intervention or to exorcise illness-producing demons. Just as food, drugs, and other ingestibles took center stage in early Chinese longevity and medical rituals, music was sometimes compared to a kind of food or tonic that not only nourished the body but could bring about therapeutic results as well.

In this chapter, I argue that the power of music in medical practice and thought lay in its power to transform bodies according to beliefs about cosmic harmony, resonance, and balance that became especially prevalent during the early imperial period. The history of the connection between medicine and music is much longer, however, extending back to the early Warring States period, when notions of proper and excessive music emerged as a means of distinguishing good and bad types of music. That musical type should determine the medical effects of music reveals much about how musical harmony was intimately linked to notions of balance in the human body from early in the textual record.

We begin our discussion of music and medicine by looking at Warring States discourses that attempt to canonize or codify music. We see how some early authors employed spiritual and cosmic explanations for why one should discriminate among certain types of music, which directly implicated the human body and its medical condition. Next, we examine the link between music and ascetic regimens of maintaining bodily health and finally, the ways in which music was considered to be either a tonic or pathogen, depending on its type. All of these aspects of musical discourse help reveal how music was thought to be a material aid in boosting individual health and curing illness, precisely because of its material and spiritual powers for re-integrating or re-aligning the human body with the proper balance of the cosmos.

EMERGING CONCEPTS OF "PROPER" VS. "EXCESSIVE" MUSIC

In the later chapters of the *Analects*, Confucius purportedly blames the "tunes of Zheng" (*Analects* 15.11 and 17.18) for "disordering" (*luan* 亂) the Elegantiae. Other texts from approximately the fourth through third centuries BCE join in helping create a more definite canon of music by singling out certain types of music as taboo, such as that from the states of Zheng, Wei, and Song, while extolling the virtues of certain Odes—in particular, the Elegantiae and Lauds. While it is a straight-forward matter to find out which style of music was condemned and which praised in any given text, it is not so apparent what the underlying rationale behind such distinctions was. Why, for example, were certain music, tones, and sounds considered to be taboo, or "excessive," "ignoble," and "depraved" (to use early Chinese terms on the matter, from such phrases as *yi yue* 溢樂 , or *yin sheng* 淫聲, *jian sheng* 賤聲, and *xie yin* 邪音), while others were extolled as "proper" (*zheng* 正)? Below, I show how discourses on "proper" vs. "excessive" music reflect a much larger cultural concern with holistic notions of harmony and balance among one's body, mind, and environment, which was also the basis for ideas about health and medicine. Through our discussion of styles of music, therefore, we arrive at a better understanding of the medical ideas associated with the musical arts.

What, one might wonder, was specifically wrong with certain styles of music, such as that from the state of Zheng, that they should elicit such a critical attitude from many of the learned elite? In one passage from the *Zuo zhuan*, we learn that musical sounds might be linked to conditions of ease and disease of the heart-mind, so that there is a medical basis for discriminating between different types of music:

二十一年春，天王將鑄無射，泠州鳩曰：「王其以心疾死乎！夫樂、天子之職也。夫音、樂之輿也；而鐘、音之器也。天子省風以作樂，，。物和則嘉成。故和聲入於耳而藏於心，心億則樂。窕則不咸，槬則不容，心是以感，感實生疾。今鐘槬矣，王心弗堪，其能久乎！」

In the spring of his twenty-first year of rule, the Heavenly King was going to cast the Wu Yi bell. Music Director Zhou Jiu states: "Will not the king die from an illness of the heart-mind! As for music, it is the duty of the Son of Heaven. Musical tones are the vehicle of music, while the bells are the instruments for the musical tones. The Son of Heaven examines the customs [of the people] in creating music ... When things are in harmony, then well-being prevails. For this reason, when harmonious sounds (*sheng*) enter the ear and nest themselves in the heart-mind, the heart-mind will be at ease and thus, joyous. If [however] the instrument is insubstantial, then [the heart-mind] cannot grasp the entirety; if it is oversized, then [the heart-mind] cannot fully embrace it. One's heart-mind will thereby become deluded. The manifestation of delusion manifests gives birth to illness. Now, the bells are oversized, and the king's heart-mind will not bear it. How can he continue in this manner for long?"[3]

Insofar as the king listens to musical sounds that are "too large" for his own heart-mind and, possibly, position as king, he is committing a ritual offense of some sort. However, the main reason for the king's disease does not merely concern ritual offense. Rather, the thrust of the criticism launched here concerns the relationship between the king's desires and his ultimate health: the king has expensive taste and engages in an endless search for luxury of the senses. Hence, this criticism mainly concerns abuses of the human body rather than abuses of ritual protocol.

Through a physiological dissection of the situation, Zhou Jiu outlines how music of a certain type—that performed on instruments either too small or too large—might adversely harm the health of the listener. While he does not single out particular styles of music as bad, Zhou Jiu nonetheless associates sounds that issue from expensive and ostentatious instruments (as many bell sets during the period were wont to be) with an individual's emotional and mental deterioration. Unnecessary extravagance is viewed as a form of excess that throws one's body out of balance. Music is an object of physiological benefit or harm, described in terms of medical diagnostics.

We might begin to understand why musical styles are relevant to the health of the body by examining the cosmic rationale behind the relationship between music and medicine. Such a rationale is introduced in the following passage in the *Zuo zhuan*:

天有六氣，降生五味，發為五色，徵為五聲。淫生六疾。六氣曰陰、陽、風、雨、晦、明也，分為四時，序為五節，過則為菑：陰淫寒疾，陽淫熱疾，風淫末疾，雨淫腹疾，晦淫惑疾，明淫心疾。

There are the Six Qi of Heaven, which descend to produce the Five Flavors, expand to make the Five Colors, manifest themselves in the Five Tones, and in excess, produce the Six Illnesses. [These aspects of Heaven] are said to be Yin, Yang, Wind, Rain, Obscure, and Bright. They divide to make the four seasons and form a sequence to give the Five Modes.[4] If there is too much [of any one of them] then disaster strikes: excessive Yin corresponds to illnesses of cold, excessive Yang, to illnesses of heat; excessive Wind, to illnesses of the extremities; excessive Rain, to illnesses of the gut; excessive Obscurity, to illnesses that entail confusion; and excessive Brightness, to illnesses of the heart-mind.[5]

Deriving all illness from imbalances of the primary Six *Qi* upon one's body, this author maps Heaven's basic components onto their corresponding parts of or influences on the body. For example, Yin, which in itself represents and manifests all that is dark, hidden, and cold, is correlated with the cold aspects of the body. For this reason, if there are excessive quantities of it interacting with the body, the body will respond to the imbalance by producing an "illness of cold." In such a way, essential aspects of the cosmos, which come together to form meteorological and seasonal patterns, might also influence the body just as they would act upon the Earth.[6] To elaborate on the meteorological metaphor: tonal imbalance in one's immediate environment affects the seasons of the body just as cosmic imbalance affects the seasons of Earth.

What is especially of interest to us is the author's reference to the Five Modes and Five Tones in relationship to the cosmos. Indeed, the Five Tones are characterized as an essential creation of cosmic *qi*—and therefore, they are as much a natural and permanent part of the universe as the

Six *Qi* themselves. Though the reference to the Five Modes is obscure and somewhat of an anomaly in the context of later Chinese musical theory, we might try to understand them from the parallel provided with the four seasons in the text.[7] Accordingly, the Five Modes appear to be but a temporal aspect of the ordering or sequencing of the Six *Qi*. Just as the four seasons are fundamentally different from each other yet dependent on each other according to a sequential, patterned, and somewhat regularized cycle, the Five Modes each possess fundamentally different characteristics from each other yet also depend on a specific sequence determined by the cosmos itself. The fact that there exists such a foundational connection between musical elements such as the Five Tones and the Five Modes and the cosmos on the one hand, and between such cosmic elements and human illness on the other, clearly shows that one's basic health is dependent on the "cosmic correctness" of the music to which one listens. As such, balance in music is not just important because it directly impacts the balance of the body; it is also important because it signifies the degree to which an individual is balanced in relationship to what is right for the cosmos as a whole.

In the *Zuo* passage leading up to this segment on cosmology, we find another comment that illuminates how concepts of musical pace and modality help in regulating human health:

晉侯求醫於秦，秦伯使醫和視之，曰：「疾不可為也，是謂近女，（室）〔生〕疾如蠱。非鬼非食，惑以喪志。良臣將死，天命不祐。」公曰：「女不可近乎？」對曰：「節之。先王之樂，所以節百事也，故有五節；[遲速本末以相及]，中聲以降。五降之後，不容彈矣。於是有煩手淫聲，慆堙心耳，乃忘平和，君子弗聽也。物亦如之。至於煩，乃舍也已，無以生疾。君子之近琴瑟，以儀節也，非以慆心也．

The Marquis of Jin requested a doctor from the state of Qin. The Earl of Qin sent Physician He to see him, who said: "I cannot cure this illness. It is called 'being too close to women,' and it produces an illness much like a *gu* 蠱 type of poisoning.[8] Not due to either ghosts or food, it brings on such confusion that one loses track of one's intent. Not even Heaven's blessing can stop the fact that a virtuous minister is going to die."[9]

The Duke asked, "May one not get close to women?"

Physician He replied, "Regulate it. The music of the Ancient Kings was used to regulate the hundred affairs. For this reason there are the Five Regulations [of the Five Tones], in which slow and fast, fundamental and subsidiary succeed each other, and modal changes would occur [only] from the central range of tones.[10] After five rounds of [such] modal changes, one should stop the performance. If at this point one's fingers are vexed and the tones are excessive, glutting the heart-mind and

congesting the ears, then one will forget [all sense of] balance and harmony. The gentleman does not listen [to such music]. It is the same with
[all] things: when they reach a point of overindulgence, then he refuses
[them], so that there is no way for illness to arise. When the gentleman
nears the *qin* and *se* zithers, he does so in order to ritually regulate [him-
self], not to glut his heart-mind."[11]

Though the Marquis' illness involved an excess of sexual relations with
women and not an excess of music, Physician He makes it a point to show
that the act of overindulging in either can bring on dire consequences for
one's health.

The analogy of music in this passage is informative, not least because it
outlines precisely how regulating music in certain ways might be beneficial
or harmful to the human body. We learn that this process involves not
merely restricting how much music is performed, but making sure that the
music one hears is music whose very modal structure and changes proceed
according to certain contemporary rules of balance and harmony. Music
whose "center of gravity" lies mostly within the modalities of the "central
tones" (which I follow commentators in interpreting as the Five Tones),
and which does not deviate from this modal range according to a measured
five rounds, is music that maintains a sense of balance and harmony within
itself. Similarly, music is considered to be good, or healthy, if its pace of fast
and slow is regulated so as to alternate one after the next and not continue
at any single pace for an inordinate amount of time. If musical modalities and pace are balanced properly, then music affects the individual in a
similar manner—an individual's body becomes tempered, paced, and well
balanced just like the music to which he listens.

The opposite musical situation also brings about a corresponding condition in the human body. Though the text speaks of "overindulging," "congesting," or "glutting" one's mind and ears, the problem that Physician He
presents is not one of quantity of music but of style. Indeed, the overindulgence of one's senses and vexing of one's fingers stems from an infraction
committed by listening to forbidden styles—styles which stray dangerously
far from the central modes without returning in due measure or according
to culturally stipulated rules of modal change.[12] Musical deviations from
what is considered to be central, balanced, and harmonious bring about
delusion, anxiety, and confusion in the listener because his sense organs,
heart-mind, and even various parts of his body (such as the fingers) will
take on the traits of the music to which he listens. Thus, since music that
deviates from notions of proper balance and harmony is necessarily "over-
indulgent," "congested," and "glutting," the body too can be so described
when in the presence of such music.

This cautionary, medicalized evaluation of music—linking musical styles to physiological excesses and imbalances—continues during the Warring States. The author of the XZMC, for example, warns not just of certain sounds in general, but of the specific dangers of the "music of [the states of] Zheng and Wei." The danger is real, he claims, because "[even though] one deems them unfit to be heard, [one] nonetheless [feels compelled] to follow them 非其聽而從之也."[13] In describing the inevitable influence of musical sounds on human psychology, the author continues to differentiate between two types of music, both of which have the power to affect humans.[14] First, there is "ancient music (*gu yue* 古樂)," which "favors the heart-mind 龍心."[15] Then, there is "excessive music (*yi yue* 益 (溢)樂)," which "favors the extremities 龍指."[16] Here, two areas of the body are linked up with two different types of music: ancient and excessive. One type of music nourishes one's central core, the heart-mind, while the other serves the interests of the more superficial parts of the body.

The hierarchy drawn between what lies at the center versus the periphery, or at the core versus the extremities of the human body, highlights values associated with some contemporary hierarchies of bodily functions.[17] For example, bona fide, proper cogitation, intention, aims, and emotions are often considered to be the domain of the heart-mind (the text of the XZMC itself attests to this), while desires are mostly associated with the sensory areas of the body, notably situated away from the heart-mind and on the surface of the body (nose, eyes, ears, mouth, fingers—for touch).[18] Thus, the author's point is clear: ancient music is proper and necessary for one's moral edification because it elevates and nourishes the most important part of the body: the heart-mind, or the core. Excessive music, on the other hand, is dangerous because it stimulates the extremities only (the domains in which the desires can come to dominate)—which are considered to be secondary and capable of throwing the entire body off balance.

Other writings also stress the dichotomy between the body's core and periphery on the one hand, and proper and excessive music on the other. In his "Discourse on Music," Xunzi condemns "barbarian customs and depraved tunes," while praising the Elegantiae and Lauds in the following manner:

使其聲足以樂而不流，使其文足以辨而不　諰，使其曲直、繁省、廉肉、節奏足以感動人之善心，使夫邪汙之氣無由得接焉．

They [the former kings] made their sounds sufficient to take delight in without getting carried away; made their lyrics sufficient to yield discernment without leading thoughts astray; made their [variations in terms of] winding or straight, intricate or sparse, austere or robust, and restrained or progressive sufficient to set into motion people's virtuous heart-minds, so that perverse, muddy energy would have no means by which to attach itself therein.[19]

Here, the heart-mind is again contrasted with secondary aspects of human physiology: here, the desires are not associated with one's extremities *per se*, but with one's *qi* (material force). If one's "virtuous heart-mind" is not activated, negative, chaotic, and depraved external energies (*xie yu zhi qi* 邪汙之氣) could introduce turbulence into the human body.

Such refined music, which Xunzi prefers simply to refer to as "Music" (*yue* 樂; I highlight this normative usage by capitalizing the term), is vital to the moral and spiritual health of a person because of its ability to bring what is at the center or core of the body (the heart-mind) to a state of harmony and equilibrium (*qi* 齊). This notion of equilibrium, I believe, refers to the straightening out or putting into alignment of particular motions (in the dance), sounds (in music), and emotions (in the heart-mind). For example, Xunzi at one point refers to the orderly equilibrium of dancers who "advance and retreat" according to a musical rhythm.[20] Interpolating from such a concrete, visual image, we might understand what Xunzi means by equilibrium when he applies it to a person's emotions, especially in his comment, "the joy and anger of the former kings were therein both able to obtain a state of equilibrium 先王〔之〕喜怒皆得其齊焉."[21] One might imagine such emotions being felt in proper time and measure, being expressed more formally as refined joy or anger, and not as a chaotic mix of various types of uneven energies. Indeed, this explanation coheres with Xunzi's descriptions of how Elegantiae and Lauds help control the heart-mind so that perverse and chaotic forms of *qi* do not disturb it. Presumably, such musical forms provide a ritualized protocol, much like that of a dance, that helps bring control, balance, and equilibrium to one's various, often opposing, emotions.

The language of centrality, harmony, and equilibrium pervade Xunzi's "Discourse" and characterize the effects of Music on individual physiology and moral psychology: "Thus, when Music is performed then one's intent is pure, when Ritual is cultivated then one's conduct is complete. One's ears and eyes are perspicacious and clear; one's blood and *qi* are harmonized and balanced 故樂行而志清，禮脩而行成，耳目聰明，血氣和平."[22] The restorative and nourishing applications of Music in this passage are clear: when one listens to Music, not only do one's senses reach their highest potency, the dynamic processes of blood and *qi* become synchronized and measured so as to provide an overall sense of well-being to the person. True, proper Music, in Xunzi's eyes, takes on the role in the body of what we would now ascribe to serotonin or endorphins.

Music helps bring about not only such physiological boons to the individual; it also helps achieve a larger, shared sense of community harmony and mutual respect:

故樂在宗廟之中，則君臣上下同聽之，莫不和敬；閨門之內，則父子兄弟同聽之，莫不和親；鄉里族長之中，則長少同聽之，莫不和順

Thus, when Music is in the midst of the ancestral temple, and the ruler and ministers, the high-ranking and the low, listen to it together, there are none who are not harmonious in their respect. When it is within the doors of chambers, and father and sons, elder and younger brothers, listen to it together, there are none who are not harmonious in their affection. When it is in the midst of towns, villages, and hamlets, and the old and young listen to it together, there are none who are not harmonious in their accord.[23]

The three Chinese terms used in this excerpt to depict different kinds of social harmony are *he jing* (和敬), *he qin* (和親), and *he shun* (和順), each of which points to the types of emotional feelings expected to obtain through idealized interactions between members of specific social groups. Subordinates apperceive of a more distant but uplifting type of respect for their superiors; lower-ranking kinsmen feel a special bond of closeness towards elder relatives; and the young appreciate a feeling of obedient harmony towards the village elders. In every case, the expression of musical harmonies translates into an appropriate feeling of social harmony elicited from the audience. We thus see how Xunzi extends his account of the medical, moral, and spiritual effects of music to encompass the larger well-being of the community. The notion of harmony links bodily and communal feelings in an integrated system of equilibrium and health.

Xunzi also speaks of Music as vital to the health of the entire state.[24] Such large-scale well-being in turn helps bring about the orderliness of one's military and the satisfaction of one's ruler, so that achieving harmony and equilibrium is a desired goal for individuals, communities, and states alike.[25] But lest we think that Xunzi limits himself to human societies, let us examine how his language of harmony, equilibrium, and centrality implies a larger sphere as well. At one point, Xunzi states that Music "is the Great Straightener of all under Heaven (i.e., the people of the world), and the Aligner of centrality and harmony 故樂者、天下之大齊也，中和之紀也."[26] Here, though the statement is vague and open to interpretation, I believe Xunzi claims that music not only straightens things out for individuals, communities, and kingdoms, it also aligns all things "under Heaven" according to the very definition of centrality and harmony. Once again, the qualities of centrality, harmony, and equilibrium—characteristic of Music for Xunzi—are thought to spread their fine qualities throughout the world, implicating individual heart-minds, state bodies, and the world in a holistic vision of world health.[27]

As the epitome of orderliness and harmony, Music holds supreme importance in keeping the world functioning properly as a single bodily system. Just as care must be taken to promote good personal health and avoid extremes within the body, Music must be approached so as to promote a salubrious balance in the body politic. It should come as no surprise, then, that Xunzi should make a calculated distinction between Music and "sounds and music" (*sheng yue* 聲樂), which includes both good and bad types of music.[28]

But what constitutes bad music for Xunzi? One of Xunzi's relevant distinctions is that between "depraved tones" (*xie yin* 邪音) and "Ritual and Music" (*li yue* 禮樂). Depraved tones incorporate certain types of sounds, such as "excessive sounds" (*yin sheng* 淫聲) or "ignoble sounds" (*jian sheng* 賤聲). To give specific, contemporary examples of what he means by such sounds, Xunzi follows the author of XZMC in denouncing the tones of [the states of] Zheng and Wei (note that he is careful not to call such things, "music"), accusing them of presenting "dazzlingly seductive appearances 姚冶之容" and "causing a person's heart-mind to go to excess 使人之心淫."[29] Indeed, the reputation of such states for beautiful, seductive women (who perform these seductive sounds) appears to have been widespread by the third century BCE.[30] He subsequently cautions the nobleman to avoid unbalancing his heart-mind in such a manner by asking him specifically to avoid dangerous inputs, including "excessive sounds," and "sexual feelings for females 女色," as well as harmful outputs, such as "uttering foul language 不出惡言."[31] The very language of excess in relationship to the body points to the underlying medical epistemology that we have been outlining so far: one that views health in terms of harmonious processes and balanced systems both within and outside of the body. Clearly, the presence of an overabundance of women or women who dressed and behaved themselves in what was considered a more sexually explicit way—i.e., not in accordance with standard, Zhou ritual protocols—were considered to be things that could upset the bodily equilibrium of viewers. Such statements attest to the predominantly male audience of not just official musical performances but of these writings as well.

Seen above, Xunzi stresses the idea that depraved sounds can wreak havoc on an individual's psychic equilibrium, well-being, moral fiber and, ultimately, on the rest of society and the world itself. What is not so obvious is that he claims a one-to-one correlation between the style and mood of a certain type of music and the various mindsets, behaviors, and levels of health that such music brings about: "When music is dazzlingly seductive by being headlong, then the people will be disrespectful and lowly. Disrespectful, they will bring about disorder; lowly, they will be contentious 樂姚冶以險，則民流慢鄙賤矣。流慢則亂，鄙賤則爭."[32] This one-to-one correlation between music and the individual body is possible because, Xunzi contends, music interacts with humans at the most basic levels of *qi*:

> 凡姦聲感人而逆氣應之，逆氣成象而亂生焉；正聲感人而順氣應之，順氣成象而治生焉。唱和有應，善惡相象
>
> In general, when depraved sounds stimulate a person, then a wayward *qi* responds to it, and when this wayward *qi* takes an outward form, then chaos is born therein. [On the contrary,] whenever upright sounds stimulate a person, then a compliant *qi* responds to it, and when this compliant *qi* takes an outward form, then order is born therein. Lead voices and harmonies each have their respective responses, and good and bad each produces its outward form.[33]

Describing a system of stimulus and response (*gan ying* 感應), a notion of causation that reaches maturity in the early imperial period, Xunzi explains the mechanics of musical influence on the human psyche, thereby linking his moral claims about musical style to contemporary, medical beliefs about natural/spiritual law and the human body.

So far, it seems clear that the relevant distinction for Xunzi between different types of musical sound lies in the extent to which certain sounds might elicit a harmonious, peaceful, and orderly response in humans, as opposed to a wayward, unbalanced, and chaotic response. Music, or that which stimulates the former, thus becomes nothing more than a critical, psycho-physiological tool for attaining the moral Dao, as well as a profound state of well-being, much as one would describe the effects of yoga or meditation practices today: "Thus, Music (*yue* 樂) is happiness (*yue* 樂). The nobleman finds happiness in obtaining his Dao, while the petty man finds happiness in his desires 故曰：「樂者、樂也。」君子樂得其道，小人樂得其欲."[34] Here, Xunzi brings in the moral rhetoric of the nobleman—associated with the Dao—and the petty man—associated with base ways—to reinforce the dichotomy between true Music and depraved sounds. Happiness through the moral Dao is distinguished from happiness through one's desires, which presumably correspond to a lesser happiness linked to the fulfillment of the senses. This shows how music associated with moral cultivation might qualitatively change the type of happiness one perceives.

From these descriptions of music in the *Zuo zhuan*, XZMC, and *Xunzi*, we see that processes of musical canonization were part and parcel of a growing interest in medicalizing self-cultivation towards the end of the Warring States period. Quite possibly, the process by which music was canonized was linked to physical practices—such as meditation or yogic stretching—said to link the moral goals of virtue and refined, gentlemanly behavior with the spiritual, physiological, and medical goals of an equanimous heart-mind. The practice of "not-moving the heart-mind," described in *Mencius* 2A2 and associated with a physical practice pursued by both Mencius and Gaozi to achieve higher levels of moral awareness, comes to mind as a possible example of such physical techniques. Indeed, since at least the fourth century BCE, the theme of depraved excess of the body and a disordered state or age became almost pervasive in literature on music, especially in writings stemming from Ru traditions.

As the frame of reference for discussing music came to involve the cosmos and not merely the individual and state, we see how conceptions of health were expanded to include individual bodies as microcosms of an entire universe. Music came to have a robust effect upon ever larger spheres of the environment. In the following citation attributed to the Zhou Jiu 伶州鳩 in the *Guo yu*, we see how the entire cosmological complex of music, the human body, the governmental apparatus, and one's natural environment are implicated in a single macrocosmic vision of health:

「夫政象樂，樂從和，和從平. 聲以和樂，律以平聲 ... 物得其常曰樂極 ... 如是，而鑄之金，磨之石，繫之絲木，越之匏竹，節之鼓而行之，以遂八風. 於是乎氣無滯陰，亦無散陽，陰陽序次，風雨時至，嘉生繁祉，人民龢利，物備而樂成，上下不罷，故曰樂正.

Government adopts the image of music: music comes from harmony, and harmony comes from balance ... [35] When things have obtained their constancy, we call this "the crowning of music" ... In such a way, the casting of metal, the polishing of stone, the attaching of silk and wood, the boring of holes in gourds and bamboo, and regulating the size of drums all carries it [music] forth, so as to follow along with the Eight Winds. And so, [the surrounding] *qi* will harbor no obstructed Yin or scattered Yang. Yin and Yang will proceed in an orderly fashion, and wind and rain will arrive at the appropriate times. There will be favorable growth and bountiful blessings, the people will benefit and be in accord, things will be complete and music perfected, and neither superiors nor inferiors will be overworked. Thus we say that music is has been rectified. [36]

Here, harmonious music follows along with the diversity of sounds in the cosmos—as expressed through the Eight Winds—allowing natural cycles and systems to proceed without monotony and obstruction. It creates a thriving environment of *qi* in which people, animals and plants, winds and weather conditions, and governmental systems might all thrive. A balance of *yin-yang* forces obtains, as neither overwhelms the other in excess.

In this idyllic picture of music, cosmic flourishing is omnipresent, extending to individual bodies and social life as well as the natural world. Music must meet a certain standard in order to be cosmically efficacious, and so, only proper music accords with natural processes, harmonies, and balance. For this reason, the rectification of music according to the harmony and balance of the cosmos is nothing short of the perfect solution to the imbalances and pitfalls of human, social, and cosmic bodies.[37] Through such passages, we see clearly how the discourse on proper and excessive music was intimately linked to a medicalized understanding the human body in terms of a system of balances in the cosmos at large.

MUSICAL ASCETICISM AND MODERATION

In chapter one, we examined ways in which music was thought to bring down a state by contributing to the physiological and moral demise of its ruler. In such contexts, music resembled a dangerous substance that must be strictly regulated and used in moderation, lest it get the better of the individual. In this section, we highlight the role of music in ascetic health practices, making note of how authors promoted moderation as a method of achieving bodily and cosmic balance. Our focus here is therefore not on music as a type of medicinal substance per se, but on music as that which must be used, understood, and appreciated as part of an ascetic regimen of body and mind.

In *Zuo zhuan* (Xiang 10.2), incorrect use of music can bring about sickness associated with evil spirits. The Duke of Song entertains the Marquis of Jin with a musical dance called "Sang Lin 桑林," which was traditionally the sole prerogative of the Son of Heaven and not the state of Song (where it was customarily performed—in defiance of Zhou ritual protocol).[38] The Marquis, a proper gentleman, demonstrates his virtue by effectively hiding out in an adjacent room until the musical performance was completed, thereby avoiding having to witness or be present for an improper act. When the Marquis subsequently falls ill and consults the tortoise shell to find out about his sickness, the spirit of Sang Lin appears. Rather than pray to appease it, a spokesperson for the Marquis insists on the latter's innocence in the matter, declaring: "We declined the ceremony; they were the ones to perform it. If indeed this were an appearance of the spirit, then the punishments should be heaped on them [the state of Song] 我辭禮矣，彼則以之。猶有鬼神，於彼加之。"[39] After this, the Marquis recovered from his illness.

In this story, we see how illness is deeply intertwined with morality and one's proper use of the rites. Though it is a spirit who acts here as the pathogenic agent and mistakenly makes the Marquis sick, music plays a role in the process. The Marquis represents the moralist whose upright behavior and appropriate use of ritual helps ward off ills. Musical performance, as a type of rite, stands as the primary subject of moral scrutiny. Proper regulation of what one hears thus represents a critical method of both insuring one's moral integrity and keeping the body healthy and free of pathogens.

In the following passage from the *Zhanguo ce*, we see how music might be might signify a life of luxury and the senses. Like a dazzling female beauty, one must approach this potentially dangerous medium with discipline, taking care not to fall into its alluring traps:

魏文侯與田子方飲酒而稱樂. 文侯曰:「鍾聲不比乎,左高。」田子方笑。文侯曰:「奚笑?」子方曰:「臣聞之,君明則樂官,不明則樂音。今君審於聲,臣恐君之聾於官也。」文侯曰:「善,敬聞命。」

Marquis Wen of Wei drank and listened to music together with Tian Zifang when he said [to him]: "The sounds of the bells are not in tune; the ones on the left are sharp." Tian Zifang laughed. When Marquis Wen asked "Why do you laugh?" the latter replied, "Your servant has heard it said that when a ruler is enlightened, then he takes pleasure in offices; when he is not enlightened, then he takes pleasure in tones. Now My Lord pays attention to sounds, and so your servant fears that he is deaf to offices." The Marquis replied, "Good. I respectfully ask to hear [your opinion of] my fate."[40]

Here, it is neither the style nor quantity of music that is at issue. The very fact that Marquis Wen pays attention to music is read by Tian Zifang as a sign of sensual indulgence at the expense of more important matters of the state, which, in turn, will affect the Marquis' general fate (along with the fate of his state). Certainly, that music symbolizes only luxury and pleasure, and that it stands in a mutually exclusive relationship with official business is an extreme stance that one would expect from a Mohist or conservative moralist. Yet for the story at hand to make sense, such an attitude must also have been embraced at some level by a wider audience, such as the expected readership of the *Zhanguo ce*. We might therefore assume that music could be perceived as dangerous material in and of itself, which warranted use but not overzealous attention. According to this view, moderate use of music involves a dispassionate, rather sanitized use of music in which one might show one's appreciation without displaying great interest in or knowledge about it.

The relationship between medicine and music in this passage is less clear, though implicit. That the Marquis promptly asks Tian Zifang to discuss his fate (*ming*) for him reveals the common belief that a ruler's attitude towards music could expose the condition of both his personal health and the wider health of the state. The concept of *ming* is used in early China to designate not just a personal destiny, which is often understood in terms of one's health, illnesses, and life-span (e.g., an untimely death from illness would be attributed to *ming*). If the ruler's *ming* were under scrutiny, such a *ming* could also include the broader health and destiny of the state, since the health of the ruler was seen as a conduit for the larger whole. Thus, the fact that the Marquis' *ming* was to be discussed in the wake of this criticism suggests that personal and state health was thought to be directly correlated with a ruler's attitudes towards music.[41]

A similar situation arises in another section of the *Zuo zhuan*, where a certain Yue Qi predicts the deaths of a ruler and his listening companion based on their uses of and attitudes towards music:

宋公享昭子，賦《新宮》。昭子賦《車轄》。明日宴，飲酒，樂，宋公使昭子右坐，語相泣也。樂祁佐，退而告人曰：「今茲君與叔孫其皆死乎！吾聞之：『哀樂而樂哀，皆喪心也。』心之精爽，是謂魂魄。魂魄去之，何以能久？」

The Duke of Song fêted Zhaozi, singing him the poem, "New Palace," to which Zhaozi responded with the poem, "Chariot Linchpins."[42] The next day when they feasted, drank liquors, and enjoyed musical performances, the Duke of Song made Zhaozi sit to his right, and when they talked they wept among themselves. Yue Qi was assisting [at the feasts], and retreated to report to others, saying "At present our Lord and Shusun are both likely to die! I have heard it said that sadness in the midst of joy and joy in the midst of sadness both signal the loss of one's heart-mind. The quintessential vigor of the heart-mind lies in what are known as the *hun* and *po* [spirits]. When the *hun* and *po* leave a person, how can he last for much longer?"[43]

This passage parallels the previous one found in the *Zhanguo Ce*, except that it is much more explicit in terms of what is meant by the fate of the Duke and his companion. Here, the manner in which one engages in music-making signals an entire way of life—one of luxury and overindulgence of one's senses and appetites. The effect of such unregulated indulgence of the senses and appetites results in an unleashing of strong passions such as joy and sadness. Such a torrent of untempered emotions is considered to be harmful and bring on illness and even death not because of the power any individual emotion might unleash. Rather, the issue again revolves around the notion of what is appropriate, and what is appropriate involves the balancing and harmonizing of the emotions.

Here we see that the mixing of two potent and opposite emotions such as joy and sadness was thought to violate a fundamental sense of balance. Although individual emotions are not to be shunned, they are to be expressed properly—according to regulations of some sort. But what might such regulations be? Judging from the context of this passage, emotions should be expressed one at a time, just as the Five Modes mentioned above were to be performed one at a time without mixing. And just as the manner in which one changed musical modes was strictly regulated, one could not just willy-nilly switch from one emotion to the next (as did the Duke of Song and Zhaozi). Whether emotions or modes, individuals and music had to be kept in balance and timed according to an awareness of what was befitting of the context. This parallels situations described in the *Analects* in which Confucius made certain not to sing on days on which he had already wept.[44]

In a lengthy *Zuo zhuan* passage that explains the merits of ritual—and music as a part of ritual—we further see the link between musical sounds and one's health, well-being, and even long life. I cite a portion of it here:

夫禮、天之經也，地之義也，民之行也。天地之經，而民實則之。則天之明，因地之性，生其六氣，用其五行。氣為五味，發為五色，章為五聲。淫則昏亂，民失其性。是故為禮以奉之

As for ritual, it is the warp of Heaven, the rightness of Earth, and the conduct of the people. It is the warp of Heaven and Earth, yet it is the people who realize and regulate it. Regulating the brightness of Heaven and following the nature of Earth, [the people] produce the Six Qi (of Heaven and Earth) and employ its five phases. These Qi form the Five Flavors, go forth as the Five Colors, and are displayed as the Five Tones. When in excess, then there is confusion and disorder, and the people lose hold of their natures. For this reason [people] created ritual to respectfully present it [to Heaven and Earth?].[45]

In the same way that authors speak of moderating music so as to balance one's emotions and desires and attain good health, the author of this passage proclaims that ritual helps balance the sensory intake of humans. A balanced sensory load allows people to hold on to their basic natures (*xing* 性) and achieve a sense of clarity and order. Conversely, the opposite effect is produced by a disruption of this balancing act, which requires tempering one's intake of the Five Flavors, Colors, and Tones. This passage gives us a sense of the extent to which the discourse on music and health was a part of the larger rationale behind sumptuary and ritual regulation in ancient Chinese society.

In passages like these found in the *Zuo zhuan* and *Zhanguo ce*, we see how music was something to be enjoyed or appreciated in specific, regulated ways. While the notion of moderation was interpreted differently in different texts and passages, all of the passages examined seem to agree that the moderation of music could help prevent illness, confusion, and even death. Notions of extravagance concerning conspicuous opulence converged with notions of extravagance concerning musical style and harmony. Thus, ideas about musical style and its effects on the human body were grounded in larger, more generalized conceptions—often including the realm of ritual—of what was considered to be extravagant, unnecessary, excessive and unbalanced in one's lifestyle. In such cases, music was harmful because it provided one with opportunities to deviate from cultural and ritual forms, instead overindulging the senses with frivolous entertainment.

Many of passages examined highlight the importance of maintaining balance and harmony inside and outside one's body. Cosmos and body are intertwined in a sphere of mutually influencing *qi*. Just as the *qi* of the cosmos act upon the Earth in the form of weather patterns and seasons to help determine the conditions for life, they act upon and influence the human body to help determine the latter's health and well-being. And, just as such *qi* need to be in balance to provide the ideal conditions for life on Earth, they also need to find balance and harmony to provide for one's basic health. Since music serves as a vehicle that can either nourish or upset the ideal, balance and harmony of *qi* in one's body, the ascetic moderation of music becomes a matter of survival: of health and life over death. The ideal of balancing and harmonizing one's body with the larger cosmos is in principle very similar to the goal of sagely, cosmic attunement described in the last chapter. One main difference is that the goal of tempering bodily *qi* in these passages is not so much an exclusive spiritual goal for the sage as it is a medical goal for the people at large or the moral gentleman specifically.

MUSIC AS MEDICINE OR TONIC

Another way in which music served in a medical capacity was as a medicine or tonic that transformed the body through direct "ingestion" of it. Such instances are similar to the recommended use of music as a means of achieving bodily balance and harmony just examined, especially insofar as the passages described above imply that music has a certain effect on the body, just as would a medicine or tonic. The main difference, however, is that in the passages to be analyzed below, the analogy of medicine as a form of medicinal is much more obvious and often stated explicitly. Discussions of music as a medicinal also revolve around the solution to simple or temporary imbalances or bodily needs, and so they often do not take large-scale cosmic and bodily harmony as the ultimate goal. Such discussions show how music could help fight disease or otherwise boost human health and the spirit. In such a way, they belong more to the genre of therapeutic recipes for specific ailments and problems rather than philosophical, moral rhetoric and cosmological theorizing about society's and a ruler's ills.

In previous chapters, we saw how Xunzi links music to the robustness of one's *qi* and emotional and moral stature. The *Zuo zhuan*, as well, attests to the value of music as nourishment for a proper fighting spirit:

晉侯將伐虢。士蒍曰:「不可。虢公驕,若驟得勝於我,必棄其民。無眾而後伐之,欲禦我,誰與?夫禮、樂、慈、愛,戰所畜也。夫民讓事、樂和、愛親、哀喪,而後可用也。虢弗畜也,亟戰,將饑。

Now, ritual, music, compassion, and affection are the means by which one nourishes oneself for battle. Only after the people [are taught to be] yielding in their affairs, to take pleasure in harmony, to love their kin and grieve the loss of them can they be used [to fight in battle]. Guo does not nourish these. He sends his people frequently into battle, and [so] they will starve.[46]

At first glance, this passage does not necessarily speak directly of cultivating the people's health through music. The phrase, "nourishing oneself for battle" could refer to the type of moral education thought necessary to maintain discipline and organization in the army, as referenced in *Analects* 13.29 and 13.30. However, the particular juxtaposition of the verb, "to nourish (*xu* 畜)," on the one hand, with "starvation," on the other, suggests that the lack of one may cause the other. Even if this were a metaphorical use of the term "nourish," as some commentators suggest, the point of the passage is to say that the people become unhealthy or sickly when not properly nourished, so that health—metaphorical or not—is ultimately the issue.[47] Understood more literally, the notion that people might starve from a lack of proper ritual, musical, and emotional nourishment—simply because they will have to engage in a behavior (going to war frequently) that weakens them instead—suggests that these forms of nourishment actually provide a tangible means for protecting one against such blights as starvation. In either case, music is one element of many that serves as a tonic for human health and boon for battle, at the very least because it promotes healthy behaviors that help lead to military success.

In a somewhat different vein, the following passage in the *Zuo zhuan* shows that music, and especially the louder sounds of brass and drums, might be used to uplift the spirit, or even to energize one's troops—much to the same effect as a jolt of caffeine seems to energize and arouse people for work today: "The three armies use sharp [weapons to fight], while bronze instruments and drums are utilized to 'sound out' the men's *qi*. It is appropriate sharpen one's weapons and thus use them when fighting in a strategic pass; while it is appropriate for the loudest sounds to drum up fighting spirit when launching a surprise attack 三軍以利用也，金鼓以聲氣也。利而用之，阻隘可也；聲盛致志，鼓儳可也."[48] While the object of discussion in this passage is not music *per se* but sounds played rhythmically to either signal fighting or drum up spiritual support for it, such sounds derive in part from bronze instruments that were associated primarily with ritual performances at court. Clearly, the sounds of drums and bronzes could have a clear effect on the morale, spirit, and aim of one's troops. Because of their effects on the physiology of the body, such sounds could therefore be used to enhance the general health of a military body as a unit.

It is in the spirit of rousing troops and training them to focus on a shared objective that we might understand music as presented in the next passage, also found in the *Zuo zhuan*:

楚令尹子元欲蠱文夫人，為館於其宮側而振萬焉。夫人聞之，泣曰：「先君以是舞也，習戎備也。今令尹不尋諸仇讎，而於未亡人之側，不亦異乎！」御人以告子元。子元曰：「婦人不忘襲讎，我反忘之！」

The chief minister of Chu, Zi Yuan,[49] wished to seduce Lady Wen (the widow of King Wen of Lu), so he constructed a large hall by the side of her palace, where he had dancers perform the Wan dance.[50] When the lady heard it, she wept and said, "My deceased Lord used this dance to train his troops for battle. But now the Minister, rather than use it against our enemies, is having it performed by the side of one who is not yet dead—is this not outlandish?"[51] One of her attendants told Zi Yuan about her remarks, whereupon, he exclaimed: "The Madame does not forget [the importance of] surprising one's enemies, whereas I on the contrary have forgotten it!"[52]

Though the exact function of the Wan dance still eludes commentators, many agree that it was commonly used at ritual sacrifices to ancestors and that it could incorporate both military and civil (or "refined") elements.[53] Here, we learn that it was used by some rulers to "train troops for battle," and that such a usage of it was considered valuable precisely rulers could "surprise one's enemies" with it. From such descriptions, we might surmise that the dance helped discipline troops to work together in rhythmic unison—so as to function as a single, effective unit rather than a mass of incoherent individuals. Another interpretation—one that is certainly not mutually exclusive with the previous one—is that the dance was understood to help "rouse" the fighting spirit and optimism of the troops, which would boost their courage and chances of success on the battlefield.

Both this passage and the previous one in the *Zuo zhuan*, Duke Xi, 22.8, mention music in relationship to the practice of launching surprise attacks on enemy. Only when an enemy lacks coherence, organization, and a unified spirit or sense of direction and purpose, might one speak of a "surprise attack." To say that music is especially effective in launching such attacks on an enemy suggests that music helps instill precisely those traits that help distinguish coordinated troops from chaotic troops under attack. Furthermore, it is surely no coincidence that the term for performing the Wan dance in the last passage is not "to perform," but "to rouse (*zhen* 振)"—a verb that is often used in connection with drum beats and rhythms. That both passages should speak of sound or music and, in particular, drum beats as a means of rousing troops for a surprise attack suggests that such musical sounds were not just valued for the discipline they might achieve. They were thought to be capable of unifying the intent and spirit of an entire brigade, of creating a single, resolute body out of several tens or hundreds of individual bodies and of exciting such a body to the point that it is capable of serving a formidable blow to any troops that might be unprepared for it. In other words, both contexts suggest that the spirit of one's troops could be roused and unified by drum music, thereby lending one's army coherence and unity that will aid them in battle.

Though not used to ward off or cure illnesses, this particular usage of music might be understood as "medical" insofar as it helps boost the effectiveness, purpose, and commitment of troops that might otherwise be characterized by disarray and a general malaise of the spirit. It is "medical" in the sense of being "nutritional" to the body in some way. That early Chinese rulers and thinkers would recognize such nutritional aspects of music and how they might be applied in the society is not surprising and entirely in keeping with what we have seen thus far about their beliefs concerning music and the heart-mind, *qi*, and body. What might appear surprising, perhaps, is the military context in which music brings about its beneficial results. Evidence of musical instruments in tombs suggests that there was a "frequent association of musical instruments with weapons and chariots."[54] Precisely what such evidence means is subject to debate: that musical instruments should be buried in the same compartment with objects of war may merely point to the ancients' desire to both protect and entertain themselves in the afterlife.[55] Given what appears to have been a tradition of using musical instruments as alerts or signals to troops as well as a means of divining the outcomes of battles (seen in chapter three), we might see this particular deployment of musical elements (certainly not *yue* in its full glory) in military training as a natural development in the discourse on the benefits of music on bodily health.

In a lengthy *Zuo zhuan* passage on ritual examined briefly above (Zhao 25.3), the author provides a very informative account of one's natural, emotional responses to ritual and the Five Tones. It is in this discussion that we find the directive to moderate one's emotions according to a pattern that helps humans fit themselves appropriately within the cosmic triad of Heaven-Earth-human: "'[Only] when sadness and happiness do not lose [their proper places] might one harmonize with the natures of Heaven and Earth. This is the way in which one can exist for a long time.' Jianzi exclaimed, 'Mighty indeed is Ritual!' 哀樂不失，乃能協于天地之性，是以長久. 簡子曰：「甚哉，禮之大也」."[56] Though the author speaks most directly here about ritual, his medical discussion of its benefits appears as though it could be drawn directly from discourses on music that we have been looking at so far. Here, ritual contributes to bodily cultivation and serves as a tonic for long life. It helps one achieve these things by optimizing one's emotional balance so that it accompanies and even accentuates the basic natures of Heaven and Earth—or the cosmos.[57] Interestingly, achieving a certain type of unity with the basic nature of the cosmos is said to affect the human lifespan. Humans might thus join the symphonic processes of Heaven and Earth by finding their own "cosmic groove" and ultimately attaining an enhanced, long life because of it.

Music brings about salutary effects on the body might primarily because of its harmonious qualities, which allow individuals to tune themselves to the harmonies of the cosmos, thereby tapping into its life-giving qualities of health. In a previously cited passage from the *Zuo zhuan*, we see how harmony serves as a prerequisite for a gentleman's peace of heart-mind. It helps to consider the fuller context here so as to understand how the author links cosmic harmony with individual benefits, medical, spiritual, and moral:

先王之濟五味、和五聲也，以平其心，成其政也。聲亦如味，一氣，二體，三類，四物，五聲，六律，七音，八風，九歌，以相成也；清濁、大小、短長、疾徐，哀樂、剛柔，遲速、高下，出入、周疏，以相濟也。君子聽之，以平其心。心平，德和。故《詩》曰：『德音不瑕』。今據不然。君所謂可，據亦曰可；君所謂否，據亦曰否。若以水濟水，誰能食之？若琴瑟之專壹，誰能聽之？同之不可也如是。」

The former kings enhanced the Five Tastes and harmonized the Five Sounds so as to steady their heart-minds and establish government. The sounds are similar to the tastes. [In music, for example], there is the Single

Qi, the Two Dances, the Three Genres [of Odes], the Four Objects [for performance], the Five Tones, the Six Pitch-standards, the Seven Melodies, the Eight Winds, and the Nine Songs—all of which mutually interact and complete [the music]. There is also the turbid and the clear, small and large, short and long, fast and slow, sad and happy, hard and soft, delayed and hastened, high and low, the departing and the coming, and the dense and the sparse—all of which mutually enhance each other.

The gentleman hears such music and steadies his heart-mind. When his heart-mind is steadied, his virtue becomes harmonious. Hence the Odes say: "His virtuous reputation [literally: "the tone of his virtue"] has no flaw."[58] Now, Ju is not like this. Whatever the ruler says is permissible, he also says is permissible. Whatever the ruler rejects, he also rejects. If one were to enhance water with water, who would be able to eat it? If one were to [play on] *qin* and *se* zithers of only a single note, then who would be able to listen to them? The impossibility of "sameness" is like this."[59]

The ostensible point of this passage is to demonstrate the merits of harmony, as understood by the fruitful coming together of many diverse elements, rather than the voicing of things in unison.[60] As in many passages that describe a sage's attunement to the cosmos through the calming and balancing of his heart-mind, this passage also stresses the balancing of one's psyche so as to achieve a steady, equanimous state of being. And, similar to many Ru texts that connect music to moral psychology and cultivation, this passage goes on to link a tranquil state of mind with one's Virtue (*De* 德), whose quality will be superior as it emanates from one's person. The health benefits of music on an individual therefore do not merely involve the physical steadying of one's heart-mind, they also help spawn the development of other positive aspects of a person, like one's superior Virtue, sense of empathy, knowledge of another, cosmic connectedness, etc.

Archaeological evidence demonstrates the prevalence of tiny jade figures of dancing women with long sleeves and curving, bent bodies, dating to the Western Han.[61] Indeed, these may simply be figures of everyday musicians placed in the tomb to entertain its occupant. Tentatively identified by some art historians as "jade maidens," which refer to the names of dancing female spirit mediums mentioned in the *Chu ci* and other Han *fu* (poems), these figures may underscore the importance of music and dance in shamanic rituals associated with the South during the early imperial period.[62] Aimed at summoning the spirits in order to aid humans in some way, such dancing might have been associated with the act of exorcizing illness-causing spirits. Whether or not such dances would have been referred to as *yue* (music) is uncertain, just as it is unclear whether dancers of these types would have been placed in tombs for exorcistic, spirit-related purposes or merely for entertainment. In any case, the prevalence of such figures suggests an appreciation of a specific type of musical event that likely played a role in bringing benefit, health, and well-being to humans, in addition to spiritual and aesthetic enjoyment.[63]

One finds music as a source or cause of illness among a state's population as well. For example, in the *Han shu*, music coming from the states of Zheng, Wei, Song, and Zhao was said to have made people sick on the inside and live shorter lives while contributing to a chaotic government and injuring the people in society at large.[64] Here the author appeals to a type of environmental determinism that causally links sounds from certain cultures and states to the physiological well-being of the people who live in those regions. His argument is based on a science of physical influence supported by the concept of *qi*, which is linked to sound and wind. Clearly, the theme of musical influence on the physiological state of humans constitutes a robust belief even through the Han imperial era.

Similarly, in the *Huainanzi*, an author goes so far as to link both doomed states and depraved music with diseased people:

及至亂主，取民則不裁其力，求於下則不量其積，男女不得事耕織之業以供上之求，力勤財匱，君臣相疾也。故民至於焦脣沸肝，有今無儲，而乃始撞大鍾，擊鳴鼓，吹竽笙，彈琴瑟。。 失樂之所由生矣。

When it comes to chaotic rulers, they do not properly gauge the labor of their population, and they place demands on their inferiors without first measuring their capacities. Men and women cannot manage their farming and sewing work so as to meet the demands of taxation from above. Labor is hard and resources are squandered, and ruler and minister are antagonistic toward each other. Thus, the people reach a stage of having parched lips and boiling livers; they have enough for now but nothing saved up.[65] And yet [such rulers] begin to strike the big bells, beat their resonant drums, blow into their reed pipes and pan pipes, and pluck the large and small zithers . . . The loss of happiness starts from this.[66]

According to the statements preceding this passage, music provides a means for people to adorn and outwardly express their feelings of happiness (*yue*). In the same way, ritual vessels call forth the people's goodness, military weapons and gear decorate their anger, and mourning garments give outward expression to their sadness within.[67] As such, music is but an outward manifestation of certain internal—even medical—conditions in humans. So when humans experience bitterness and turmoil, such feelings are necessarily revealed through the sounds they make.

Since the music that is implied in this passage most likely refers to the ruler's music—and not the music of the diseased people themselves—a ruler's internal chaos and lack of personal measure translates into music that is inappropriate for the given conditions and circumstances of his rule. Thus, the fact that diseased people "lose their happiness" corresponds to the fact that their chaotic ruler performs music inappropriately and does not care about the proper measures of ruling his people.[68] As this passage bears out, prestigious musical performances that are not accompanied by proper state rule are symptoms of a diseased ruler and society, and they bring about the further loss of happiness among the population.

The appropriate flow of the cosmos, expressed through musical performances, promotes the health of a society and its individuals. Consider the following passage, from the *Lüshi chunqiu*, which reconstructs the origins of a particular dance that brings health and environmental benefits to society:

昔陶唐氏之始，陰多滯伏而湛積，（水）〔陽〕道壅塞，不行其（原）〔序〕，民氣鬱閼而滯著，筋骨瑟縮不達，故作為舞以宣導之

In the past, at the inception of the Yinkang clan, the Yin had coagulated in great amounts and accumulated excessively.[69] The watercourses were blocked and obstructed, and water could not flow out from springs. The ethers of the people became thick and clogged up, and their muscles and bones tight and constricted. They therefore invented a dance with which to spread and guide the Yin.[70]

Here, the principle of harmony and the balance of *yin-yang* forces in the world is one and the same as the principles of balance within the Yinkang clan and the individual human body. Just like Yu the Great, who tamed and controlled the waterways of ancient times, the dance mentioned here represents the power of humans to intervene in the natural world in a harmonious way. The physical movement of the dance helps unclog and relax watercourses and vessels in the human body just as the act of dredging canals and diverting water helps direct water through the veins of the Earth. The dance is thus a rhythmic exercise that nourishes and restores the proper cosmic flow in the body.

CONCLUSION

In this chapter we have seen how music serves not just as a vehicle for benevolent government rule, moral cultivation, or cosmic attunement; it acts as a potent medical intervention as well. Certain types of music and sounds were singled out as unfit for audiences, and especially, heads of state, because of the ill effects they had on the health and the well-being of various types of bodies: the individual, the social, and, sometimes, the cosmic. The "tunes of Zheng and Wei," "excessive music," or "depraved sounds" are all references to styles and types of music denounced by many writers, and especially the Ru, by around 400 BCE.

Discussions of proper and excessive styles of music came to adopt a medical language that described how sounds and tunes affected the proper balance of the body and heart-mind and, in an isomorphic manner, how they affected the state and cosmos. This medical language was grounded in a religious cosmology, which came to the fore in the middle and late Warring States period, that underscored the belief in an idealized, macrocosmic-microcosmic harmony between the human body and cosmos. In texts dating to 300 BCE and later, authors began to view the workings of the cosmos and the human body, as well as the relationship between the two, in terms of a type of musical harmony. This harmony shaped the construction and transformation of certain forms of ethical cosmology, serving as the primary means by which notions of the taboo were built and styles of music were contested. In effect, the notion of the "taboo" became enmeshed in a larger discourse on man's physico-spiritual, or medical, relationship to the cosmos.

With the onset of cosmologies of resonance and macro-microcosmic harmony, musical types was distinguished from each other not on the basis of a dichotomy of secular entertainments vs. religious ritual, but according to an evaluation of its effects on the natural balance and equilibrium of component parts of the cosmos. Proper music came to be perceived as spiritually uplifting and good for one's health not because "God deemed it so" but because it resonated with the patterns, rhythms, and overarching harmony and balance of the sacred cosmos. Similarly, excessive music such as the tunes of Zheng interfered with such a balance, introducing disruptive, chaotic elements not only deep into the psyche of individuals who listened to it, but into their bodily health and ethical well-being, not to mention the health and well-being of society, the state, and cosmos.

In our analysis of texts in this chapter, we located instances in early Chinese literature that pointed to a connection between music and medicine, and music and health/disease. We built upon previous discussions of music in both beneficial and detrimental relationship to the body so as to draw up an account of the specifically medical uses of music in these texts. Though medical connections with music have always been implied through the dominant idea that music helps one cultivate the body, the passages examined here understood music to act in explicitly potent, physiological ways. Music, indeed, could serve as a pathogen, tonic, elixir, or vehicle of health or disease, depending on the type of music and the way it was used or performed.

In our examination of many narratives from the *Zuo zhuan* and a few other sources, we learned how a notion of musical asceticism arose in conjunction with larger beliefs about the importance of ritual in helping regulate human behavior and health. We saw how discourses that encouraged moderation of sensory inputs fit into an overall, cosmic conception of human health. According to such a conception, human health should mimic the ideal, natural balance and patterns of *qi* in the cosmos. Any disruption to such a balance and to the regularities of its patterns has the potential to bring about death, disease, and other disorders such as delusion, anxiety, and mental "congestion."

Music was also used as a tonic for curing illness, warding off disease, and generally improving health. It appears as though this connection between music and medicine could be age-old: according to Shizuka Shirakawa, the etymology of the term for "physician" (*yi* 醫) refers to the sounds of exorcistic beating.[71] Admittedly, while "music" as *yue* includes much more than mantic rituals or incantations, one cannot deny the relationship between such forms of rhythmic and, possibly, melodic manipulations of sound and what develops into *yue*-music. So while the *yi* were not considered to be musicians in any specialized sense of what was viewed as *yue* in China, medicine that incorporated certain elements of music (such as drum beats), along with medical interpretations of music appear not to have been uncommon throughout early times.

Conclusion

This book narrates a development concerning ancient Chinese views on music that is at once spiritual and political: the growth of a belief that music serves as the basic modality of the cosmos—as its mode of operation, so to speak. What might explain the emergence of music as a central human link to the cosmos? The most convincing answer, I show, calls for a rather simple explanation, or "single thread" that ties together many early diverse conceptions of music and the cosmos. It is the idea that harmony, along with other integral concepts like balance and resonance, emerged as a concept intrinsic to the operations and functioning of the cosmos. In an age when accounts of naturalistic, systematic cosmologies appeared differently from text to text and author to author, one striking consensus regarding the core nature of the cosmos seems to have surfaced: the cosmos functioned according to harmonious patterns and resonant synchronicities. From the start, such concepts were all tightly linked to music.

That the cosmos functioned according to harmonious patterns and resonant synchronicities is reflected clearly in what came to be known as Five Phases cosmology, which laid out an elaborate system of correspondences among objects of the world. Such a cosmology of correspondences not only expressed the goal of regularity, system, and cause and effect through mere correlation—or, perhaps better expressed, through a belief in the resonance between certain remote objects–it epitomized the orderly coming together of many variegated types of objects and forces. As such, it came to embody an early Chinese concept of harmony, as that which brings many disparate elements together in a seamless, orderly fashion.

The movements and activities of astral bodies, meteorological phenomena, and even human bodies were all considered to be integral to the harmonious, resonant cosmos. Many of the texts examined in this book presented the cosmos—also sometimes referred to as the Dao of Heaven—in terms of felicitous and balanced patterns expressed through the circulation of *qi* through winds, the human body, the seasonal cycle, and the weather. Every text examined here seems to agree that the harmony and balance of these cosmic phenomena would allow for the regular and orderly flourishing of things, individuals, and societies in the world, while their disharmony would cause the opposite. With such an image of cosmos in mind, it stands to reason that the concept of harmony, including all that it encompassed (e.g., such things as resonance, order, regularity, and balance), helped place music at the center of cosmological discourse, raising its status from that of an exercise, enjoyable activity, cultural form, or commemorative and sacrificial ritual, to something that mimicked the cosmos and also constituted an integral aspect of cosmic operations.

As concepts of the body emerged in congruence with new cosmologies of resonance, and as they were considered in isomorphic relationship to the cosmos, notions of harmony helped define operations of the body as well. Kenneth DeWoskin has highlighted the importance of a "cosmos-music-mind triad," in discussions about music.[1] Indeed, as this book has shown, while it is perhaps more accurate to refer to a triangular relationship among the cosmos, music, and the human body—and not just the "mind"—such a triad certainly played an important role in the values and meanings associated with music. The fact that a developing discourse on medicine cast the human body in terms similar to those describing both the cosmos and music suggests that bodily functions were also defined ideally through the concept of harmony and ideals of balance and resonance.

The two sections of this book—music and the state, and music and the individual—highlight converging themes. One theme, common especially in Ru circles, is that human relationship to the cosmos is creative and engendering, rather than passive and conforming. Current literature on correlative cosmologies sometimes underscores a common assumption that humans were to "fit in" and "align" themselves by allowing cosmic operations and patterns to direct their behaviors and worldviews. The common saying, "Heaven and human come together to form one 天人合一"—a saying simplified from a Han Dynasty treatise—is often understood in terms of how humans should alter their behavior to conform to Heaven's natural and inevitable laws.[2] My analysis shows that there is no single narrative or assumption that humans are to "fit in" in such a way. Indeed, in many texts, humans are presented as integral agents who—often through music—might add to and change the course of the cosmos itself. Even in clearly non-Ru texts, often influenced by *Zhuangzi* or the *Daodejing*, music brings one back to one's original, unobstructed cosmic self, which would interact with the cosmos according to its own creative and transformative impulses. In either case, humans are not passive in the sense that they give themselves over to the laws of the cosmos. Rather, they join into a unique relationship that not only elevates themselves and enhances the cosmos, but brings peace, harmony, and prosperity to the world around them as well.

This book thus underscores the active role individuals—and especially imperial rulers and sages—were thought to play in using music to insure the proper movements of the cosmos, or the "granting of the seasons," as Nathan Sivin puts it when describing a ruler's imperial prerogative.[3] Some authors thought that by paying meticulous attention to the type of music performed or the quality of the sounds emitted, humans might not only gain access to cosmic forces and powers, but they might also add to, create, and even perfect such powers by virtue of such activities. In such a way, humans could act as a vital link in a mutually defining process of cosmic-human interaction. The constant, additional cosmic input of human beings—as beings who complete the harmonies of nature in their own capacity as unique beings or as humans in general—gives meaning to human activity and endeavor in relationship to the musical arts.

In our discussion on the effects of music on the individual psyche and body, we saw how certain Ru authors contributed to an entirely new, emerging discourse on psychology that placed music in a position of chief importance. Music was discussed in terms of its powers to affect the emotions and qi, helping to transform such basic components of the self into refined feelings of virtue and righteousness, appropriate for a Ru gentleman. Certain Ru authors went so far as to claim that music was the most effective vehicle in helping tame and shape our emotions in such a manner.

Authors of more non-Ru leanings tended not so much to speak about music in the cultivation of a moral psychology as about music in the attainment of sagely knowledge and attunement with the most authentic processes of the natural cosmos. In such writings music played a key role as the quintessential manifestation of the cosmos. Only he who could tap into and understand the true nature of such music could be considered to be a sage. If successful, such an individual would be considered to be spiritually uplifted as well as empowered to help move and shape the cosmos as it unfolds. Music in such contexts served as a conceptual standard for joyful, insightful, emotionally balanced, and cosmically integrated living.

MUSICAL AESTHETICS AS SPIRITUALITY
IN EARLY CHINA

The role of music in the culture of early China was closely linked not just to the aesthetic appreciation of an art form; it entered the realm of the spiritual as well. Whether one considers music in relationship to the state or individual body, music had the power to uplift audiences, societies, government, bureaucrats, and rulers in ways that no other art form could. It was thought to have the power to speak to the living and dead alike—living clans and dead ancestors—and to unify their attitudes or even moral sentiments. Later, in early imperial discourse, music provided a means of tapping into cosmic harmonies and balances, so that whatever or whoever controlled and moderated music could partake in some fashion in the spiritual workings of the entire world.

Precisely because music was a spiritual tool, it could be used by a variety of people for different purposes. The end goal in each case usually had some spiritual element associated with it. For example, when a ruler aspired to better unify his state and concentrate power in his own hands, what better vehicle than music for bringing together cultural mores and claiming legitimacy as the axial agent in control of cosmic operations? Just as the ruler needed to pay the sacrifice to Heaven and Earth at the correct intervals and in the correct way, he also needed to play music that was attuned to cosmic patterns and harmony. Similarly, he needed to establish and maintain an accurate calendar that could effectively guide farmers and peasants through the progress of the seasons. Also important in reinforcing his spiritual status was the ruler's ability to predict, avoid, and lessen the impact of anomalous occurrences such as eclipses and natural disasters. All of these aspects of being a ruler, and, especially, the Son of Heaven, helped establish his spiritual legitimacy as a primary conduit between the spiritual realm of the cosmos—which under ideal circumstances would move forward with harmony and flowing grace—and a realm mired by problems, imbalances, struggles, and difficulties.

With respect to the individual, music was thought to be a primary means of moral and spiritual attainment. While the link between music and the goal of gentlemanly cultivation as outlined in Ru circles has been well established in scholarship on musical aesthetics, the goal of sagely attunement with Heaven has not been widely discussed. Yet this goal perhaps marks one of the most unadulterated attempts at connecting music with the cosmos, which turned music not just into a mechanism for spiritual attainment, but into a goal of attainment as well. The goal of cosmic attunement—a goal of achieving "True" or "Heavenly Music," as some texts put it—exemplifies how music had become representative in itself of the pinnacle of spiritual cultivation. In such a light, one's involvement with music was perceived as much more than an aesthetic pursuit, since the process of listening to and understanding music was not merely about appreciating the music and the feelings or insights it may bring. It was seen as a journey to the core of the cosmos, with stops along the way that would convey the true emotional, physiological, and spiritual make-up of musician and composer alike. Such an endeavor was fit for the sage, the most spiritual of humans as outlined in early Chinese literature.

Even in Ru circles, music came to represent more than just an expression or means of moral cultivation. At the dawn of the early imperial era, Ru authors (as early as Xunzi) proclaimed an awesome role for music. They spoke of its ability to transform the psyche and lead it from raw emotions to moral virtue and what is right. Beyond this, they spoke of its role in helping create social harmony in the clan and in the culture more broadly. State order was not just implicated through the correct use of music; indeed, the entire movement of the cosmos could be affected through it. So while Ru authors did not promote a sage's spiritual identity with the music of the cosmos, they sometimes went so far as to recommend that wholesome and balanced music be employed so that humans might plug into and help complete the cosmos itself. Such, I would argue, was an eminently sacred goal of cosmic connection as well.

Music was also sometimes understood as an agent that could help dispel evil spirits or recapture the correct cosmic balance in one's body. Such spiritual uses for music belonged more generally to the realm of complex medical diagnostics, which included but was by no means limited to musical components. Nonetheless, it is important to view these discussions of music and medicine in terms of more fundamental, cosmic notions of balance and harmony that underpinned both realms of knowledge. Once we grasp that music was often chosen to be the primary exemplar or representative manifestation of the harmonious cosmos itself, we find it easier to comprehend how bodily systems, morality, social and state order, and cosmos intersected in essential ways. We arrive that much closer to a more comprehensive understanding of both discourses on ancient Chinese music and early imperial spiritual orientations regarding human relationship to the cosmos.

Notes

PROLOGUE

1. Michael Wines, "A Dirty Pun Tweaks China's Online Censors," *New York Times*, March 11, 2009.

2. Yang Bojun 楊伯峻, *Chunqiu Zuozhuan zhu* 春秋左傳注 (Beijing: Zhonghua shuju, 1995), 10.20.8, 1419. Similar notions of harmony are presented in other parts of the text, such as 10.25.3, and also in the *Guo yu* ("Zhengyu"), in a passage in which Scribe Bo discusses the Zhou decline. For a translation of the latter passage, see Wai-yee Li, *The Readability of the Past in Early Chinese Historiography* (Cambridge: Harvard University Asia Center, 2007), 119.

3. The traditional Six Arts included the rites, music, charioteering, archery, composition, and arithmetic.

INTRODUCTION

1. Sun Xidan 孫希旦, *Liji jijie* 禮記集解 (Beijing: *Zhonghua shuju*, 1998), 19 ("Yue ji 樂 記, Part I"), 993.

2. See A. C. Graham, *Disputers of the Tao: Philosophical Argument in Ancient China* (La Salle, IL: Open Court, 1989), 314–15.

3. Michael Puett writes of the arbitrary powers of spirits and their agonistic natures. Puett, *To Become a God* (Cambridge: Harvard University Asia Center for the Harvard-Yenching Institute, 2002), 78–79.

4. Nathan Sivin, "State, Cosmos and the Body in the Last Three Centuries B.C.," *Harvard Journal of Asiatic Studies* 55.1 (1995): 6–7.

5. Michael Nylan has recently put forth a very interesting argument stating that the systematic synthesis of *yin-yang* and Five Phases discussions with cosmic systems of *qi* may have occurred as late as the last years of the first century BCE (late Western Han). See Michael Nylan, "Yin-yang, Five Phases, and *qi*," in *China's Early Empires: A Re-appraisal*, eds. Michael Nylan and Michael Loewe (Cambridge: Cambridge

University Press, 2010), 398–414. While Nylan may indeed be onto something important, namely, that the systematization into a single discourse of all three vital cosmic components—*yin-yang*, Five Phases, and *qi*—occurred relatively late, it is still quite possible to demonstrate a late Warring States interest in drawing resonant correspondences between one or two of these cosmic aspects. My claim for the existence of many different competing cosmologies of resonance during the late Warring States and early imperial periods therefore does not conflict with Nylan's narrower claim that a single, unified "*yin-yang*, Five Phases" cosmology of *qi* may not have existed before the late Western Han.

6. For a description of the "naturalistic turn," or a move from "religion" to "naturalism," or "religion" to "philosophy," see Michael Puett, "Violent Misreadings: The Hermeneutics of Cosmology in the *Huainanzi*," in "Special Issue: Reconsidering the Correlative Cosmology of Early China," *Bulletin of the Museum of the Far Eastern Antiquities* 72 (2000): 45. An account of anthropological and sinological perspectives on the nature of correlative cosmology can be found in the same article, 29–47. Nylan provides a summary of key definitions of correlative cosmology and thinking in her Appendix to "Yin-yang, Five Phases, and *qi*," 409–14.

7. Jenny So, ed., *Music in the Age of Confucius* (Washington, D.C.: Freer Gallery of Art and Arthur M. Sackler Gallery, 2000), 29.

8. David Schaberg, *A Patterned Past: Form and Thought in Early Chinese Historiography* (Cambridge: Harvard University Press, 2001), 116.

9. See Jamie James, *The Music of the Spheres: Music, Science, and the Natural Order of the Universe* (New York: Copernicus Books, 1995).

10. For comparison of early Chinese thoughts on the matter with ancient Greek notions of the "harmony of the spheres, see G. E. R. Lloyd, *Adversaries and Authorities, Investigations into Ancient Greek and Chinese Science* (Cambridge: Cambridge University Press, 1996), 165–89.

11. Scott Cook, "Unity and Diversity in the Musical Thought of Warring States China," (Ph.D. diss., University of Michigan, 1995), 103.

12. See chapter four. For an excellent summary of the related terms and their various meanings, see John Knoblock, *Xunzi: A Translation and Study of the Complete Works*, 3 vols. (Stanford: Stanford University Press, 1988–1994), Vol. 3, 74–76.

13. See *Mozi*, Chapter 32, Sun Yirang, ed., *Mozi Jiangu*, (Taipei: *Hua qu shu ju*), 227.

14. Private communication with David Schaberg, December 2002. For more information on the social and political contexts of music, see Wu Hung, "Art and Architecture of the Warring States Period," in Michael Loewe and Edward Shaughnessy, eds., *The Cambridge History of Ancient China* (Cambridge: Cambridge University Press, 1999), 739. See also John Major and Jenny So's introduction, "Music in Late Bronze Age China," in So, *Music in the Age of Confucius*. For the socio-political contexts of chime-bells during the Bronze Age, see Lothar von Falkenhausen, *Suspended Music: Chime-Bells in the Culture of Bronze Age China* (Berkeley: University of California, 1993), 23–65.

15. The extent to which acrobatics were included in musical dance performances (*yue*) is still unclear for the early period in China.

16. There are notable exceptions to this, as will be demonstrated in my presentation of the literature on music, discussed below.

17. Cai Zhongde 蔡仲德, *Zhongguo yinyue meixue* 中國音樂美學史 (Beijing: Renmin yinyue chubanshe, 1995); and Tian Qing 田青, *Zhongguo gudai yinyue shihua* 中國古代音樂史話 (Shanghai: Shanghai wen yi chu ban she, 1984).

18. Wang Zichu 王子初, *Zhongguo yinyue kaoguxue* 中國音樂考古學 (Fuzhou: Fujian jiaoyu chubanshe, 2003).

19. Zhao Feng 趙渢, ed. *Yueji lunbian* 樂記論辨 (Beijing, Renmin yinyue, 1983); and Mizuhara Iko, "Chugoku kodai ongaku shiso kenkyu 中国古代音樂思想研究," *Toyo ongaku kenkyu* 10 (June 1965): 207–31.

20. For the Wei-Jin period, see Howard L. Goodman's works: *Xun Xu and the Politics of Precision in Third-Century AD China* (Leiden: Brill, 2010); and "A History of Court Lyrics in China during Wei-Chin Times," *Asia Major* 19.1 (2006): 57–109. For the Song period, see Rulan Chao Pian, *Song Dynasty Musical Sources and Their Interpretation* (Hong Kong: The Chinese University Press, 2003). For the Ming, see Joseph Lam, *State Sacrifices and Music in Ming China: Orthodoxy, Creativity, and Expressiveness* (Albany: State University of New York Press, 1998). More contemporary, anthropological studies of ritual music or performance traditions can be found in Bell Yung, Evelyn Rawski, and Rubie Watson, eds., *Harmony and Counterpoint: Ritual Music in Chinese Context* (Stanford: Stanford University Press, 1996); and Bell Yung, *Cantonese Opera: Performance as Creative Process* (Cambridge: Cambridge University Press, 2009).

21. Steven Van Zoeren, *Poetry and Personality: Reading, Exegesis, and Hermeneutics in Traditional China* (Stanford: Stanford University Press, 1991). See also Martin Kern, *Die Hymnen der Chinesischen Staatsopfer: Literatur und Ritual in der Politischen Repraesentation von der Han-Zeit bis zu den Sechs Dynastien* (Stuttgart: Steiner, 1997).

22. Martin Kern, "Tropes of Music and Poetry: From Wudi (r. 141–87 BCE) to ca 100 CE," in Nylan and Loewe, *China's Early Empires*, eds. Michael Nylan and Michael Loewe (Cambridge: Cambridge University Press, 2010), 480–91.

23. Kern, "Tropes of Music and Poetry," 483–84.

24. Falkenhausen, *Suspended Music*. For a critical response to von Falkenhausen's study, see Robert Bagley's incisive essay, "Percussion," in So, *Music in the Age of Confucius*, 34–63.

25. Ingrid Furniss, *Music in Ancient China: An Archaeological and Art Historical Study of Strings, Winds, and Drums during the Eastern Zhou and Han Periods* (770 BCE–220 CE) (Amherst, NY: Cambria Press, 2008).

26. This dichotomy can be found throughout the book. See especially *ibid.*, 284.

27. James Hart, "The Discussion of the *Wu-Yi* Bells in the *Kuo-Yü*," *Monumenta Serica* 29 (1970/71).

28. Scott Cook, "Unity and Diversity."

29. Kenneth J. DeWoskin, *A Song for One or Two: Music and the Concept of Art in Early China* (Ann Arbor: University of Michigan Center for Chinese Studies, 1982).

30. DeWoskin, *A Song for One or Two*, 29.

31. A. C. Graham's work on *yin-yang* and correlative cosmologies provides one detailed source in English on this matter. See also Gu Jiegang's *Wude zhongshi shuoxia de zhengzhi he lishi* 五德終始說下的政治和歷史 (Hong Kong: Longmen Publishing, 1970) for a history of Five Phases formulations, as well as the recent essays on the topic of "correlative cosmology" in *Bulletin of the Museum of Far Eastern Antiquities*

72 (2000). An excellent source for understanding some of the fundamental ways of delineating this cosmology in the early Han is John Major, *Heaven and Earth in Early Han Thought: Chapters Three, Four and Five of the Huainanzi* (Albany: State University of New York Press, 1993). See also Michael Nylan's "Yin-yang, Five Phases, and *qi*," for a critical account of much of this scholarship.

32. The reader may wish to refer to a recent study by Christopher Cullen on this matter: "Numbers, Numeracy, and the Cosmos," in Nylan and Loewe, *China's Early Empires*, 323–38.

33. We are usually not privy to writings by lower-class musicians—most of our authors write about music as intellectual enthusiasts or musical directors and ritual specialists. Often, the common musician is depicted as blind.

34. Performance would most likely have been influenced as well by discussions concerning the musical repertoires of the day—what was considered to be acceptable, edifying, or illicit.

35. "Luo Gao," in Wu Yu 吳璵, ed., *Shangshu duben* 尚書讀本 (Taipei: Sanmin Publishing, 1985), 126.

36. "Wu Yi," in *ibid.*, 139.

37. "Jun Shi," in *ibid.*, 144.

38. Edward Shaughnessy, "*Shang shu* 尚書 (*Shu ching* 書經)," in *Early Chinese Texts: A Bibliographical Guide*, ed. Michael Loewe (Berkeley: University of California Press, 1993), 377–80.

39. Cook, "Unity and Diversity," 72.

40. *Analects*, 7.32. Adapted from the translation by D. C. Lau, *Confucius: The Analects* (London: Penguin, 1979), 90.

41. See also *Analects* 1.12, and 13.23 for more instances of harmony as a social ideal.

42. *Analects* 16.1. Yang Bojun 楊伯峻, ed., *Lunyu yizhu* 論語譯注 (Hong Kong: Zhonghua shuju, 1984), 172.

43. Many scholars date the earliest portions of this text to around the fourth century BCE. See the recent summary of positions in Karen Desmet, "The Growth of Compounds in the Core Chapters of the *Mozi*," *Oriens Extremus* 45 (2005/6): 99–118. See also A. C. Graham, *Divisions in Mohism Reflected in the Core Chapters of Mo-Tzu* (Singapore: Institute of East Asian Philosophies Occasional Paper and Monograph Series 1, 1985); and Loewe, ed., *Early Chinese Texts*, 336–41.

44. *Mozi*, annot. Sun Yirang 孫詒讓, *Mozi jiangu* 墨子閒詁 (Taipei: Huaqu shuju, 1987), 10 ("Elevating the Worthy, *Xia* 尚賢下"), 19 ("Against Aggressive Warfare, *Xia* 非攻下"), and 27, ("Heaven's Will, *Zhong* 天志中").

45. I follow David Schaberg's dating of the text: Schaberg, *A Patterned Past*, 8. The term *he* occurs too many times in this text to analyze it here in the detail it deserves. Thus, I only provide a general outline of the usage of the term in this text. Also, given the text's the relatively late date (~fourth century BCE), it is likely that the transformations I outline were already beginning to take place in a limited fashion. Therefore, even if there exist a few textual citations in which harmony is applied to the cosmos, my theory could still hold.

46. Yang Bojun 楊伯峻, *Chunqiu Zuozhuan zhu* 春秋左傳注 (Beijing: Zhonghua shuju, 1995), "Duke Zhao 20.8," 1419.

47. See *Zuo zhuan*, "Duke Xi 24.2," "Duke Xiang 11.10," and "Duke Xiang 29.8," among other passages. While some of the references using the term *he* in the *Zuo zhuan* point to aesthetic contexts of music and the harmony of the "five sounds" (*wu sheng* 五 聲) like the one just quoted, most examples refer to the "harmony of the people/masses" (*he min/zhong* 和民/眾) as a social ideal. See for example *Zuo zhuan*, "Duke Yin 4.4," "Duke Xi 5.9," and "Duke Xuan 12.3."

48. Commentators are unsure of what these designations in early Chinese texts mean, as they do not appear to be stable or consistent from text to text. In other parts of the text, the Winds refer to the music that originates from various geographic directions and regions (see *Zuo zhuan*, "Duke Xiang 18.4," for Music Master Kuang's comments on Northern and Southern Winds). For more on the relationship between the Eight Winds and sound, see the "Sound and Acoustics" section of Needham, Wang, and Robinson, *Science and Civilisation in China*, ed. Joseph Needham, Vol. 4.1 (Cambridge: Cambridge University Press, 1962), 126–228. For a discussion of the Eight Winds and their correlations to musical tones in the early Han period, see John Major, "Notes on the Nomenclature of the Winds and Directions in the Early Han," *T'oung Pao* 65.1–3 (1979): 66–80.

49. *Zuo zhuan*, "Duke Xiang, 29.13," 1164.

50. *Ibid.*, "Duke Zhuang, 22.1," 221.

51. See chapter two for more on this.

52. The Five Modes seem to refer either to rhythmic structures or the modal structures of sounds.

53. *Zuo zhuan*, "Duke Zhao, 1.12," 1222.

54. For more on the relationship between music and the winds and seasons, see Mark Lewis, *Sanctioned Violence in Early China* (Albany: State University of New York Press, 1990), 218–21.

55. For an account of actual debates over nature and artifice during the Warring States period, see Michael Puett, *The Ambivalence of Creation: Debates Concerning Innovation and Artifice in Early China* (Stanford: Stanford University Press, 2001).

56. Even though this development occurs, this is not to say that the other uses of harmony ceased to exist as such. What I describe is an additional overlay of meaning that gradually began to dominate the semantic range of the term.

57. I choose this date because it marks not only the approximate dating of such texts as the *Mengzi* and *Zhuangzi*, but also because the newly excavated texts from Guodian were buried (at the earliest) around such a time. While there is not enough data to infer when most of the Guodian texts were composed, judging from intellectual concerns and vocabulary, sometime during the fourth century BCE seems to be a fair guess.

58. Guo Qingfan 郭慶藩, *Zhuangzi jishi* 莊子集釋 (Taipei: Wanjuan lou, 1993), 2 ("Qi Wu Lun 齊物論"), 45–50.

59. A similar passage in *Laozi* points to a more metaphorical interpretation of the cosmos as music. Wang Bi's reading of *Laozi* 5 reads, "The space between Heaven and Earth, is it not just like a bellows or a mouth organ!" Richard Lynn, trans., *The Classic of the Way and Virtue: A New Translation of the Tao-te ching of Laozi as Interpreted by Wang Bi* (New York: Columbia University Press, 1999), 60, and 61–62, note 3. Here, the cosmos is likened to the space in a mouth organ that serves as the locus for the instrument's production of sound.

60. Lü Buwei 呂不韋, comp., annot. Chen Qiyou 陳奇猷, *Lüshi chunqiu jiaosshi* 呂氏春秋校釋 5.2 ("Da Yue 大樂"), 255. Translation adapted from Lü Buwei, *The Annals of Lü Buwei (Lüshi chun qiu): A Complete Translation and Study*, trans. and ed. John Knoblock and Jeffrey Riegel (Stanford: Stanford University Press, 2000), 136–37.

61. See Cai Zhongde 蔡仲德 on the how music relates to the wind, *Zhongguo yin yue mei xue shi* 中國音樂美學史 (Taipei: Landeng, 1993).

62. Lü Buwei, *Lüshi chunqiu jiaosshi* 5.2 ("Da Yue 大 樂"), 256. Translation by Knoblock and Riegel, 138.

63. *Ibid.*, 5.5 ("Gu Yue 古 樂"), 285. Translation by Knoblock and Riegel, 149.

64. Sun Yirang 孫詒讓, *Mozi jian gu* 墨子閒詁 (Taipei: Huaqu shuju, 1987), 6 ("Ci Guo 辭 過"), 34–35.

65. Much debate concerning the textual history of *Laozi* has been spawned by the discovery of Laozian fragments in the tomb from Guodian, datable to ~300 BCE. *Jingmen shi bowu guan* 荊門市博物館, ed., *Guodian Chu mu zhu jian* 郭店楚幕竹簡, (Jingmen: Wen wu, 1998). What these debates suggest is that, while it seems likely that oral traditions espousing Laozian types of thought were in existence during the late fourth century BCE, the compilation of the text "in 5000 characters" as was transmitted throughout the centuries, as well as the prevalence and impact of these notions on contemporary intellectual currents, is likely not to have occurred before the third century BCE. See Harold Roth, "Some Methodological Issues in the Study of the Guodian *Laozi* Parallels," in *The Guodian Laozi: Proceedings of the International Conference, Dartmouth College, May 1998*, eds. Sarah Allan and Crispin Williams (Berkeley: Society for the Study of Early China and the Institute of East Asian Studies, University of California, 2000), 71–88.

66. *Laozi*, Chapter 42.

67. For an in-depth discussion of the concept of *wu-wei* as a metaphor for early Chinese thought, see Edward Slingerland, *Effortless Action: Wu-Wei As Conceptual Metaphor and Spiritual Ideal in Early China* (Oxford: Oxford University Press, 2003).

68. *Huainanzi*, "Chuzhen 俶真訓," in *Huainanzi honglie jijie*, eds. Feng Yi 馮逸 and Qiao Hua 喬華 (Beijing: Zhonghua shuju, 1989), 44.

69. Sun Xidan 孫希旦, *Liji jijie* 禮記集解, 19 ("Yue ji 樂記, Part I"), 993.

70. This text, along with another one of the Four Books, the *Great Learning* (*Da xue* 大學), originally appeared in the ritual compendium the *Li ji, Book of Rites*. For some brief comments on the provenance of the *Zhong yong*, see Loewe, ed., *Early Chinese Texts*, 296. See also the prefatory materials in Andrew Plaks, *Ta Hsüeh and Chung Yung (The Highest Order of Cultivation and On the Practice of the Mean)* (New York: Penguin Books, 2003), vii–xxxii.

71. Xie Bingying 謝冰瑩 et al., eds., *Xinyi sishu duben* 新譯四書讀本, *Zhong yong xinyi* 中庸新譯 (Taipei: Sanmin shuju, 1991), 22.

72. Sun Xidan, *Liji jijie*, 990.

73. *ibid.*

74. *ibid.*, 993.

75. *ibid.*, 992–93.

76. *ibid.*, 992.

77. This perspective provides a lasting backdrop to discourses concerning music throughout the Han Dynasty. DeWoskin cites at least two passages from Han

apocrypha which assume that music underlies the operations of the cosmos. See DeWoskin, *A Song for One or Two*, 166 and note 22.

78. Cook does not describe this change in terms specific to Chinese history, but he does suggest that such a view arose in direct relationship to the attainment of knowledge about relationships between musical harmonies and numerical perfections, as also expressed in the natural world. Implicitly, Cook explains the association of music and the cosmos to the growth of an explicit knowledge in musical harmonies. Cook, "Unity and Diversity," 103–105.

79. For interesting contemporary theories on how metaphors help constitute the operations of our brains, see George Lakoff and Mark Johnson, *Philosophy in the Flesh: The Embodied Mind and its Challenge to Western Thought* (New York: Basic Books, 1999); Mark Johnson, *The Body in the Mind: The Bodily Basis of Meaning, Imagination, and Reason* (Chicago: University of Chicago, 1987); and Gilles Fauconnier and Mark Turner, *The Way We Think: Conceptual Blending and the Mind's Hidden Complexities* (New York: Basic Books, 2002). I am thankful to Edward Slingerland for pointing me to these sources and for his work on metaphor theory in early Chinese thought.

CHAPTER ONE. MUSIC IN STATE ORDER AND COSMIC RULERSHIP

1. "Sang Jian" refers to a locale in the state of Wei 衛, and the "upper banks of the Pu River" is associated with music linked to the evil King Zhou of the Shang Dynasty.

2. Wang Liqi 王利器, ed., *Fengsu tongyi jiaozhu* 風俗通義校注 (Beijing: Zhonghua shuju, 1981), 6 "Sheng Yin 聲音," 267.

3. Five of these Six Classics were transmitted through the ages, while that of music was allegedly "lost." For more on the history of the Five/Six Classics, see Michael Nylan, *The Five "Confucian" Classics* (New Haven: Yale University Press, 2001), 19–41.

4. The Odes are also often translated as Songs or Hymns, and even Poems, and should be distinguished from the *Canon of Odes*, which constitutes a discrete text, as opposed to an oral repertoire.

5. The Six Arts included the rites, music, charioteering, archery, composition, and arithmetic.

6. See Furniss, *Music in Ancient China*, 256–59.

7. *Ibid.*, 154–55; 286–87.

8. I adopt Steven Van Zoeren's translations of these terms. See Van Zoeren, *Poetry and Personality*, 7–8.

9. See Arthur Waley, trans., *The Book of Songs* (New York: Grove Press, 1960).

10. Cheng Junying 程俊英 and Jiang Xianyuan 蔣見元, *Shijing zhuxi* 詩經注析 (Beijing: Zhonghua shuju, 1991): Mao 274.

11. *Zhouyi zhushu* 周易注疏 (Taipei: Taiwan xuesheng shuju, 1984): Hexagram 16, "Yu" 豫, 208.

12. Martin Kern, "*Shi Jing* Songs as Performance Texts: A Case Study of 'Chu Ci' (Thorny Caltrop)," *Early China* 25 (2000): 66.

13. Cheng Junying and Jiang Xianyuan, *Shijing zhuxi*, Mao 242, 787–90. Translation slightly altered from Waley, *The Book of Songs*, 260. The "sightless and eyeless" 矇瞍 refer to the musicians, who were often blind.

14. The term "*yong* 雝" in this proper name refers to harmonious sounds.

15. *Shun dian* 舜典, 1.11. Translation altered from Robert Eno, *The Confucian Creation of Heaven: Philosophy and the Defense of Ritual Mastery* (Albany: State University of New York, 1990), 196. For an interesting link between the ancient graph for the royal Music Master Kui 夔 and the graph, *nao* (an ape and ape-masked dancer with one great foot), see Eno's discussion on 195–97.

16. These last two statements refer to a stanza from "Thick grows the artemesia," an Ode, now appearing in the Lesser Elegantiae (Mao 176), which had just been recited by Duke Xiang of Jin at a feast for Duke Wen of Lu. The stanza in question celebrates the sighting of one's lord, which results in his pleasure and great courtesy 既見君子, 樂且有儀.

17. Note that he states this to cover up the humiliating treatment of Lu by Jin a year prior to this meeting. See Yang Bojun, *Chunqiu Zuozhuan zhu*, 531.

18. Dukes of almost equal rank were not supposed to receive each other's bows.

19. Yang, *Chunqiu Zuozhuan zhu*, 6.3.7: 531. The Ode in question is Mao 249, Greater Elegantiae.

20. Waley, *The Book of Songs*, 181.

21. Such anthropomorphic behaviors could include things like sending down blessings and curses at will, consulting with humans through divination practices, accepting sacrifices that would appease them and ask for blessings, etc.

22. See the discussion of "correlative cosmology" in the Introduction. According to the predominant vision of such a cosmos, the causal mechanism of such a cosmos was one of "resonant affiliation." In other words, various types of *qi* would possess a genetic, intrinsic relationship to each other on the basis of kind. *Qi* of similar quality and kind could rouse each other to prominence and action, so that change could occur almost spontaneously by mere fact of association.

23. Note, for example, texts such as *Inner Training* and portions of the *Dao De Jing*, both dating roughly to the fourth century BCE, which contain passages concerning the physiological health of the body. For discussions on regulating the imperial body, see Elizabeth Hsu, ed., *Innovation in Chinese Medicine* (Cambridge: Cambridge University Press, 2001).

24. Nathan Sivin, "State, Cosmos, and the Body."

25. *Ibid.*, 7.

26. Yang Bojun, *Chunqiu Zuozhuan zhu*, 9.11.5; 993–94.

27. The term bu 布 is difficult to translate here. I take liberties to interpret it as "set up," meaning, "to administer," from one of its meanings: "to proclaim."

28. Yang Bojun, *Chunqiu Zuozhuan zhu*, 8.12.4; 858. Of special note in this passage is the stress on the virtues of reverence and economy, as such a statement might be understood as a response to early Mohist critiques of the effects of lavish music on state coffers and human productivity. Such would explain narratives like these that take pains to draw a connection between ostensibly extravagant ceremonies and the daily ins and outs of governance.

29. Yan Changyao 顏昌嶢, *Guanzi jiaoshi* 管子校釋 (Changsha: Yuelu shushe, 1996), 211; Allyn Rickett, trans., *Guanzi: Political, Economic, and Philosophical Essays from Early China, a Study and Translation*, rev. ed., vol. 1 (Boston: Cheng and Tsui Company, 2001), 353.

30. Yan Changyao, *Guanzi jiaoshi*, 213. Translation by Rickett, *Guanzi*, 356. Here, indeed, Rickett is correct to translate *yue* as "pleasure," as this term is contrasted earlier in the chapter with sadness and is taken as a point of discussion. Nonetheless, though "pleasure" is the primary meaning in this context, "music" is cleverly implied as well.

31. I have benefited greatly from consideration of Scott Cook's translations of the entire "Yue lun," in Cook, "Unity and Diversity," 413–28. In addition to Cook's dissertation on music, I have benefited from an unpublished work by Eric Hutton on this topic, as well as the translation by John Knoblock, *Xunzi: A Translation and Study of the Complete Works*, 3 vols. (Stanford: Stanford University Press, 1988–1994). In my translations of the "Yue lun," I have consulted both Knoblock and Cook's version and often simply offer slight emendations of their translations.

32. Xiong Gongzhe, *Xunzi jinzhu jinyi*, Chapter 20, 415. This same passage, with slight differences, can be found in the "Yue ji." Sun Xidan 孫希旦, *Liji jijie* 禮記集解, 19 ("Yue ji 樂記, Part 2,"), 1005.

33. Chen Qiyou, *Lüshi chunqiu jiaoshi*, "Da Yue," 255.

34. *Ibid.* The entire introduction to the chapter "Great Music," begins not with music per se but with a cosmogony that is similar to the text, "*Taiyi* gives birth to water [Taiyi sheng shui 太一生水]," discovered at Guodian.

35. A later passage in the same chapter refers to "Great Music" as that which brings about a state of equilibrium comparable to the Dao. For this reason, the phrase "to work at music" perhaps simply refers to the acts of practicing and performing it. *Ibid.*, 256.

36. *Ibid.*

37. *Ibid.*

38. Michael Puett presents this relationship in terms of that of the "adept" and the Dao; I would read the entire passage as referring more exclusively to the ruler of a state. Nonetheless, Puett highlights the fact that such an adept helps moderate and fulfill cosmic processes, so that he is not a mere bystander or passive link in a chain of events. See Puett, *To Become a God*, 175.

39. Chen Qiyou, *Lüshi chunqiu jiaoshi*, "Da Yue," p. 256.

40. *Guoyu* (Shanghai: Shanghai guji publishing, 1995): 14.7, 460. I am following the citation of this passage in the *Taiping Yulan* 太平御覽 section on music, which reads *meng* 萌 for *ming* 明. Cited in *Ibid.*

41. It appears as though musical sound was strongly linked to winds—perhaps because sound was thought to have been carried by wind, or because sound was thought to have been contained in it. For more on the intriguing linkages between music, meteorological events, and the agricultural cycle, see Lewis, *Sanctioned Violence*, 218–21. As we will explore in chapter three, the divinatory role of sound in early Chinese culture seems to be largely dependent on its associations with wind and, subsequently, *qi* (which was also associated with air and wind).

42. A complete translation and interpretation of this important passage can be found in Li, *The Readability of the Past*, 136–47. See also Schaberg, *A Patterned Past*, 86–95, for another discussion.

43. Yang Bojun, *Chunqiu Zuo zhuan zhu*, 9.29.13; 1161–65. Also Sima Qian, *Shi ji* (Beijing: Zhonghua shu ju, 1992), 31; 1452–53.

44. Yang Bojun, *Chunqiu Zuo zhuan zhu*, 9.29.13; 1161–65.

45. We will encounter some of these criticisms in texts examined throughout this book.

46. Yang Bojun, *Chunqiu Zuo zhuan zhu*, 9.29.13; 1161–65.

47. While the sequence mentioned here is on the whole somewhat similar to the sequence in the Mao version, some significant differences exist. For example, the Airs of Bin are listed at the end of the Wind section in Mao, while they appear just after the Airs of Qi in this *Zuo* reference. Also, the Airs of Qin take their place after the Airs of Bin in this passage, but only after the Airs of Tang in the Mao sequence. Because of such sequential discrepancies, and because we have no way of knowing whether there were other Airs from small states that simply did not make it into the Mao version, it is impossible to tell which Airs Jizha refused to comment on.

48. Unfortunately, the passage does not elaborate further on this type of music. We can only assume that such music was contrary to the other ancient styles of music that demonstrated resolute but moderated expression of the passions.

49. Li, *The Readability of the Past*, 146.

50. *Ibid.*

51. Yang Bojun, *Chunqiu Zuozhuan zhu*, 1643.

52. *Ibid.*, 3.20.1; 215.

53. Zhong Zhe 鍾哲, *Han Feizi jijie* 韓非子集解 (Beijing: Zhonghua shuju, 1998), 3 ("Shi Guo 十過"), 63.

54. *Ibid.*

55. Chen Qiyou, *Lüshi chunqiu*, "Da Yue," 256.

56. Chen Qiyou, *Lüshi chunqiu*, "Chi Yue," 265–66. Translation altered from Riegel and Knoblock, 141. According to commentators, this translation of the three creations corresponds to what the author describes in the preceding sentences as "considering the large to be beautiful and the many to be wonderful," not to mention seeking after the "strange and exotic."

57. *Ibid.* Significantly, it is the sage who determines whether music has lost its nature by "not producing pleasure 其樂不樂."

58. We discuss this in more detail in chapter five.

59. Chen Qiyou, *Lüshi chunqiu*, "Da Yue," 256. Translation adapted from Knoblock and Riegel, 138.

60. Such a claim attempts to differentiate between types of music in the strongest possible manner—in terms of a difference of species (music vs. not music) instead of type or style of music. In accordance with the practice of rectifying names, or defining words in terms of their ideal forms and not just in terms of a general concept, the author discards disorderly music as not even worthy of being called music. Indeed, while Xunzi implied this very notion by somewhat consistently referring to bad music as "musical sounds" or other names, the author of this passage articulates this radical

separation between proper music *qua* music and "musical sounds" clearly and explicitly. We see such a distinction carried on throughout the chapter on music in the *Li ji*, or *Book of Rites*, as well.

Notably, in this latter text, the reference for proper music is "Great Music (*da yue* 大樂)," though there are many instances where the author merely refers to "music" to describe his ideal type. The author of the *Book of Rites* also makes sure to distinguish explicitly between "sounds (*sheng* 聲)," "tones (*yin* 音)," and "music (*yue* 樂)." See Sun Xidan, *Liji jijie*, 19 ("Yue ji 樂記, Part I"), 982.

CHAPTER TWO. A CIVILIZING FORCE FOR IMPERIAL RULE

1. *Analects*, 7.18.

2. As Arthur Waley points out, the *Mozi* refers to the third section of the Odes as "Da Xia," rather than "Da Ya," the title by which it is known in the received tradition. Using citations from the *Xunzi*, the commentator Yu Yue demonstrates that indeed the terms *ya* 雅 and *xia* 夏 were interchangeable in ancient times. The *Shuowen jiezi* 說文解字 however, makes no mention of the connection. Intriguingly, the excavated text, "Kongzi shi lun 孔子詩論" ("*Confucius' discussion of the Odes*") also contains an older form of *xia* 夏 for *ya* 雅. See Sun Yirang, *Mozi jiangu*, 28 ("Tian Zhi, Xia 天志下"), 199; Arthur Waley, *Confucius: The Analects* (New York: Alfred A. Knopt, 2000, originally published 1938), 230–31; and Ma Chengyuan 馬承源, ed., *Shanghai bowuguan cang Zhanguo Chu zhushu* 上海博物館藏戰國楚竹書, vol. 1 (Shanghai: Shanghai Guji Publishing Co., 2001), "Kongzi shilun," 127.

3. Jenny So mentions the link between correct music and civilization, as opposed to non-Xia immorality. See So, *Music in the Age of Confucius*, 26–27.

4. Yang, *Chunqiu Zuozhuan zhu*, 5.24.2, 425.

5. Furniss, *Music in Ancient China*, 117. For another archaeological account of non-Zhou music, see Lothar von Falkenhausen's writings on Chu music, "Chu Ritual Music," in *New Perspectives on Chu Culture during the Eastern Zhou Period*, ed. Thomas Lawton (Washington, D.C.: Arthur M. Sackler Gallery, Smithsonian Institution; Princeton: Princeton University Press, 1991), 47–106.

6. See also passages in *Zuo zhuan* 10.4.8 and 3.21.2 for other examples of music as an accompaniment to the ritual act of transferring of power and/or favor to another.

7. Yang, *Chunqiu Zuozhuan zhu*, 9.11.5, 993. For another translation of this passage, see Wai-yee Li, *The Readability of the Past*, 128–29.

8. As Wai-yee Li points out, however, because the musical gifts in question are tainted by their association with the excessive music of Zheng, Wei Jiang must hold off on accepting these gifts until he is convinced of the propriety of the entire situation. Li, *The Readability of the Past*, 130–32.

9. We examine this connection in greater detail in chapter four.

10. Xiong Gongzhe, *Xunzi jinzhu jinyi*, 20, 415. This same passage, with slight differences, can be found in the "Yue ji," ["Record of Music"]. *Li ji*, 19 ("Yue ji 樂記, Part 2,"), 1005. See also Knoblock, *Xunzi*, and Cook, "Unity and Diversity."

11. Xiong Gongzhe, *Xunzi jinzhu jinyi*, 20, 413. Translation adapted from Knoblock, *Xunzi*, vol. 3, 82.

12. Xiong Gongzhe, *Xunzi jinzhu jinyi*, 20, 415.

13. The supposition that the text referred to here is the title of a chapter of Xunzi's own writings derives from commentator Wang Xianqian 王先謙 (1842–1918), in Xiong Gongzhe, *Xunzi jinzhu jinyi*, 20, 413.

14. *Ibid.* Wang Xianqian changed *zhu shang* 誅賞 to read *shi shang* 詩商, where *shang* is read *zhang* 章, or the written portions of the *Odes*.

15. *Ibid.*, 409. Translation adapted from Cook, "Unity and Diversity," 415.

16. Xiong Gongzhe, *Xunzi jinzhu jinyi*, 20, 410.

17. *Ibid.*, 413. Translation adapted from Cook, "Unity and Diversity," 419.

18. Sun Xidan, *Liji jijie*, 977.

19. Sima Qian, *Shi ji*, 3 ("Yin ben ji 殷本紀,"), 105.

20. Wu Zeyu 吳則虞, *Bohutong shuzheng* 白虎通疏證 (Beijing: Zhonghua shuju, 1994), "Li Yue 禮樂," 96–97.

21. Liu Wendian 劉文典, *Huainan honglie jijie* 淮南鴻烈集解 (Beijing: Zhonghua shuju, 1989), 20 ("Taizu Xun 泰族訓"), 670.

22. I am thankful to Michael Puett for first pointing out to me the distinctive approach to unity and diversity in the *Huainanzi*. For more on the text's advocacy of the feudal kingdoms and diverse types of thinking over the Qin political model and Confucian orthodoxy, see Griet Vankeerberghen, *The Huainanzi and Liu An's Claim to Moral Authority* (Albany: State University of New York Press, 2001), 144.

23. The term *shao* 韶 is difficult to translate. Later commentators take it as a loan word for *shao* 紹, which refers to continuity and transmission. They explain such a choice of words by claiming that the name suggests Yao's transmission and handing down to Shun of his virtue and right to rule. I prefer to translate *shao* 韶 according to the "tone" radical that is already present in the graph. Such a term in itself refers to harmony and beauty; hence, my translation as "euphonia."

24. Liu Wendian, *Huainan honglie jijie*, 20 ("Fan lun xun 氾論訓"), 425.

25. See especially *Analects* 2.1 and 12.19.

26. *Guo yu*, 14.7 ("Shi Kuang lun yue 師曠論樂"), 460–61.

27. Ban Gu, *Han shu* (Beijing: Zhonghua shuju, 1995), 22 ("Li yue zhi 禮樂志"), 1043. This type of music is discussed in Kern, *Die Hymnen der Chinesischen Staatsopfer*, 56.

28. *Ibid.*

29. Emperor Wudi in particular raised the status of music and musical forms at court by establishing the Music Bureau (to which he appointed Li Yannian as "Director of Harmonizing the Pitch-pipes"); having the Odes chanted at night, having ditties performed from the former states of Zhao, Dai, Qin, and Chu; employing scores of famous poets such as Sima Xiangru 司馬相如 to write poems and *fu* 賦, supporting discourse on the pitch-standards, and for bringing into consonance the eight timbres of music. See Ban Gu, *Han shu*, 22 ("Li yue zhi"), 1045.

30. Sima, *Shi ji* 18 ("Feng Shan Shu 封禪書,") 1396. Translation by Burton Watson, *Records of the Grand Historian of China, Vol. II: The Age of Emperor Wu 140 to circa 100 BCE* (New York: Columbia University Press, 1961), 55. Commentators

think that Emperor Wudi commissioned a musician named Hou Diao 侯調 to invent the *konghou* 空侯 instrument.

31. Martin Kern, "Tropes of Music and Poetry," 484.

32. Li Yannian was the brother of Wudi's favorite consort, and is reputed to have included Central Asian tunes to the military music of the age. See *ibid.*, 484–85, especially notes 12 and 15. The concepts of "new" and "changing" tunes appear to be most relevant to Han times, and, in particular, the periods during and after Emperor Wudi's reign.

33. Creative in the sense that the sage is attuned to the patterns of the ultimately creative cosmos.

34. One recalls his efforts to standardize objects in every aspect of life: weights and measures, the written language, axle lengths, tools, currency, etc.

35. Kern, "Tropes of Music and Poetry," 485.

36. *Guodian Chumu zhujian*, 180. See chapter six for more on this.

37. Kern, "Tropes of Music and Poetry," 485.

38. Zhong Zhe, *Han Feizi jijie* 3 ("Shi Guo 十過"), 63. Translation by Burton Watson, *Han Fei Tzu: Basic Writings* (New York: Columbia University Press, 1964), 55.

39. The "pure *jiao*" mode is associated with Music Master Kuang in this text and again in the *Liezi* ("Tang wen" chapter), perhaps because of its link to the Yellow Emperor ("pure *jiao*" was the name given to the Yellow Emperor's *qin*-zither.) The tone is likened in the *Huainanzi* to "white snow." See DeWoskin, *A Song for One or Two*, 163, note 11. I think that there must be some link between its position as third (and hence, representing intervals of a third) tone and the notion of clarity or purity.

40. *Xiao jing* 孝經, 12, "Guang Yao Dao Zhang," 廣要道章 6.18b.

41. Xiong Gongzhe, *Xunzi jinzhu jinyi*, 20, 414–15.

42. *Ibid.*, p. 413. Translation based on Cook, "Unity and Diversity," 419–20. Like Cook, I follow Wang Xianqian's emendation of the text from "*shen zhu shang* 審誅賞" to "*shen shi shang* 審詩商," and then his subsequent reading of "*shang* 商" as "*zhang* 章," referring to "stanza." See the commentary in Xiong Gongzhe, *Xunzi jinzhu jinyi*, 20, 413.

43. For more on how Xunzi links music to the individual psyche and *qi*, see chapter four. Since *qi* as a concept was not confined to individuals or the human body, it makes sense that the transformations of one's *qi* brought about by music could extend beyond the individual to the greater social sphere as well.

44. Eno, *The Confucian Creation of Heaven*, 190–97.

45. One will note, for example, the *Lüshi chunqiu* comment about the "Shaman tones" of Chu, which were created when the state was in decline. Chen Qiyou, *Lüshi chunqiu jiaoshi*, "Chi Yue," 266.

46. For Confucius' vision of Zhou as an "ethnicity" defined through cultural goods, see Erica Brindley, "Barbarians or Not? Ethnicity and Changing Conceptions of the Ancient Yue (Viet) Peoples (~400–50 B. C.)," *Asia Major* 16.1 (2003): 1–32.

47. Liu Wendian 劉文典, *Huainan honglie jijie* 淮南鴻烈集解 (Beijing: Zhonghua shuju, 1997), 9 ("Zhu Shu Xun 主術訓,"), 275.

48. *Ibid.*

49. *Shangshu dazhuan*, 1 ("Yao Dian,"), 11b.

50. The pitch-standards and their general correlations are as follows: Yellow Bell (*Huangzhong* 黃鐘), Forest Bell (*Linzhong* 林鐘), and *Taicou* 太簇 correspond to

Heaven, Earth, and humans, respectively; *Guxian* 姑洗, *Ruibin* 蕤賓, Southern Lü (*Nanlü* 南呂), and *Yingzhong* 應鐘 correspond to the beginnings of spring, summer, autumn, and fall, respectively. Wang Yingling 王應麟, Xiaoxue gan zhu 小學紺珠, "Lü li 律曆" [Song Dynasty]. Cited in Luo Zhufeng 羅竹風, ed., *Hanyu da cidian* 漢語大詞典, vol. 1 (Shanghai: Hanyu da cidian chuban, 1994), 157.

CHAPTER THREE. REGULATING SOUND AND THE COSMOS

1. The "Treatise on the Pitch-standards and Calendar" opens by claiming that what follows is an edited version of Liu Xin et. al.'s writings on the uses of music in administrative harmony, recorded on the occasion of a grand, imperially sponsored conference during Wang Mang's reign. This suggests that the ideas on music and sound presented in this section of the *Han shu* slightly predate the Eastern Han. For a discussion of early Chinese harmonics in the *Shi ji* and *Huainanzi* and a comparison of these to some early Greek notions, see G. E. R. Lloyd, *The Ambitions of Curiosity: Understanding the World in Ancient Greece and China* (Cambridge: Cambridge University Press, 2002), pp. 56–60.

2. For an outline of the resonant relationship between certain sounds and other cosmic phenomena in the Five Phases system, see Needham, Wang, and Robinson, *Science and Civilisation in China*, 51.

3. Such causality is characterized by one object influencing or inducing the spontaneous eruption of another object. Two objects need not be directly in contact with each other, as spontaneous resonance works remotely as well.

4. The type of cosmology that prevails in the early imperial periods involves the "Five Phases" of metal, wood, water, fire, and earth. The foremost thinker to have promoted a cosmology based on these five phases was Zou Yan, active around 250 BCE. For some histories of Five Phases cosmology, see A. C. Graham's work on *yin-yang* and correlative cosmologies, along with Gu Jiegang, *Wude zhongshi*. For recent essays on the topic of correlative cosmology, see *Bulletin of the Museum of Far Eastern Antiquities*, "Special Issue: Reconsidering the Correlative Cosmology of Early China," Vol. 72 (Stockholm: Fälth and Hässler, 2000). For the correlation between the number five and Heaven (Tian 天], which appears in Han sources, see Mark Csikszentmihalyi, *Material Virtue: Ethics and the Body in Early China* (Leiden: Brill, 2004), p. 168. The claims in this chapter concur with the notion that such a correlation dates to early imperial times.

5. Cook, "Unity and Diversity," 49–53; and DeWoskin, *A Song for One or Two*, 33.

6. Martin Kern, "A Note on the Authenticity and Ideology of *Shih-chi* 24, 'Yue shu,'" *Journal of the American Oriental Society* 119.4 (1999), p. 676.

7. Cook and DeWoskin often translate *yin* as "tone," and DeWoskin also uses the term "voice," when speaking of the eight voices 八音 (*A Song for One or Two*, 52). Kern translates *yin* as "sound" ("Authenticity and Ideology of *Shi-Chi* 24," 677). For a fuller discussion of the various nuances in usage of these terms, see Cook, "Unity and Diversity," 49–53. In general, Cook defines *yin* as "patterned" or "ordered" sound, and *sheng* as unqualified sounds, often vocal, "ranging from human cries and sobs to bird chirpings, animal howls, and the like."

8. For example, the *Laozi* refers to the *wu yin* (Five Tones) while the *Han shu* refers to them as the *wu sheng* (Five Sounds). One can be fairly sure that both texts are referring to the same thing, as they not only mention the number five, but associate them with the same five intervallic relationships as well: *gong* 宮, *shang* 商, *jue* 角, *zhi* 徵, and *yu* 羽. These five should be understood in terms of the five relative pitches in a pentatonic mode, rather than as fixed tones.

9. See Xunzi's "Discourse on Music" for a good example of *sheng* in such contexts. In that chapter, Xunzi uses the term *sheng* to denote sounds in general, while *yin* is reserved for musical forms—even the lascivious tones from the states of Zheng and Wei. For *yin* as animal noises, see *Zhuangzi*, chapters two and eleven, in which the authors speak of the sounds of chickens and dogs (*ji gou zhi yin* 雞狗之音), as well as that of baby birds (*kou yin* 鷇音).

10. The *lü* has been studied and discussed extensively by Lothar von Falkenhausen in chapter eight of Falkenhausen, *Suspended Music*. He also evaluates the semantic distinctions between the traditional *lü* names in von Falkenhausen, "The Rise of Pitch-standards," 433–39.

11. This development occurred sometime during the late Warring States and early imperial era. Each pipe was a tuning device, constructed so as to produce a single, standard pitch. For more on this, see Falkenhausen, "The Rise of Pitch-standards," 433–39.

12. Falkenhausen intriguingly contends that the pitch-standards "were a means of defining musical notes, but were not musical notes themselves ("The Rise of Pitch-standards," 436). In this chapter, however, I understand the pitch-standards to refer to an actual acoustic pitch. The fact that the meanings of *lü* as pipes and pitch-standards could at times be interchanged suggests that authors often intended for the *lü* to be both pitches and a means of defining them.

13. See the article titled, "Shen Kua," in Sivin, *Science in Ancient China*, vol. 3, 1–53. In this article, Sivin gives a helpful synopsis of how mathematical harmonics was related to cosmology and astronomical endeavors. He points in particular to the binome "*lü lü* 律呂," which refers in later texts to the general set of twelve pitch-standards—some of which are designated with the word "*lü* 呂" in the name.

14. See A. C. Graham, *Later Mohist Logic, Ethics and Science* (Hong Kong: The Chinese University Press, 2003), p. 179.

15. *Ibid.*, 325.

16. Heaven is clearly anthropomorphized in many writings from early China. It has a will; it expresses emotions and can be vindictive; and it consistently passes judgment on humans. See especially the descriptions of Heaven provided in the early Mohist treatises, not to mention portions of the *Analects*, *Documents*, *Odes*, and *Yijing*.

17. This is especially the case in the *Analects* 12.11, where Confucius speaks of the normative roles for the names "ruler," "minister," "father," and "son."

18. Sun, *Mozi jiangu*, 285. See also Graham, *Later Mohist Logic, Ethics and Science*, 325.

19. What remains of their writings is fragmentary and mostly substantiated through contemporary discussions of their ideas by the later Mohists, Zhuangzi, and other late Warring States writers. For more about the *ming jia* "School of Names," whom A. C. Graham calls "The Sophists," see Graham, *Disputers of the Tao*, 75–94.

See also Chad Hansen, *A Daoist Theory of Chinese Thought: A Philosophical Interpretation* (Oxford: Oxford University Press, 1992), 233–64. For the question of whether or not "schools" of thought even existed in early China and how the concept of "schools" developed in Han history, see Smith, "Sima Tan," 129–56. See also Nylan and Csikszentmihalyi, "Constructing Lineages and Inventing Traditions," 59–99.

20. Ma Chengyuan 馬承源, ed., *Shanghai bowuguan cang Zhanguo Chu zhushu* 上海博物館藏戰國楚竹書, vol. 7, (Shanghai: Shanghai guji chubanshe, 2009), 287–99, especially 293.

21. Chen Guying 陳鼓應, ed. *Laozi zhuyi ji pingjie* 老子註譯評介 (Beijing: Zhonghua shuju, 1984), 106.

22. The materialistic, but nonetheless "transcendent" view of self-cultivation put forth in the *Guanzi* "Nei Ye" and "Xin Shu (Techniques of the Heart)" chapters should be considered along with the developments in materiality discussed by Mark Csikszentmihalyi in *Material Virtue*. See especially chapter five on the developments of material virtue in the early Chinese empire. For more on early Chinese concepts of the body, see also Sivin, "State, Cosmos, and the Body," 5–37.

23. Yan, *Guanzi jiaoshi*, 323. The dating of this chapter of the *Guanzi* is, like many other chapters of the text, not known. Allyn Rickett surmises that the chapter might have been compiled rather late, at the court of Huainan in Liu An's time (~130's BCE). This does not mean that the quotations or ideas from the chapter date to this period. Indeed, as Rickett points out, much of this chapter seems to have been influenced by the "Nei Ye," which he dates to around the fourth century BCE, or to the time of the earliest portions of the *Laozi*. See Rickett, *Guanzi*, 2, 15–39; 2, 65–70.

24. Yan Changyao 顏昌嶢, ed., *Guanzi jiaoshi* 管子校釋 (Changsha: Yuelu shushe, 1996), 242.

25. Xiong, *Xunzi jinzhu jinyi*, 373.

26. *Ibid.*

27. See especially *Jingmenshi bowuguan* 荊門市博物館, *Guodian Chumu zhujian* 郭店楚幕竹簡 (Jingmen: Wen Wu, 1998), p. 179, strips 23–26. 28. For more on the role of music in cultivating the human emotions and psyche, see chapter four.

29. Sun Yirang, *Mozi jiangu*, "Jing shuo shang 經說上." Mark Csikszentmihalyi provides an excellent discussion of the significance of these (bronze) bell and (jade) chime stone sounds in Csikszentmihalyi, *Material Virtue*, 169–72.

30. Wang, *Fengsu tongyi*, 293–94. Ying Shao is also known for making the explicit link between sagehood and aural ability. On this latter topic, see DeWoskin, *A Song for One or Two*, 31–37. See also Csikszentmihalyi, *Material Virtue*, 169–72.

31. Kenneth Dewoskin translates this phrase as the "tone-wise companion." See DeWoskin, *A Song for One or Two*, 197.

32. Guo Qingfan 郭慶藩. *Zhuangzi jishi*, 160; Burton Watson, trans. *The Complete Works of Chuang Tzu*. New York: Columbia University Press, 1968), p. 61.

33. I explore the notion that music is a legitimate medium for conveying emotional and intentional authenticity in Erica Brindley, "Music and 'Seeking One's Heart-mind' in the 'Xing Zi Ming Chu,'" special publication on moral psychology in *Dao* 5.2 (June 2006), pp. 247–55.

34. I read *fu* 負 as *bai* 敗 here. Sima, *Shi ji*, 1239; Rickett, *Guanzi*, 25.

35. Sima, *Shi ji*, 1239; Rickett, *Guanzi*, 25.

36. For more recent work on the dating of the *Zuo zhuan*, see Yuri Pines, "Intellectual Change in the Chunqiu Period: The Reliability of the Speeches in the *Zuo zhuan* as Sources of Chunqiu Intellectual History," *Early China* 22 (1997): pp. 77–132. See also Schaberg, *A Patterned Past*, 315–24. Schaberg places the *Zuo zhuan* primarily into the context of fourth century BCE Ru traditions of thought.

37. The text literally states, "pushing from the first month of spring down to the third month of winter (i.e., the whole year, consisting of four sets of three months)." On the helpful advice of John Major and a reviewer, I take these seasonal terms as a shorthand for the pitch-pipes that are correlated to each month (cf. "Yin lü" chapter of the *Lüshi chunqiu*, as summarized in Cook, "Unity and Diversity," 106.) The pitch-pipes associated with the first month of spring down and the third month of winter refer to *taicou* 太族 and *dalü* 大呂, the longest and shortest pipes respectively, so that one would begin by blowing the longest and then cycle through each seasonal pipe to the shortest. See Needham, Wang, and Robinson, *Science and Civilisation in China*, 140.

38. While it is unclear to us what this prognosis meant, remaining in the key of the tonic appeared to be an auspicious sign for King Wu. Thanks to members of the Early China Seminar (Columbia University, February 9, 2008) for suggesting that it could have been related to the association of the Zhou house with the tonic.

39. Sima, *Shi ji*, 1240.

40. Sima Qian claims the lengthy history of such practices in a statement that follows upon this passage: "[This] has been the unchanging way for hundreds of [generations of] kings" *bai wang bu yi zhi dao ye* 百王不易之道也." Sima, *Shi ji*, 1240. It is likely that Sima Qian retells a later embellishment of the Zhou conquest that projects more recent beliefs about sound and divination onto the distant past. That Sima Qian would have been in a unique position as Grand Astrologer (*Tai Shi* 太史) to know about the history of divination practices and interpretation of natural signs gives us reason to believe that the practices Sima describes here are not without some historical merit. For a summary of the divinatory role of the *Tai Shi*, see Lloyd, *The Ambitions of Curiosity*, 9–10.

41. The role of sound as a subtle manifestation of the condition of the body can also be observed in the practice of "watching the ethers," described below. Huang Yi-long and Chang Chih-ch'eng cite the Song mathematician and scientist, Shen Gua, who compares "watching the ethers" using pitch-pipes of varying lengths to acupuncture and probing the body with needles of different lengths. See See Yi-long Huang and Chang Chih-ch'eng, "The Evolution and Decline of the Ancient Chinese Practice of Watching for the Ethers," *Chinese Science* 13 (1996): p. 84, note 8. I am indebted to Miranda Brown for her discussion of the role of "clues" [*wei* 微] in early Chinese medical thought. Private conversation, 2009.

42. That sound might also have revealed information about mundane, human affairs is, in fact, entirely congruent with its potentially special relationship to the spiritual realm. After all, early Chinese military diviners would not have been interested in the distinction between spiritual and mundane aspects knowledge, as they sought to understand the whole picture of the enemy's situation. The so-called spirit

world would to them have represented just another aspect of the total information to be garnered about a given state of cosmic affairs.

43. The Northern and Southern Winds refer to the musical sounds that emanate from those very geographic regions.

44. Yang, *Chunqiu Zuozhuan zhu*, 1043. One may also read the last statement of this passage as a proclamation not of a causal relationship between a ruler's virtue and these ominous, natural signs, but of the special power of the ruler to trump other methods of prediction, such as the wind-reading just described. I find this reading less fitting because the statement about the ruler's power is quite abrupt and seems to be predicated on what came before it. Indeed, if the author had wished to speak of the ruler's virtue in contrast to the above-mentioned methods of divination, it seems as though he would have presented his case by using more words that connote negation of what came before.

45. The correlation between musical sounds and virtue is especially prominent in the story about Prince Jizha of Wu in Duke Xiang, 29.13. Yang, *Chunqiu Zuozhuan zhu*, 1161–67.

46. For more on the relationship between winds and music, see Lewis, *Sanctioned Violence*, 218–21.

47. The text remarkably links sumptuary law with musical instrumentation and meteorological phenomena by giving primacy to the number eight, which allegedly characterizes the natural diversity of things in each area: eight rows of dancers (for the Son of Heaven), eight instruments, and eight winds. Yang, *Chunqiu Zuozhuan zhu*, 46.

48. Sound was also used by military men to divine about the outcomes of battle in a passage in the *Zhou Li*, which likely dates to the Han period. It appears that the connection between cosmos and sound is firm by this later time, insofar as the text mentions that the pitch-pipes were used to match human sound with the inner harmonies of the cosmos. See the commentaries about this in Sima, *Shi ji*, 1240.

49. By Han times, it seems, the connection between *qi* and sounds was clearly cosmic in nature. For example, Wang Chong explained the creation of prophetic children's songs in terms of young boys who would become vehicles for Yang *qi*. Prophetic songs were nothing more than cosmic manifestations of *qi* channeled through young boys (*yang* in nature). See Anne Behnke Kinney, *Representations of Childhood and Youth in Early China* (Stanford: Stanford University Press, 2004): 160–61.

50. I understand the term *jian* 兼 here according to the Mohist use of the term: connoting universality, or at the very least, that which is shared and not particular to any single object.

51. Following the comment by Wang Yinzhi 王引之 regarding a corrupt previous usage of the phrase *xiao he* 簫和, it is likely that the presence of these two terms in the list of instruments is also a later editorial mistake. I therefore do not translate these terms here. See Xiong, *Xunzi jinzhu jinyi*, 418, note 4.

52. Xiong, *Xunzi jinzhu jinyi*, 418. Translation slightly adapted from Cook, "Unity and Diversity," 425–26. For more information on the large and small mouth organs, *yu* 竽 and *sheng* 笙, respectively, see Feng Guangsheng, "Winds," in *Music in the Age of Confucius*, ed. Jenny F. So (Washington D. C.: Freer Gallery of Art and Arthur M. Sackler Gallery, 2000), pp. 87–99.

53. The dating of this text is obscure, though it is generally attributed to the late Warring States and early imperial periods. I would suggest that it is not likely to be a Warring States text, as its incorporation of the cosmology of spontaneous resonance is fairly thorough and suggests a more mature stage in the development of such systems of thought.

54. See Ralph Sawyer (with Mei-chün Sawyer), trans., *The Seven Military Classics of Ancient China* (Boulder: Westview Press, 1993), 72–73. I am grateful to Kenneth Swope and his unpublished paper dealing with music in late Ming military operations for pointing me to this source.

55. For example, *jiao* tones indicate a white tiger; *jue* tones indicate a black martial; *shang* tones indicate a vermillion bird; *yu* tones indicate a hooked formation; and *gong* tones indicate a green dragon. See Sawyer, *The Seven Military Classics*, 72–73.

56. Such timbres and visual cues include the sound of a particular type of drum; the flashing of lights from a fire; the sounds of bronze, iron, spears, and halberds; the sound of people sighing; and even silence. Sawyer, *The Seven Military Classics*, 72–73.

57. Lü Wang 呂望, *Liu tao* (Six Secret Teachings 六韜) (Beijing: Zhonghua shuju, 1991), 20. Chapter 3.12, "Military Portents" (Bin zheng 兵徵), 20. Translation adapted from Sawyer, *The Seven Military Classics*, 74.

58. Lü, *Liu tao*, 20.

59. In general, this text is dated to the Han period, but scholars do not deny the possibility that much of the information in it, and indeed, many of its passages, stem from earlier sources, such as Xunzi's "Yue lun." For more on the relationship between the "Yue ji" text and the treatise titled "Yue shu," found in Sima Qian's *Shi ji*, see Yu, "Liji Yueji," 56–67. See also Kern, "Authenticity and Ideology of *Shi-Chi* 24," 673–77.

60. Sun, *Liji jijie*, 988. Sima, *Shi ji*, 1189.

61. Sun, *Liji jijie*, 994. Sima, *Shi ji*, 1196.

62. Chen, *Lüshi chunqiu jiaoshi*, 255.

63. *Ibid.*

64. One is tempted to draw a connection between this emergent view of music and the cosmos and Pythagoras' notion of the "music of the spheres," or heavenly bodies. As far as I know, there is no evidence of mutual influence between the ancient Greeks and Chinese on this topic. G. E. R. Lloyd shows how such concepts differ from each other in Lloyd, *Adversaries and Authorities*, 186–89.

65. The *Bohu tong* is perhaps one of the first texts to explicitly link the *sheng* of sounds with the *sheng* of the sage. See Csikszentmihalyi, *Material Virtue*, 170. See also DeWoskin, *A Song for One or Two*, 32, where he cites Ban Gu's commentary to the *Bohu tong* passage. For more on the notion of sagely "attunement" with the cosmos as a "psychology of attunement," see Erica Brindley, "Music, Cosmos, and the Development of Psychology in Early China," *T'oung Pao* 92 (2006): 39–47. Indeed, it appears that from the late Warring States to the early Han, the sage becomes increasingly defined through his connection to the cosmos and his extraordinary ability to know, perceive, and create models of it.

66. According to DeWoskin, this comment is attributed to the *Fengsu tongyi* but is not in the present version of it. DeWoskin, *A Song for One or Two*, 33, note 7. Csikszentmihalyi remarks that the *Yiwen leiju* 20.1a and *Taiping yulan* 104, 1855

both associate this statement with the text. Csikszentmihalyi, *Material Virtue*, 170, note 20.

67. Li Ling and Keith McMahon, "The Contents and Terminology of the Mawangdui Texts on the Arts of the Bedchamber," *Early China* 17 (1992), pp. 158–59.

68. *Ibid.* These sounds likely constituted evidence of a person's (specifically, a woman's) harmonization, both with one's partner and with the cosmos at large. See Donald Harper, *Early Chinese Medical Literature: The Mawangdui Medical Manuscripts* (New York: Keegan Paul International, 1998), 389–90 (especially note 9); 411 and 434. On this last page, a Mawangdui text explicitly lists the Five Sounds as throaty breathing, panting, continual moaning, blowing, and biting.

69. For more on the relationships between cosmology and the regimes of the late Warring States and Han eras, see Aihe Wang, *Cosmology and Political Culture in Early China* (Cambridge: Cambridge University Press, 2000).

70. For a discussion of the political ramifications of using the pitch-standards, see Falkenhausen, *Suspended Music*, 310–18.

71. Notably, this treatise is separate from Sima's "Treatise on the Calendar" (*Li shu* 曆書), which is placed immediately after it. In the *Han shu*, on the other hand, the two topics are collapsed into one chapter in the "Treatise on the Pitch-standards and Calendar." The authenticity of Sima's "Treatise" is in doubt, although its compliance with the principles laid out in the *Han shu* treatise suggests a Han date. Ban Gu 班固, the author of the *Han shu*, admits to copying the entire section on pitch-standards from Liu Xin's 劉歆 (32 BCE–23 CE) memorial to the throne (written between 1 CE and 5 CE). See Qiu Qiongsun 丘瓊蓀, *Lidai yuezhi lüzhi jiaoshi* 歷代樂志律志校釋 (Beijing: Zhonghua shuju, 1964): 1–14. See also B. J. Mansvelt Beck, *The Treatises of Later Han: Their Author, Sources, Contents and Place in Chinese Historiography* (Leiden: E. J. Brill, 1990): 56–63. A recent discussion of this chapter that does not discuss music at length can be found in Christopher Cullen, "Numbers, Numeracy, and the Cosmos," in Nylan and Lowe, *China's Early Empires*, 323–38.

72. That Sima Qian links the terms *yin* to the Five Tones and *sheng* to the pitch-standards is revealing of their possible differences, and can be seen in the citations, "For this reason, the tones (*yin*) begin with *gong*," (Sima, *Shi ji*, 1251) and "When King Wu of the Zhou attacked the Shang tyrant Zhou, he made use of a practice of blowing the pitch-pipes and listening to their sounds (*sheng*)" (Sima, *Shi ji*, 1240). For the correlative and mathematical linkages mentioned, see 1243–51. Much work still needs to be done on the cosmology behind these linkages and on the significance of number in relationship to cosmology. For more on this matter, see the chapter entitled "Heavenly Harmonies," in Lloyd, *Adversaries and Authorities*, 165–89.

There are many almanacs (*ri shu* 日書) uncovered in the recent past from tombs that date to the Warring States and early imperial periods. These types of texts differ from the treatises of Sima Qian in that they mostly provide concrete, detailed information about the auspiciousness of particular days and times. Sima's accounts are intended to rationalize the system so that the most basic mathematical interrelationships and cosmic patterns might be understood. For a discussion of these almanacs, see Mu-chou Poo, *In Search of Personal Welfare: A View of Ancient Chinese Religion* (Albany: State University of New York Press, 1998), pp. 69–101.

73. See especially Sima, *Shi ji*, 1243–48. Notably, on page 1249, the text correlates the Five Tones with certain multiples of six, eight, and nine; and each of the twelve pitch-pipes is then mathematically correlated to one of the Five Tones. For more on pitch-standards, see Derk Bodde, "The Chinese Cosmic Magic Known as Watching for the Ethers," in *Essays on Chinese Civilization* (Princeton: Princeton University Press, 1981), pp. 352–61. Bodde introduces the notion of pitch-standards as scales or sequences, which can be misleading. He arrives at this conclusion by inquiring into the Han practice of expanding the basic twelve pitch-standards into sixty pitch-standards. In order for the twelve pitch-standards to be combined meaningfully with the Five Tones of the pentatonic scale (thus arriving at the number sixty), Bodde claims, the pitch-pipes themselves had to refer not just to their pitches, but to a scale associated with each one.

One should realize that a scale represents a mode, or set sequence of intervals (such as the pentatonic mode of *gong, shang, jue, zhi, yu*) that begins on a particular pitch. If the pitch-pipes each represented different modes, while the Five Tones their starting pitches, then early Chinese music would not have been pentatonic but dodecatonic. Bodde clearly does not wish to state this. Rather, the reader should not think of the Five Tones in terms of fixed tones but in terms of five relative tones in a pentatonic mode, possessing a fixed interval between each of the tones. There would thus be five possible modal permutations for any given fundamental tone. If one were to play each possible mode beginning on each possible pitch-standard, one arrives at the possibility of sixty different scales, or five modal permutations times twelve. Hence, a scale is different from the pitch-pipes or pitch-standards themselves. For Bodde's argument, see Bodde, "The Chinese Cosmic Magic," 354.

Also, according to Bodde, the pitch-pipes of the twelve pitch-pipes "cover a range of exactly one octave," thereby providing "the twelve half notes of the untempered chromatic scale." Given that the pitch-pipes can refer to pitches, this is certainly possible, and likely the case. Bodde, "The Chinese Cosmic Magic," 352.

74. The Eight Rectitudes appear to be the categories of wind, subsequently outlined by Sima Qian according to their characteristic interactions of *yin-yang* and *qi*. Sima, *Shi ji*, 1243. For more on the relationship between the Eight Winds and sound, see the "Sound and Acoustics" section of Needham, Wang, and Robinson, *Science and Civilisation in China*, 126–228.

75. Sima, *Shi ji*, 1239.

76. According to commentators who wish to reconcile this text with that of the "Treatise on the Pitch-standards and Calendar" of the *Han shu*, the "six pitch-standards," are supposed to refer to six of each Yin and Yang types of pipes, thus making twelve total. Sima, *Shi ji*, 1239.

77. Ban, *Han shu*, 959, note 1.

78. Indeed, the relationship between wind and music is very tight in ancient China. It would appear that the ancient Chinese viewed wind as the medium through which sound traveled. While sound would by Han times come to be viewed as implicit in wind and the *qi* of wind, it had not always been equated with such natural, cosmic phenomena, as this chapter will show.

79. Ban, *Han shu*, 956. For the association of the Yellow Bell with the number nine, see 958.

80. *Ibid.*, 966. The Chinese phrase reads, "The length of the Yellow Bell is equal to [the length of] ninety average-length kernels of black sticky rice measured out [side-by-side] 以子穀秬黍中者黍之廣，度之九十分，黃鐘之長." I base my translation on Yan Shigu's 顏師古 comments that 子穀 zigu refers to kernels of rice, and *jushu* 秬黍 refers to a type of black, sticky rice. Ban, *Han shu*, 967.

81. Ban, *Han shu*, 966.

82. *Ibid.*, 967–70.

83. This is a pun on the term "lü 呂" (mode), which finds a homophone in "lü 旅" (travel).

84. This is because Yin reaches its maximum during the twelfth month, the month associated with this pitch-pipe.

85. I am grateful to John Major for pointing out that this reference to months denotes not just time, but, more specifically, the months as they are expressed physically as points on the horizon. See especially Major, *Heaven and Earth in Early Han Thought*, 109.

86. This is another pun, linking the phonically related terms, *cou* 族 and *zou* 奏.

87. Ban, *Han shu*, 959.

88. Note that the type of each action is matched phonically to the name of the pitch-standard. Discussions that attempted to justify the meaning of a term by referring to meanings associated with linguistic cognates of the term became common practice during the Han period.

89. Ban, *Han shu*, 959.

90. The author takes it for granted that the pitch-standards are direct manifestations of the sounds of the cosmos, transmitted through the sounds of birds to humans. They are therefore of the same kind, whether in their audible form as sound, or in their more invisible form as cosmic wind. It is important to note here that sound is manifestly audible for all to hear and represents the very material operations of the cosmos.

91. For information on the decline of this practice, see Huang and Chang, "Evolution and Decline."

92. Bodde, "The Chinese Cosmic Magic," 355. The *Later Han Shu* treatise is discussed in Mansvelt Beck, *The Treatises of Later Han*, 58–61.

93. Bodde, "The Chinese Cosmic Magic," 353.

94. *Ibid.*

95. Recent archaeological evidence suggests that the names of the pitch-standards were originally derived from the names of individual bells, not pipes. This possibly upsets the entire notion that pitch-pipe sounds had from early on been linked to the *qi* of the cosmos, making it unlikely that such a belief ever existed in pre-Warring States and Han times. See Falkenhausen, "The Rise of Pitch-standards," 437.

96. One might ask how sound can be primary, if it is not audible. Since one ascertains cosmic functioning by watching how *qi* has manifested itself directly through the pitch-pipes—musical instruments that normally produce sound upon the blowing of *qi* through their hollows—it is fair to say that the early Chinese understood the displaced ashes as an expression of cosmic sound. Although they detected this sound through visible and not aural cues, it remains sound, for it emerged from instruments that normally produce audible sound.

97. Such a connection was not lost on later commentators to the practice. As mentioned before, Shen Gua (1030–94) compared the practice of "watching the ethers" with acupuncture, insofar as both practices used probes of some sort to make contact with *qi* (either that of the human body or of the Earth). See Huang and Chang, "Evolution and Decline," 84, note 8. The role of *qi* in pulse diagnostics is also analogous to the practice of "watching the ethers." Physicians—like the ritual specialists who paid attention to the types of *qi* beneath the surface of the earth—read pulses along the arm and wrist to distinguish between types of *qi* just under the surface of the skin. In each case, vital information about body of humans or the "body" of the cosmos lay hidden from the layman's view. For a brief summary of pulse diagnostics, see Charlotte Furth, *A Flourishing Yin: Gender in China's Medical History, 960–1665* (Berkeley: University of California Press, 1999), pp. 50–51.

98. Indeed, one might go so far as to claim that this form of imperial religiosity was part and parcel of the rise of proto-scientific methods—relating to correlative systems of spontaneous resonance—during the Han period.

99. Needham, Wang, and Robinson, *Science and Civilisation in China.*

100. In particular, it agrees with the reference to *ming* (name) in the *Taiyi sheng shui*, to the Zhuangzian notion of blowing of the pan-pipes of Heaven, and to the Laozian notion of the soundless sound of the Dao.

101. I am grateful to William Baxter for pointing out that this is only part of the story. There were at least two different ways to write "wind" in the oracle bones: with a pictograph depicting a sail, and with a phonetic compound that combined such a pictograph for "sail" with the graph for "bird" (*niao* 鳥). It is this latter phonetic compound that was also used to write "phoenix." For more details, see Karlgren, *Grammata Serica Recensa.*

102. Lewis, *Sanctioned Violence*, 221. For connections among wind, music, and *De*, see also Jane Geaney, *On the Epistemology of the Senses in Early Chinese Thought* (Honolulu: University of Hawaii Press, 2002), 22–30.

103. One might wish to consider the analogous links between music and pipes, on the one hand, and the body and its vessels or channels, on the other. Though this analogy is not explicit in the early texts we have examined in this book, the fact that both types of vessels (musical pipes and bodily vessels) serve to transport *qi* lends itself to an easy comparison taken up by later commentators. Pipes and channels convey wind and *qi*, the necessary components of the cosmos and the body. Once music and the basis for harmony become primarily associated with the pitch-pipes and *qi* cosmology rather than bell sets and a sacrificial cosmology of the spirits, the relationship between music and the cosmos seems to have become tighter than ever.

104. Lothar von Falkenhausen has shown that pitch-standard variations (not *yin*-tones) are culturally specific, and has speculated that such standards are derived from bells, and not pipes, in the early Zhou period. Archaeological evidence has confirmed the notion that pitch-standard names were "nothing more or less than names of individual bells, and that there was no stringent system in which the pitches of the different bells were correlated." (Falkenhausen, "The Rise of Pitch-standards," 437.) See also Falkenhausen, *Suspended Music*, chapter nine.

105. In addition one might wish to examine how music theory embraced certain traditions in numerology and divination, such as the significance of the number nine,

and numbers that are multiples of the numbers six, eight, and nine, into its system. See especially Sima, *Shi ji*, 1249.

CHAPTER FOUR. MUSIC AND THE EMERGENCE OF A PSYCHOLOGY OF THE EMOTIONS

1. More private, chamber music was likely to have been quite different from that of ritualized music for grand, central halls and outside areas. Ingrid Furniss has suggested that the placement of instruments in tombs may indicate whether such instruments were used for ceremonial or private purposes. This is because the instruments found in the central tomb tended to be ensembles that included bell and chime stone sets as well as other ritual vessels (sometimes bronze, and not merely ceramic), while the instruments buried in side chambers were usually not bell and chime stone sets, and were often buried together with other personal accents. Furniss, *Music in Ancient China*, 154–156, 285–288. Furniss also shows that the solo string tradition had begun to develop by the Eastern Zhou period. Furniss, 97. Further archaeological evidence suggests that small musical ensembles may have been the common ritual form of music in southern regions like that of contemporary Zhejiang. See So, *Music in the Age of Confucius*, 21, 27–28.

2. Xunzi may have been the first thinker to have explicitly claimed that "music is joy" and to have brought renown to such a phrase. See Xiong, *Xunzi jinzhu jinyi*, 20 ("Yue lun 樂論"), 409.

3. The words for "joy," (OC: *rawk) and "music" (OC: *ngrawk) share both the same graph and phonetic root. Each was differentiated from each other on the basis of context, and the pronunciation would differ in accordance to such semantic differentiation, much as one differentiates between *le* and *yue* in modern usage. William H. Baxter, *Handbook of Old Chinese Phonology* (Berlin: Mouton de Gruyter, 1992), 534. Etymological ties between the characters for "music" and "joy" had existed long prior to Xunzi's assertion. See also Mizukami Shizuo's discussion of the etymological roots of *yue* in bronze bell inscriptions, where it means "to please," and "to make happy." Mizukami Shizuo 水上靜夫, "'Gaku' ji ko '樂' 字考," *Nihon Chugoku gakkai ho* 18 (1996): 28.

4. Many earlier authors allude to implicit associations between the terms, but none proclaims their equivalence, or even links them explicitly. For example, in their extant denouncement of *yue* (Chapter 32), the early Mohists implicitly connect the sounds (*sheng* 聲) of *yue* with the emotion, *yue*-joy/happiness. See Sun Yirang, ed., *Mozi jiangu*, 227. Similarly, Mencius speaks in the same phrase of "delighting in music" *le yue* 樂 樂 (*Mencius* 1B1), while authors of the *Zuo zhuan* link harmonious music and the joy that is derived from it (*Zuo zhuan*, Duke Xiang 11.5). Schaberg demonstrates for the text of the *Mencius* that "The word *yue* is one which Mencius uses along with *le* to describe pleasure of all sorts." See David Schaberg, "Social Pleasures in Early Chinese Historiography and Philosophy," in *The Limits of Historiography*, ed. Christina Kraus (Leiden: Brill, 1999), 24. From these examples, it seems clear that the linguistic connection between the two homographs was understood in terms of a semantic connection well before Xunzi's explicit remarks in the third century BCE.

5. Thus, my use of the term also does not exactly correspond to ancient Greek usage. See H. G. Liddell and Scott, *An Intermediate Greek-English Lexicon* (Oxford: Oxford University Press, 1997), 903.

6. Donald Munro, "The Origin of the Concept of *De*," in *The Concept of Man in Early China* (Stanford: Stanford University Press, 1969), 185–97.

7. Geaney, *On the Epistemology of the Senses*, 25. For an interesting account of the relationship between music and the harmony of *De*, see 22–30.

8. *Ibid.*, 25. See, for example, *Mencius* 2A2.

9. *Zhuangzi*, Chapter 5, 214–15. Cited in Geaney, *Epistemology of the Senses*, 26.

10. *Ibid.*, 191. Geaney, 27.

11. The citations from the *Shu* are not present in the transmitted version but found in a text called *Cai Zhong zhi ming* 蔡仲之命 (*The Commands of Cai Zhong*). See Yang, *Chunqiu Zuozhuan zhu*, 309–10.

12. *Guo yu*, 4.93 ("Shikuang lun yue 師曠論樂"). Cited and translated in Schaberg, *A Patterned Past*, 118.

13. *Ibid.*

14. *Mencius* 5B1. Yang Bojun, ed., *Mengzi yizhu* 孟子譯注 (Hong Kong: Zhonghua shuju, 1998), 232.

15. For more on the eight winds and their correlations to musical tones, see John Major, "Notes on the Nomenclature of the Winds and Directions in the Early Han," *T'oung Pao* 65.1–3 (1979): 66–80.

16. Csikszentmihalyi, *Material Virtue,* 181–87.

17. *Zhouyi zhushu* 周易注疏 (Taipei: Taiwan xuesheng shuju, 1984): Hexagram 16, "Yu" 豫, 208.

18. Sun Xidan, *Liji jijie*, 19 ("Yue ji, Part II"), 1036. The same text claims that "music is that which gives form to *De* 樂者所以象德也," 19 ("Yue ji, Part I"), 997; and defines music in terms of "virtuous tones" (德音之謂樂), 19 ("Yue ji, Part II"), 1015.

19. Van Zoeren, *Poetry and Personality*, 17–51. See also Martin Kern, "*Shi Jing* Songs as Performance Texts: A Case Study of 'Chu Ci' (Thorny Caltrop,)" *Early China* 25 (2000): 49–111.

20. This is what Martin Kern, citing Jan Assmann, refers to as "normative cultural memory." Kern, "*Shi Jing* Songs," 67.

21. *Ibid.*, 66.

22. *Shi jing*, Mao 109. Trans. Waley, *The Book of Songs*, (New York: Grove Press, 1960), 308.

23. *Shi jing*, Mao 204. Trans. Waley, *The Book of Songs*, 139.

24. *Shi jing*, Mao 162. Trans. Waley, *The Book of Songs*, 151.

25. Van Zoeren, *Poetry and Personality*, 7.

26. By "school," I am not necessarily referring to an actual physical school house, but to the abstract notion of the lineage school, in which Confucius was the master of a group of disciples (*dizi* 弟子) at his door, otherwise known as "door disciples (*mentu* 門徒)." The commentarial tradition that follows alternate versions of this anecdote in Liu Xiang's *Shuo Yuan* interprets Confucius' criticism as not directed towards the actual placement of the instrument but at the style of Zilu's playing as well as the content of the music. See : Edward Slingerland, *Confucius: Analects* (Indianapolis:

Hackett Publishing Company, 2003), pp. 116–117. D. C. Lau interprets the passage more literally in terms of the physical placement of Zilu's instrument. While this latter interpretation is suggestive, I discount it because of the presence of the verb, "to do/play (wei 為)," which implies one's action upon the grand zither.

27. *Analects*, 11.15.

28. Furniss, 77–98; 288–92.

29. *Analects*, 11.15.

30. *Ibid*.

31. Note that this is different from saying that what is aesthetically pleasing is defined in terms of what is morally good. *Analects* 3.25 quickly dispels us of this latter notion, with the comment: "The Master said of the *shao* that it was both the perfection of beauty and goodness. Of the *wu* he said that it was the perfection of beauty but not of goodness."

32. *Analects*, 1.1.

33. See for example, *Analects* 4.2, 6.11, and 11.4.

34. *Analects*, 6.20.

35. *Analects*, 7.14:

36. *Analects*, 7.10.

37. *Analects*, 17.21.

38. See Van Zoeren, *Poetry and Personality*, 29–30 for an interpretation that claims Confucius' concern regards the musical performance of the Odes, and not merely the words.

39. *Analects*, 3.2.

40. *Analects*, 17.11.

41. *Analects*, 3.3.

42. Ma Chengyuan, *Shanghai bowuguan cang Zhanguo Chu zhushu*, vol. 1.

43. Ma Chengyuan, *Shanghai bowu guan*, 225.

44. For an interesting account of the implications of such textual similarity, see Martin Kern, "The Odes in Excavated Manuscripts," in *Text and Ritual in Early China*, ed. Martin Kern (Seattle: University of Washington Press, 2000), 157. Kern claims that such similarities among texts, especially those without transmitted counterparts, suggest a remarkable stability in transmission.

45. *Jingmenshi bowuguan*, GDCMZJ, 179, strip 1. The same line from XQL uses the word "regulated" (*zheng* 正) instead of "fixed" (*ding* 定). Ma Chengyuan, *Shanghai bowuguan*, 220–21. The same graph in XZMC can also be transcribed as *zheng*. Since either graph could be a lexical variant for the other, I have chosen to take it as "fixed" on the basis that this term best underscores the author's problematic of using the heart-mind to make the correct decisions out of an array of possible ones.

In translating from this text, I use the current Chinese transcriptions provided by the editorial teams of both the Guodian and Shanghai Museum strips. My interpretations are thus completely based on the foundational work of these editors and not on my own paleographical reading of certain graphs in their pure, untranscribed state. I have also benefited from reading and considering translations or partial translations of this text by Paul Goldin and Sarah Queen (unpublished work). See Paul Goldin, "Xunzi in the Light of the Guodian Manuscripts," *Early China* 25 (2000): 113–46.

46. *Analects*, 17.2.

47. If the "Nei Ye" is indeed a fourth century BCE text, as scholars such as Luo Genze, Guo Moruo, A. C. Graham, Harold Roth, and W. Allyn Rickett suggest it is, then it is perhaps the only text besides XZMC and the *Mencius* to enter at length into discussions of the human psyche. Even then, the "Nei Ye" does not really focus on interrelationships between the external and internal realms as does the XZMC. See Rickett, *Guanzi*, vol. 2, 15–39; and Harold Roth, *Original Tao: Inward Training and the Foundations of Taoist Mysticism* (New York: Columbia University Press, 1999), 26.

48. Donald Harper has pointed out the possibility that the graph for *qu* 取 might actually refer to the lexical meaning of its cognate, *ju* (聚 "to gather together," "concentrate") (private conversation, May, 2004). This would change the meaning of the text considerably, lending it a more internal focus that clearly maintains the integrity and power of the human psyche in itself. See Ma Chengyuan, *Shanghai bowuguan*, 222; Li Ling 李零, *Guodian Chujian jiaodu ji* 郭店楚簡校讀記 (Beijing: Beijing daxue, 2002), 112; and Chen Wei 陳偉, *Guodian zhushu bieshi* 郭店竹書別釋 (Wuhan: Hubei jiaoyu, 2003), 182–83. I stand by my reading of *qu* as "to grab, to take," because such a meaning better accentuates the external nature of teachings and their powers over the self.

49. For a critique and description of currently prevailing blank slate theories, see Steven Pinker, *The Blank Slate: The Modern Denial of Human Nature* (New York: Viking, 2002).

50. *Jingmenshi bowuguan*, GDCMZJ, 179, strips 2–3.

51. For an in-depth account of emotions as presented in the text, see Michael Puett, "The Ethics of Responding Properly: The Notion of *Qing* in Early Chinese Thought," in *Emotions in Chinese Culture*, ed., Halvor Eifring (Leiden: Brill, 2004), pp. 37–68.

52. Yang, *Mengzi yizhu*, 6A1, 253.

53. *Jingmenshi bowuguan*, GDCMZJ, strips 50–51, 181. The *Shanghai bowuguan* notably skips over the sentence about the people believing you even though you have not yet acted. See Ma Chengyuan, *Shanghai bowuguan*, 252.

54. In order to understand the special position of music as part of the normative Dao over humans, it is important to realize that the term "Dao" sometimes refers in the text to many different paths, all of which might exert some kind of deterministic force over human nature and behavior. This can be seen in the fact that teachings in the XZMC possesses two basic meanings: 1) the specific teachings of the sages (including music), and 2) any determining force in one's environment which gives rise to adaptive learning (including sounds). According to the latter, more general usage, "teachings" can be taken as "environmental influences," or even, "upbringing."

55. The phrasing of these statements is confusing. Literally, the author states something to the effect that hardness is "of a bowl" and softness is "of a rope."

56. *Jingmenshi bowuguan*, GDCMZJ, strips 8 and 9, 179. These strips, until the statement about the Four Seas, are missing from the Shanghai version of XQL. See Ma Chengyuan, *Shanghai bowuguan*, 225–26.

57. I am indebted to Stephen Durrant for bringing this linguistic nuance to my attention. The term "teachings" is graphically represented in both the Guodian and Shanghai strips as [HANDWRITE], which contemporary paleographers take to

represent our modern term *jiao*. According to the commentary to the Shanghai version, this graph can mean both "*xue*-to learn," and "*jiao*-to teach," and it is defined in the *Shuo Wen* specifically as "fang," which is then glossed by Duan Yucai as "Xiao, to model (oneself upon)." See Ma Chengyuan, *Shanghai bowuguan*, 226.

58. For the difficult character, *yao* 舀, I follow Li Ling's reading as *dao* 陶. Li Ling, *Guodian zhujian jiaodu ji*, 509. Quoted in Goldin 2000, 132, note 69.

59. *Jingmenshi bowuguan*, 179, strips 23–26. Ma Chengyuan, *Shanghai bowuguan*, 239–40.

60. Such a claim is justified through the statement given in the previous example whereby hardness grabs hold of a bowl and softness grabs hold of a rope. Hardness and softness are not inherent characteristics of either cups or ropes external qualities that impress themselves upon the raw materials of cups and ropes. Indeed, the possibility for such a reading is tempting, especially since later thinkers of the Wei-Jin Dynasty, such as Xi Kang (223–262 CE), discussed precisely this topic at length. Xi Kang's later essay titled, "Discourse [on the claim that] sound possesses neither sadness nor happiness 聲無哀樂論," would presumably have refuted claims—some of which might have been made by their Warring States predecessors—that emotions were physically transmitted through sound. But given the lack of explanation in the text, one cannot be sure that the author espouses such a materialistic vision.

This interpretation would need to be based in certain assumptions about *qi*-material force that are not explicit in the text. While the text does state that emotions are manifested in the world as *qi*-material force (*Jingmenshi bowuguan*, GDCMZJ, 179, strip 2), the question of whether sound actually possesses emotional *qi* or whether it is merely evocative of it remains murky.

61. I suggest that we keep an open mind about the underlying logic of causality in these texts. From scholarship on the ancient Greeks, we know that people maintained certain beliefs in the concreteness of external and internal forces and the permeability of the human body. See Ruth Padel, *In and Out of the Mind: Greek Images of the Tragic Self* (Princeton: Princeton University Press, 1992): 40–44, 49–59. We must not presume that the ancient Chinese possessed the same conceptions on the transmission and perception of sound that we possess in the present day.

62. *Jingmenshi bowuguan*, GDCMZJ, 179, strips 14 and 15. Though there are many ways to interpret the language of this section, the interpretation that makes the most sense to me reads as follows: "There are four methods of the Dao, yet only the Dao for humans is the one that can be followed (taken as a chosen path). The other three methods only lead one inexorably ahead (without choice)." The critical distinction in this reading is that between a chosen path appropriate for humankind and the more determined paths (of Heaven, Earth, and things? The three other "methods" are left unspecified in the text) that work simultaneously upon human life in this world. Interestingly, the Laozian conception of a Dao that cannot be followed (道可道非常道) appears to be a direct response to the claim here that the "Dao for humans is the one that can be followed."

63. Note that this does not refer to all types of music, but more precisely, to ritually prescribed music in the Zhou tradition that would have been deemed proper by the *Ru* ritual specialists. *Jingmenshi bowuguan*, GDCMZJ, 179, strip 15. It is unclear

from the text whether the author is referring to these as specific texts or more generally, as key aspects of a transmitted tradition that might include texts but also point to certain patterns of words, sounds, and behaviors, etc.

64. *Jingmenshi bowuguan, GDCMZJ,* 179, strips 15 and 16.

65. For more on this, see Brindley, "Music, Cosmos, and the Development of Psychology in Early China," 27–28. This statement should not be confused with the types of claims Mencius makes concerning the naturally endowed moral agencies in humans. To say that humans are inclined to act morally because moral knowledge, as well as the motivating force underlying moral action, is inherent in every human (as in the *Mencius*) is very different than to claim that humans have an endowed (intellectual) capacity to create vehicles for moral education such as music and the rites (as in the XZMC).

66. Perhaps this helps support the idea that the XZMC was an earlier text that fits in better with fourth century BCE concerns than later, more imperial concerns, but we cannot know for sure.

67. Ma Chengyuan, *Shanghai bowuguan,* 222. *Jingmenshi bowuguan, GDCMZJ,* 179, strip 4. The three missing characters in this sentence in the XZMC are completed by the text of the *Shanghai bowuguan.* As usual, Qiu Xigui's original speculation about the missing characters turns out to be correct. See *Jingmenshi bowuguan, GDCMZJ,* 182, note 3.

68. The graphs in the two versions are at odds here, and this difference changes the meaning significantly. In *Shanghai bowuguan,* the text refers to happiness (*xi* 喜) in both parts of the phrase, speaking of its extension in two different directions. In XZMC, on the other hand, the text makes use of a graph which the editorial board takes to be *li*-rites 禮, rather than *xi*-happiness. I believe the lexical meaning of *xi*-happiness makes more sense in the passage at hand. *Jingmenshi bowuguan,* 180, strips 22–23. Ma Chengyuan, *Shanghai bowuguan,* 238–39.

69. Taking *qi* 齊 as *ji* 櫅.

70. Modern paleographers are still uncertain about the meaning of some of the characters used in this passage. I insert use questions marks to indicate areas of uncertainty. *Jingmenshi bowuguan, GDCMZJ,* 180, strips 26–27.

71. *Jingmenshi bowuguan, GDCMZJ,* 179, strips 2–3.

72. Texts to the "Lai" and "Wu" can be found in the extant *Book of Odes.* They are numbers 295 and 285, respectively. The "Shao" is a music associated with the legendary Emperor Shun, while the "Xia" is associated with Emperor Yu the Great, the legendary founder of the historically dubious Xia dynasty.

73. The term "*jiu* 舊" is tentatively read by the commentator to XQL as "*jiu* 久." Ma Chengyuan, *Shanghai bowuguan,* 244.

74. *Jingmenshi bowuguan, GDCMZJ,* 180, strips 26–27.

75. One might then ask: is it the psyche that perceives of morality through music, or is morality inherent in the sounds themselves? While the passage depicts music as morally evocative just as it is emotionally evocative, this does not necessarily mean that music possess morality in itself. The most one can justifiably claim from statements in the text is that musical performances express something akin to moral behavior. And, as an expression of moral behavior, music helps serve as a legitimate tool for individual cultivation.

76. Intriguingly, this statement connecting the practice of "seeking one's heart-mind" and music is not present in the XQL version of the text. In this latter version, the author discusses the value of "seeking one's heart-mind" specifically in relationship to teachings and the presence of "artifice" (*wei* 偽) in such a pursuit. He does not assert the superior and unique role of music in such a context. Ma Chengyuan, *Shanghai bowuguan*, 265–66. For a more in-depth analysis of the concept of artifice in early China, see Michael Puett, *The Ambivalence of Creation: Debates Concerning Innovation and Artifice in Early China* (Stanford: Stanford University Press, 2001). For the possible interpretations of "seeking one's heart-mind" in early Confucianism, see my article, "Music and 'Seeking One's Heart-mind' in the 'Xing Zi Ming Chu,'" special publication on moral psychology in *Dao* 5.2 (June 2006), 247–55.

77. Compare with passages which refer to this practice in *Mencius* 1A7 and 6A11. Translations read: "When I reflected [upon myself] and sought it, I did not obtain my heart 反而求之，不得吾心," and "letting go of one's heart without knowing to seek after it 有放心而不知求." Indeed, each text appears to use the term in its own way. Many thanks to J. Ivanhoe for pointing out these other usages.

78. See *Analects* 2.7, 2.8, and 3.12, which, though they all demand that some sort of inner presence accompany an action, do not really locate this inner reality in any explicit psychology or discourse on heart-mind. For more on "seeking one's heart-mind" in this text, see Brindley, "Music and 'Seeking One's Heart-mind,'" 247–55.

79. Fan Ye 范曄, *Hou Han shu* 後漢書 (Beijing: Zhonghua shuju, 1995), 50B ("Cai Yong liezhuan"), 2004–2005. For more on sagely perception and the *qin* as an instrument, see the discussion in chapter five.

80. *Xunzi*, Chapter 20. Xiong Gongzhe, trans. and ed., 414–15. I believe Xunzi uses the rare construction, "*sheng yue*" (聲樂), to highlight the component aural parts of music, as opposed to the visual parts that also would have comprised such performances.

Also, I am thankful to an anonymous reader for pointing out the similar use of the term *ye* 也 in this statement and in the XZMC (*Jingmenshi bowuguan*, GDCMZJ, 179, strips 23–26; Ma Chengyuan, *Shanghai bowuguan*, 239–40), cited above. The placement of the adverb after *ye* seems unique, and more work will need to be done to determine whether this was a standard way of writing, or whether this indicates a textual connection or a linguistic affinity between the author of XZMC and Xunzi.

81. *Xunzi*, Translation adapted from Cook, "Unity and Diversity," 416–17.

82. *Xunzi*, Chapter 20. This same passage, with slight differences, can be found in the "Yue ji," from the *Book of Rites*, discussed below. Sun Xidan, *Liji jijie*, 19 ("Yue ji, Part 2,"), 1003. The term "*xiang*" (相) in this passage is confusing. I take it to refer to good and bad each in turn, and not to the mutual relationship between them. See Cook, "Unity and Diversity," for a similar way of getting around the problem with this term, in 422, note 82.

83. The belief in causality according to stimulus and response (*gan ying* 感應) comes to dominate Han Dynasty concepts of music and social order. Though Xunzi uses this technical terminology here, the mechanics that he suggests is very similar to that described in XZMC, which is less specific or technical in its terminology. It seems likely that such terminology was just becoming popular in Xunzi's time, or that

Xunzi was one of the foremost thinkers to coin the phrase. In many ways, the psychology of influence, stemming from discourses on music and outlined by Xunzi and his predecessor in the XZMC, provide us with a template for the notion of *gan ying* that becomes popular during the Han Dynasty.

For discussions on the concept of *gan ying* in Han times, see Sarah Queen, *From Chronicle to Canon: The Hermeneutics of Spring and Autumn, According to Tung Chun-shu* (Cambridge: Cambridge University Press, 1996); and the review of this work by Anne Cheng, "From Chronicle to Canon: The Hermeneutics of Spring and Autumn, According to Tung Chun-shu, by Sarah A. Queen," *Early China* 23–24 (1998): 353–66. See also Martin Kern, "Religious Anxiety and Political Interest in Western Han Omen Interpretation: The Case of the Han Wudi Period (141–87 B.C.)," *Studies in Chinese History* 10 (2000): 1–31; and Sivin, "State, Cosmos, and the Body," 5–37.

84. One might explain this account of the mechanics of sound and sentiment as follows: emotions are transmitted through *qi* (material-force, 氣), which, while possessing a certain quality of energy, does not yet take on any specific external form. The human body might give *qi* an outward form through one's demeanor, action, sounds, aura, etc. Agreeable or disagreeable forms give rise to order and chaos in one's environment. Agreeable energies are those that produce order, while disagreeable ones are those that produce chaos.

The use of the word, *xiang* (form 象), in this description is interesting and ambiguous. Xunzi, in his precise manner of thinking, wishes to distinguish between the quality and amount of *qi* on the one hand, and its embodied manifestation in some physical form in the human body on the other. *Xiang*-form seems to refer to this physical expression of *qi*. For an interesting interpretation of the notion of outward form in the attached commentaries to the *Yijing*, see Willard Peterson, "Making Connections: Commentary on the Attached Verbalizations," in *Harvard Journal of Asiatic Studies* 42.1 (1982): 67–116.

CHAPTER FIVE. SAGELY ATTUNEMENT TO THE COSMOS

1. Kenneth DeWoskin, *A Song for One or Two*, 14. Similarly, Scott Cook has extensively researched the various textual linkages between cosmos and music, on the one hand, and music and the mind, on the other. Cook was perhaps the first to compare the early Chinese belief in a connection between music and cosmos to the Pythagorean notion of the "Harmony of the Spheres." See Cook, "Unity and Diversity," 86–87, 102–111.

2. Because of the dearth of relevant sources for early China, it is not easy to conduct a sociological study that delineates the individual elites, friends, and groups of people who promoted music as a means of aspiring to become a *junzi*, or Confucian gentleman, or a sage of some variety. Not only do we not have information about most individuals and their life histories and goals, but we are also lacking specific details concerning the ways in which music might have tangibly altered their social status. For an interesting article on the uses of music in social advancement, see Penelope Gouk's account of eighteenth century Scottish elites' participation in musical

societies. Penelope Gouk, "Music's Pathological and Therapeutic Effects on the Body Politic: Doctor John Gregory's Views," in *Representing Emotions: New Connections in the Histories of Art, Music, and Medicine*, ed. Penelope Gouk and Helen Hills (Burlington, VT: Ashgate Publishing Company, 2005), 191–207.

3. By "lineages," I mean self-conscious affiliations between teacher and disciple that developed in an extremely messy manner during the Warring States. On this topic, see Kidder Smith, "Sima Tan and the Invention of Daoism, 'Legalism,' et cetera," *Journal of Asiatic Studies* 63.1 (2003): 129–56; and Mark Csikszentmihalyi and Michael Nylan, "Constructing Lineages and Inventing Traditions through Exemplary Figures in Early China," *T'oung Pao* 89 (2003): 55–99. See also Jens Østergård Petersen, "Which Books Did the First Emperor of Ch'in Burn? On the Meaning of *Pai Chia* in Early Chinese Sources," *Monumenta Serica* 43 (1995): 1–52.

4. Cook, "Unity and Diversity," 412–13, note 54. For textual information on the "Yue shu," see the note below.

5. See Yu Jiaxi 余嘉錫, "Liji *Yueji* yu Shiji *Yueshu* 禮記樂記與史記樂書," in *Yueji lunbian* 樂記論辯, ed. Zhao Feng 趙渢 (Beijing, Renmin yinyue, 1983), 56–67. For an informative account of the similarities between these texts and the likely dating and historical context of "Yue shu," see Martin Kern, "A Note on the Authenticity," 663–77.

6. Kern, "A Note on the Authenticity, 673.

7. *Ibid.*, 673–77.

8. One is tempted to draw a connection between this emergent view of music and the cosmos and Pythagoras' notion of the "music of the spheres," or heavenly bodies. As far as I know, there is no evidence of mutual influence between the ancient Greeks and Chinese on this topic. G. E. R. Lloyd shows how such concepts differ from each other in Lloyd, *Adversaries and Authorities*, 186–89.

9. Sun Xidan, *Liji jijie*, 19 ("Yue ji 樂記, Part 1,"), 988. Sima Qian, *Shi ji*, 24 ("Yue shu 樂書"), 1189.

10. Sun Xidan, *Liji jijie*, 982. Sima, *Shi ji*, 1184. Though it is not clear here whether the author is referring to cosmic or natural principle and pattern, it makes sense in light of the statement preceding this passage to interpret principle and pattern as having to do with the inherent workings of the heart-mind.

11. The commentator to "Yue shu," Zheng Xuan, takes the term *xian* as the "hundred things," or multiplicity of earthly objects which rely on Heaven and Earth. Note that in the *Li ji* the same passage uses the term *jian* rather than *xian*. I believe Zheng Xuan is correct in filling in what is unspoken in the text, as *xian* might more literally be translated as *jian*, "between."

12. Sun Xidan, *Liji jijie*, 994. Sima, *Shi ji*, 1196. This is perhaps a reference to Confucius' quote in *Analects*, 17.11, cited in chapter four.

13. Sun Xidan, *Liji jijie*, 992. Sima, *Shi ji*, 1193.

14. This difference suggests a slight shift in preliminary assumptions. For example, while Xunzi takes pains to argue the more general case that music comprises a major form of state control, these authors begin from the assumption that this is indeed true, but that states need some means of identifying what types of music are most effective in such an endeavor. In other words, the author of "Yue ji" assumes that

the state knows about the benefits of utilizing music in state control. He therefore focuses his attention on how leaders in a state might be assured of conducting the right types of music.

15. Sun Xidan, *Liji jijie*, 989. Sima, *Shi ji*, 1189–90.

16. Sun Xidan, *Liji jijie*, 984. Sima, *Shi ji*, 1186. The "Yue ji" refers to the term the "desires" (*yu* 欲) where the "Yue shu" uses the word "expression" (song 頌). I have chosen to translate the phrase using the term "song."

17. Sun Xidan, *Liji jijie*, 984. Sima, *Shi ji*, 1186.

18. *Ibid.*

19. *Ibid.*

20. See, for example, Sun Xidan, *Liji jijie*, 995. Sima, *Shi ji*, 1197.

21. Sun Xidan, *Liji jijie*, 982. Sima, *Shi ji*, 1184.

22. Arguably, these passages on human nature seem to draw very heavily on the XZMC more than they do on Xunzi's writings. Still, the claims and terms are slightly different from the ones in XZMC, which never promoted the preservation of "Heaven's pattern" (but rather, the shaping of Heaven's nature) as an ideal of self-cultivation.

23. *Lüshi chunqiu jiaoshi* 5.2 ("Da Yue 大樂"), 255–56.

24. *Lüshi chunqiu jiaoshi* 5.3 ("Chi Yue 侈樂"), 266.

25. *Ibid.*

26. *Ibid.* Translation slightly altered from Riegel and Knoblock, 137.

27. *Lüshi chunqiu jiaoshi* 5.3 ("Chi Yue 侈樂"), 266.

28. *Zhuangzi* 13 ("Tian Dao 天道"), 458. Translation adapted from *Basic Writings of Chuang Tzu*, trans. Burton Watson (New York: Columbia University Press, 1996), 133.

29. *Zhuangzi* 13 ("Tian Dao 天道"), 463.

30. The same can be said about musical theories presented in the *Guo yu* 國語, as demonstrated in Schaberg, *A Patterned Past*, 112–20. The perfection of music, as portrayed in that text, also helps fulfill cosmic processes and bring about the psychological contentment (joy) of the people. *Ibid.*, 115. Such desirable ends require that music be nourished and promoted by only the most expert people in society.

31. See Mark Csikszentmihalyi, *Material Virtue*, 170. See also DeWoskin, where he cites Ban Gu's commentary to the *Bohu tong* passage, *A Song for One or Two*, 32.

32. According to DeWoskin, this comment is attributed to the *Fengsu tongyi* but is not in the present version of it. DeWoskin, *A Song for One or Two*, 33, note 7. Csikszentmihalyi remarks that the *Yiwen leiju* 20.1a and *Taiping yulan* 104.1855 both associate this statement with the text. Csikszentmihalyi, *Material Virtue*, 170, note 20.

33. The notion of "soundless sound" has a long history in Chinese music and aesthetics, as it is often underscored in later literature and paintings. Most likely having been rejuvenated through the "Mysterious Learning" (*Xuan xue* 玄學) movement of the Wei-Jin period, it was associated with the private musicianship of renowned poet-recluses. In literature, it is reformulated in the phrase "the absence of sound surpasses sound" (無聲勝有聲); while in art, it is often depicted in the form of a scholar-recluse (usually, an old man who resembles Laozi or Tao Yuanming) sitting behind a stringless *qin*-zither. Tao Yuanming, for example, allegedly owned a simple *qin* that had no strings. See *Jin shu*, 2463. For a simple description of the ideal, see DeWoskin,

A Song for One or Two, 138–44. For the ideal of soundless sound in literature, see especially Bo Juyi's (772–846) "Pipa xing 琵琶行 (Ballad of the Pipa.)" In art, even Wen Zhengming, perhaps inspired by Tao Yuanming's idyllic model, paints a scholar-recluse with a stringless zither in front of him. See Helene Dunne Bodman, *Chinese Musical Iconography: A History of Musical Instruments Depicted in Chinese Art* (Taipei: Asian-Pacific Cultural Center, 1987). I am grateful to David Rolston and J. Park for pointing out these possibilities in separate, unpublished papers, which were presented at the conference "Musiking Late Ming China," Ann Arbor, MI, May 5, 2006.

34. For more detailed accounts of this discourse, see Hansen, *A Daoist Theory of Chinese Thought*, 233–64; and John Makeham, *Name and Actuality in Early Chinese Thought* (Albany: State University of New York, 1994).

35. *Jingmenshi bowuguan, Guodian Chumu zhujian*, 125–26.

36. Such an interpretation is admittedly speculative and seems to run counter to the usage of *ming* in the *Daodejing* with which the text is closely associated. Nonetheless, I would like to present it here as food for thought, not least because such an interpretation might possibly reveal a more complicated relationship between the notions presented in the *Daodejing* and those of the *Taiyi sheng shui*.

37. Here, I adopt Qiu Xigui's speculation that the missing last word is *dang* 當 (appropriate). *Jingmenshi bowuguan, Guodian Chumu zhujian* 郭店楚墓竹簡, 125. Also, the phrasing for what I translate as "automatically" is "without thought" (*bu si* 不 思).

38. On the surface, this statement appears to conflict with the Laozian message that the "Dao that can be named is not the constant Dao." While the passage in *Taiyi sheng shui* accords the name of the Dao with special cosmic power that is linked to its very own operations, that name is not the same as the term "Dao," and the author does not even divulge what such a name might be. This is because the name to which he refers cannot simply be a mere appellation. Thus, the underlying meaning of this passage actually accords with the meaning in the *Laozi* that "The Dao that *can be called something* is not the constant Dao."

39. Religions for which this is true are, to name a few: Hinduism and the sound "*om*"; Pure Land Buddhism and the sound made when taking refuge in Amitabha Buddha (*Nianfo* 念佛); or Tiantai Buddhism and the sound of the words invoking the *Lotus Sutra*.

40. For more on the relationship between the *Taiyi sheng shui* and *Laozi*, see *Jingmenshi bowuguan, Guodian Chumu zhujian*. See also Allen and Williams, eds., *The Guodian Laozi*, 168–69.

41. One might wish to reject this reading on grounds that the two texts seem to contradict each other on this point. However, if names or appellations that label really are to be understood as mere substitutes for a formless Dao, then it makes no difference which label one uses to describe it. According to my argument here, the *Taiyi sheng shui* uses the term "name," while the *Laozi* uses various terms and a roundabout manner to invoke the ontological phenomenon of the Dao.

42. For more on the spiritual ideal of *wuwei*, see Slingerland, *Effortless Action*.

43. Chen, *Laozi zhuyi ji pingjie*, 228.

44. *Ibid.*, 114.

45. See Guo, *Zhuangzi jishi*, 43–113.

46. *Ibid.*, 458. Translation adapted from Watson, *The Complete Works of Chuang Tzu*, 133. For more on Zhuangzi's ideal of the pinnacle of joy, see Xiao Yumin 蕭裕民. "Zhuangzi Lun 'Yue' Jian Lun Yu 'Xiao Yao' Zhi Guanxi" 莊子論樂兼論與逍遙之關係. *Hanxue yanjiu* 23.2 (2005): 1–33.

47. Indeed, one might go so far as to claim that this form of imperial religiosity was part and parcel of the rise of proto-scientific methods—relating to correlative systems of spontaneous resonance—during the Han period.

48. The view of "soundless sound" that came to prominence in the Chinese aesthetic tradition developed out of this latter context; i.e., out of the belief that the authentic sound of the cosmos—much like the ineffable Dao—necessarily transcended concrete, measurable form.

49. Gregg Howard, "Musico-Religious Implications of Some Buddhist Views of Sounds and Music in the Surangama Sutra." *Musica Asiatica* 6 (1991): pp. 96 and 100.

50. *Lüshi chunqiu jiaoshi* 13.2 ("Ying Tong 應同"), 678.

51. *Lüshi chunqiu jiaoshi* 5.2 ("Da Yue 大樂"), 256.

52. Wang, *Fengsu tongyi*, 293–94. Ying Shao is also known for making the explicit link between sagehood and aural ability. On this latter topic, see DeWoskin, *A Song for One or Two*, 31–37. See also Csikszentmihalyi, *Material Virtue*, 169–72.

53. For another mention of Confucius and Music Master Xiang, see *Analects*, 18.9.

54. *Analects* 17.20. The *se*-zither typically has twenty-five strings, while the *qin*-zither may have anywhere from seven to ten strings. See Furniss, *Music in Ancient China*, 63–75.

55. *Ibid.*, 83–98.

56. *Ibid.*, 85–87. Furniss shows evidence suggesting that high-ranking women from the Han period could at least own, if not play, the *qin* at times. There seem to be no restrictions on or cultural tendencies limiting women's access to the *se*, however, especially in non-Zhou musical traditions. See Furniss, 85–87, and Joseph Lam, "Female Musicians and Music in China," in *Women and Confucian Cultures in Premodern China, Korea, and Japan*, ed. Dorothy Ko et al. (Berkeley: University of California Press, 2003): 97–122.

57. Sima Qian, *Shiji* 47 ("Kongzi shijia 孔子世家"), 1925. Translation from Knoblock, *Xunzi*, 78.

CHAPTER SIX. MUSIC AND MEDICINE

1. Sun Xidan, *Lijijijie* 19 ("Yueji 樂記, Part 2)," 1005.

2. Edwin Atlee, *An inaugural essay on the influence of music in the cure of diseases* (Philadelphia: Bartholomew Graves, 1804), 13–4.

3. Yang, *Chunqiu Zuozhuan zhu*, 10.21.1, 1424. Other discussions between Music Master Zhou Jiu and King Jing of the Zhou (sixth century BCE) can be found in the *Guo yu* (Zhou 3.6 and 3.7). See also James Hart, "The Discussion of the *Wu-yi* Bells in the *Kuo-yü*," *Monumenta Serica* 29 (1970–71): 391–418. Schaberg, *A Patterned Past*, 112–17.

4. I translate the Five Modes here as modal structures, following the suggestion of Joseph Lam, who claims that "*jie*" in the previous sentences on music refers to "the structuring of pitches, modes, and music compositions" (Lam, private conversation, August 30, 2007).

5. Yang, *Chunqiu Zuozhuan zhu*, 10.1.12, 1222.

6. For more on the relationship between music and the winds and seasons, see Lewis, *Sanctioned Violence*, 218–21.

7. Joseph Lam points out that theories of state sacrificial music always describe music of three, six, or nine *bian* (changes), not five *jie* (nodes/modes). Lam, private conversation, 2007. The number five is perhaps significant in this early context because of the growing emergence of a cosmology based on five essential phases. Or, if one only considers the context of this passage in the *Zuo zhuan*, the number five seems significant because everything that is produced in relationship to the human senses revolves around this number.

8. For more on *gu*, more aptly referred to as a type of witchcraft than as poisoning, see H. Y. Feng and J. Shryock. "The Black Magic in China Known as *Ku*," *Journal of the American Oriental Society* 55 (1935): 1–30. See also Kawano Akimasa 川野明正, *Chūgoku no "tsukimono": Kanan chihōu no kodoku to jujutsuteki denshō* 中国の「憑き物」華南地方の蠱毒と呪術的伝承, (Tokyo: Fūkyōsha, 2005).

9. The rhyming part of this translation is taken verbatim from Scott Cook, who attempts to write the rhyming verse of the physician into his translation. Cook, "Unity and Diversity," 83–85.

10. According to Lam, the term *jiang* implies modal changes involving pitches beyond the central range. Joseph Lam, private conversation, 2007.

11. Yang, *Chunqiu Zuozhuan zhu*, 10.1.12, 1221–22.

12. As suggested in chapter two, such music most likely included not just the experimental music of the day, but also music that derived from cultures other than that of the refined Xia peoples.

13. *Guodian Chumu zhujian*, 180. Also in "*Xing Qing Lun*," in Ma Chengyuan, *Shanghai bowuguan*, 243–46.

14. *Ibid*, 180.

15. I am reading long 龍 in terms of *chong*, "to favor," since the former graph originally implied grace and favor as well.

16. I use "excessive" here to describe the more literal connotations of *yi* 溢, as in "overflowing," or "brimming over." *Ibid*. Liu Zhao speculates that the term for "finger" (*zhi* 指) could be the term for "desires" (*shi* 嗜), which changes this sentence so that it focuses not on body parts but on bodily functions, such as the cogitation and intents of the heart-mind as opposed to its desires. Liu Zhao 劉釗, *Guodian Chumujian xiaoshi* (Fuzhou City: Fujian Renmin Publishing, 2005), 98.

17. See Geaney, *On the Epistemology of the Senses*. See also Csikszentmihalyi, *Material Virtue*.

18. Geaney notes that Xunzi confers the power to differentiate sounds to the ear, not the heart-mind. See Geaney, *On the Epistemology of the Senses*, 91.

19. Xiong, *Xunzi*, 409. Translation slightly adapted from Cook, "Unity and Diversity," 415. For another very good translation of these passages, see Knoblock, *Xunzi*, vol. 3, 30–87.

20. Xiong, *Xunzi*, 410. Translated by Cook, "Unity and Diversity," 417.

21. *Ibid.*

22. *Ibid.*, 415.

23. *Ibid.*, 409–10. Translated by Cook, "Unity and Diversity," 415–16.

24. *Ibid.*, 413.

25. *Ibid.*

26. *Ibid.*, 410.

27. The extent to which Xunzi wishes to encompass the natural world in addition to the entire social world, or "all under Heaven," will be discussed later.

28. Xunzi is also careful to oppose "Ritual and Music 禮樂" with "perverse tones 邪音"—not deigning to call the latter "music" at all. Xiong, *Xunzi*, 413.

29. *Ibid.*, 414.

30. For example, in the memorial of Qin statesman, Li Si, Li mentions that the women of Zheng and Wei as filling the palace of the king, referring to the fact that the king enjoys the finest luxuries of the world. See Sima, *Shi ji*, 87 "Li Si Liezhuan 李斯列傳," 2543.

31. Xiong, *Xunzi*, 414.

32. *Ibid.*, 413.

33. *Ibid.*, 415.

34. *Ibid.*

35. It is difficult to translate the term *xiang*, into English, as the term "image" hardly conveys the cosmological implications of the Chinese term. The German term *Gestalt* seems better to invoke something encompassing in form and manifestation, and more than just an image.

36. *Guo yu* (Shanghai: Shanghai guji, 1995): Zhou 3.6, 128. For an analysis of this section of the text, see also Schaberg, *A Patterned Past*, 113–14.

37. A relevant dichotomy between "new" and "ancient" music emerged at some point in the late Warring States to give definition to the debate on proper vs. excessive types of music, as is attested by the phrase, "new sounds" (*xin sheng* 新聲), referring explicitly in early imperial texts to the lascivious sounds of morally depraved rulers.

38. Commentators inform us that this piece was a dance used to worship the spirit of Sang Lin, where the ancient King Tang of the Shang would pray for rain. In Sang Lin there was an altar where worship to the Spirit of this sacred spot took place. Yang, *Chunqiu Zuozhuan zhu*, 977.

39. Yang, *Chunqiu Zuozhuan zhu*, 9.10.2, 977.

40. *Zhanguo ce*, vols. 1 and 2 (Shanghai: Shanghai guji, 1998), "Wei Wen Hou yu Tian Zifang Yin Jiu er Cheng Yue 魏文侯與田子方飲酒而稱樂," 780.

41. The passage ends there, without revealing what Tian Zifang told the Marquis about his fate.

42. The former Ode appears to be lost. According to commentators, "Chariot Linchpins" seems to correspond to an Ode in the "Lesser Elegantiae," Mao 218. See Cheng and Jiang, *Shijing zhuxi*, 689–93.

43. Yang, *Chunqiu Zuozhuan zhu*, 10.25.1, 1455–56. Translation altered from James Legge, *The Chinese Classics: With a Translation, Critica and Exegetical Notes, Prolegomena, and Copious Indexes*, vol. 5 [*The Ch'un Ts'ew with The Tso Chuan*] (Hong Kong: Hong Kong University Press, 1960), 708.

44. *Analects*, 7.10.

45. Yang, *Chunqiu Zuozhuan zhu*, 10.25.3, 1457.

46. *Ibid.*, 3.27.5, 236.

47. See the commentary by Yang Bojun, where he entertains this possibility. *Ibid.*, 236.

48. *Ibid.*, 5.22.8, 398–99.

49. A brother of the late King Wen of Chu.

50. This dance, a sacrificial dance, is mentioned infrequently in Zhou literature, though it seems to occupy an important place in musical history and the ancestral cult. For a brief description and summary of Zhou references to this dance, see Waley, *The Book of Songs*, 338–40.

51. Lady Wen probably refers here to the fact that the Wan was primarily a sacrificial dance performed for deceased ancestors.

52. Yang, *Chunqiu Zuozhuan zhu*, 3.28.3, 241. Translation adapted from Legge, *The Chinese Classics*, vol. 5, 115.

53. See Yang Bojun's comments in *Chunqiu Zuozhuan zhu*, 46 and 241. Arthur Waley contends that the dance was originally not a military dance, Waley, *The Book of Songs*, 339.

54. Furniss, *Music in Ancient China*, 155.

55. *Ibid.*

56. Yang, *Chunqiu Zuozhuan zhu*, 10.25.3, 1459.

57. A common interpretation of the term, *xie* 協, is to aid or assist, not just harmonize or be united with. In this sense, humans help complete or fulfill the basic natures and patterns of the cosmos—a theme that really becomes prevalent in the late Warring States and early imperial periods (especially during the Han).

58. Cheng and Jiang, *Shijing zhuxi* "Guo Feng, 1.15," Mao 160, 434.

59. Yang, *Chunqiu Zuozhuan zhu*, 10.20.8, 1420. Translation adapted from Legge, *The Chinese Classics*, vol. 5, 684.

60. Similar notions of harmony are presented in other parts of the text, such as 10.20.8, mentioned in the prologue and introduction.

61. Xiaoneng Yang, *Golden Age of Chinese Archaeology: Celebrated Discoveries from the People's Republic of China* (New Haven: Yale University Press, 1999): 426–27.

62. *Ibid.*

63. The placement of such figures in tombs, as well as the fact that they are made of jade (which had apotropaic uses) might also be significant and worth considering. Other Western Han jade maidens with long sleeves have been found in tombs not located in the South, such as that of Liu Sheng in modern-day Hebei Province. Yang, *Golden Age of Chinese Archaeology*, 427.

64. *Han shu*, "Li yue zhi 禮樂志 (Treatise on Ritual and Music)," 1042.

65. These references to body parts describe in general a state of anxiety and exhaustion that expresses itself through an imbalance of heat and moisture in these areas.

66. Liu, *Huainan honglie jijie*, 307.

67. *Ibid.*, 306–307.

68. Whether the music itself is inappropriate or the ruler's use of music is inappropriate is not entirely clear from the passage.

69. Commentators take 陶唐 to be a mistake for the Yinkang 陰康 clan. See Chen, *Lüshi chunqiu jiaoshi*, "Gu Yue," 290.

70. *Ibid.*, 284. Slightly altered from Riegel and Knoblock, 147.

71. Shirakawa, Shizuka 白川靜. *Kanji no sekai*, vol. 2 漢字の世界 (Tokyo: Heibonsha, 1976), 232–33. For an evaluation of this claim, see Donald Harper, *Early Chinese Medical Literature: The Mawangdui Medical Manuscripts* (New York: Keegan Paul International, 1998), 163–64.

CONCLUSION

1. DeWoskin, *A Song for One or Two*, p. 14.

2. The locus classicus for such a formulation is in the *Chunqiu fanlu* 春秋繁露, Chapter 10.1 ("Shen cha ming hao 深察名號,") attributed to Dong Zhongshu: "The boundaries of Heaven and humans come together into one 天人之際，合而為一."

3. Nathan Sivin, *Granting the Seasons: The Chinese Astronomical Reform of 1280, With a Study of Its Many Dimensions and a Translation of its Records* (New York: Springer, 2008).

Works Cited

Allan, Sarah, and Crispin Williams, eds. *The Guodian Laozi: Proceedings of the International Conference, Dartmouth College, May 1998*. Berkeley: The Institute of East Asian Studies and Society for the Study of Early China, 2000.

Armstrong, James. *The Art of Preserving Health: A Poem*. Dublin: L. Flin, 1767.

Atlee, Edwin. *An Inaugural Essay on the Influence of Music in the Cure of Diseases*. Philadelphia: Bartholomew Graves, 1804.

Bagley, Robert. "Percussion." In *Music in the Age of Confucius*, ed. by Jenny F. So, pp. 34–63. Washington, D. C.: Freer Gallery of Art and Arthur M. Sackler Gallery, 2000.

Ban Gu. *Han shu*. 12 vols. Vol. 4. Beijing: Zhonghua shuju, 1995.

Baxter, William. *Handbook of Old Chinese Phonology*. Berlin: Mouton de Gruyter, 1992.

Beck, B. J. Mansvelt. *The Treatises of Later Han: Their Author, Sources, Contents and Place in Chinese Historiography*. Leiden: E. J. Brill, 1990.

Bodde, Derk. "The Chinese Cosmic Magic Known as Watching for the Ethers." In *Essays on Chinese Civilization* Princeton: Princeton University Press, 1981.

Bodman, Helene Dunn. *Chinese Musical Iconography: A History of Musical Instruments Depicted in Chinese Art*. Taipei: Asia-Pacific Cultural Center, 1987.

Brindley, Erica. "Music and Cosmos in the Development of 'Psychology' in Early China," *T'oung Pao* 92, nos. 1–3 (2006): 1–49.

———. "Music and 'Seeking One's Heart-mind' in the 'Xing Zi Ming Chu,'" special publication on moral psychology in *Dao* 5.2 (June 2006), 247–255.

———. "Barbarians or Not? Ethnicity and Changing Conceptions of the Ancient Yue (Viet) Peoples (~400–50 B. C.)," *Asia Major* 16.1 (2003), 1–32.

Brooks, Bruce and Taeko. *The Original Analects: Sayings of Confucius and His Successors*. New York: Columbia University Press, 1998.

Bulletin of the Museum of Far Eastern Antiquities. "Special Issue: Reconsidering the Correlative Cosmology of Early China." Vol. 72. Stockholm: Fälth and Hässler, 2000.

Cai Zhongde 蔡仲德. *Zhongguo yinyue meixue* 中國音樂美學史. Beijing: Renmin yinyue chubanshe, 1995.

Chen Guying 陳鼓應, ed. *Laozi zhuyi ji pingjie* 老子註譯評介. Beijing: Zhonghua shuju, 1984.

Chen Qiyou 陳奇猷, ed. *Lüshi chunqiu jiaoshi* 呂氏春秋校釋. Shanghai: Xue lin Chu ban, 1995.

Chen Wei 陳偉. *Guodian zhushu bieshi* 郭店竹書別釋. Wuhan: Hubei jiaoyu, 2003.

Cheng, Anne."From Chronicle to Canon: The Hermeneutics of Spring and Autumn, According to Tung Chun-shu, by Sarah A. Queen." *Early China* 23–24 (1998): 353–66.

Cheng Junying 程俊英 and Jiang Xianyuan 蔣見元. *Shijing zhuxi* 詩經注析 Beijing: Zhonghua shuju, 1991.

Chunqiu Zuozhuan zhu 春秋左传校注. Vols. 1–4. See Yang Bojun 楊伯峻.

Confucius. *Confucius: Analects, with Selections from Traditional Commentaries.* Translated by Edward Slingerland. Indianapolis: Hackett Publishing Company, Inc., 2003.

Confucius. *Confucius: The Analects.* Translated by D. C. Lau. London: Penguin, 1979.

Confucius. *Lunyu yizhu* 論語譯注. See Yang Bojun 楊伯峻.

Cook, Scott. "Unity and Diversity in the Musical Thought of Warring States China." Ph.D. diss., University of Michigan, 1995.

———. "Yue ji—Record of Music: Introduction, Translation, Notes, and Commentary." *Asian Music*, 26.2 (Spring/Summer, 1995): 1–96.

———. "The *Lüshi Chunqiu* and the Resolution of Philosophical Dissonance," *Harvard Journal of Asiatic Studies* 62.2 (2002): 307–345.

———. 以新出楚簡重遊中國古代的詩歌音樂美學 *Zhengda zhongwen xuebao* 政大中文學報 1 (June 2004): 229–48.

Crane, Tim and Sarah Patterson, eds. *History of the Mind-Body Problem.* London: Routledge, 2000.

Csikszentmihalyi, Mark. *Material Virtue: Ethics and the Body in Early China.* Leiden: Brill, 2004.

———. "Confucius and the *Analects* in the Han." In Van Norden, 144–53. Oxford: Oxford University Press, 2002.

Csikszentmihalyi, Mark and Michael Nylan, "Constructing Lineages and Inventing Traditions through Exemplary Figures in Early China." *T'oung Pao* 89.1–3 (2003): 55–99.

Cullen, Christopher. "Numbers, Numeracy, and the Cosmos." In *China's Early Empires.* ed. by Michael Nylan and Michael Loewe, pp. 323–38. Cambridge: Cambridge University Press, 2010.

Damasio, Antonio. *Descartes' Error: Emotion, Reason, and the Human Brain.* New York: Quill, 2000.

Desmet, Karen. "The Growth of Compounds in the Core Chapters of the *Mozi*." *Oriens Extremus* 45 (2005/6): 99–118.

DeWoskin, *A Song for One or Two: Music and the Concept of Art in Early China.* Ann Arbor: Center for Chinese Studies, the University of Michigan, 1982.

———. "Music and Voices from the Han tombs: Music, Dance and Entertainments in the Han." In *Stories from China's Past: Han Dynasty Pictorial Tomb Reliefs and Archaeological Objects from Sichuan Province, People's Republic of China,* ed. by Lucy Lim et al., 64–71. San Francisco: Chinese Cultural Foundation, 1987.

———. "Early Chinese Music and Origins of Aesthetic Terminology." In *Theories of the Arts in China*, ed. by Susan Bush and Christian Murck. Princeton: Princeton University Press, 1983.

Dull, Jack. "A Historical Introduction to the Apocryphal (*ch'an-wei*) Texts of the Han Dynasty." Ph.D. dissertation, University of Washington, 1966.

Eno, Robert. *The Confucian Creation of Heaven: Philosophy and the Defense of Ritual Mastery*. Albany: State University of New York Press, 1990.

Falkenhausen, Lothar von. *Suspended Music: Chime-Bells in the Culture of Bronze Age China*. Berkeley: University of California Press, 1993.

———. "On the Early Development of Chinese Musical Theory: The Rise of Pitch-Standards." *Journal of the American Oriental Society* 112.3 (1992): 433–39.

———. "Chu Ritual Music." In *New Perspectives on Chu Culture During the Eastern Zhou Period*, ed. by Thomas Lawton, pp. 47–106. Washington D. C.: Arthur M. Sackler Gallery, Smithsonian Institution; Princeton: Princeton University Press, 1991.

Fan Ye 范曄. *Hou Hanshu* 後漢書. Beijing: Zhonghua shuju, 1995.

Fauconnier, Gills, and Mark Turner, *The Way We Think: Conceptual Blending and the Mind's Hidden Complexities*. New York: Basic Books, 2002.

Feng Guangsheng, "Winds," in *Music in the Age of Confucius*, ed. by Jenny F. So Washington D. C.: Freer Gallery of Art and Arthur M. Sackler Gallery, 2000.

Feng, H. Y., and J. Shryock. "The Black Magic in China Known as *Ku*," *Journal of the American Oriental Society* 55 (1935): 1–30.

Furniss, Ingrid. *Music in Ancient China: An Archaeological and Art Historical Study of Strings, Winds, and Drums during the Eastern Zhou and Han Periods* (770 BCE–220 CE). Amherst, NY: Cambria Press, 2008.

Furth, Charlotte. *A Flourishing Yin: Gender in China's Medical History, 960–1665*. Berkeley: University of California Press, 1999.

Geaney, Jane. *On the Epistemology of the Senses in Early Chinese Thought*. Honolulu: University of Hawaii Press, 2002.

Goodman, Howard L. *Xun Xu and the Politics of Precision in Third-Century AD China*. Leiden: Brill, 2010.

———. "A History of Court Lyrics in China during Wei-Chin Times." *Asia Major* 19.1 (2006): 57–109.

Graham, A. C. *Disputers of the Tao: Philosophical Argument in Ancient China* La Salle, IL: Open Court, 1989.

———. *Later Mohist Logic, Ethics and Science*. Hong Kong: The Chinese University Press, 2003.

Goldin, Paul. "Xunzi in the Light of the Guodian Manuscripts." *Early China* 25 (2000): 113–146.

Gouk, Penelope. "Music's Pathological and Therapeutic Effects on the Body Politic: Doctor John Gregory's Views." In *Representing Emotions: New Connections in the Histories of Art, Music and Medicine*, ed. by Penelope Gouk and Helen Hills. Burlington, VT: Ashgate Publishing Company, 2005.

Graham, A. C. *Divisions in Early Mohism Reflected in the Core Chapters of Mo-tzu* Singapore: Institute of East Asian Philosophies, 1985.

———. "The Background of the Mencian Theory of Human Nature," in *Tsing Hua Journal of Chinese Studies*, vol. 6 (1957): pp. 215–271.

———. *Disputers of the Tao: Philosophical Argument in Ancient China* La Salle, IL: Open Court, 1989.

Gu Jiegang 顧頡剛. *Wude zhongshi shuoxia de zhengzhi he lishi* 五德終始說下的政治和歷史. Hong Kong: Longmen Publishing, 1970.

Guo Qingfan 郭慶藩. *Zhuangzi jishi* 莊子集釋. Taipei: Wanjuan lou, 1993.

Guo yu 國語. Shanghai: Shanghai Guji Publishing, 1995.

Guthrie, Kenneth S., comp. and trans. *The Pythagorean Sourcebook and Library: An Anthology of Ancient Writings Which Relate to Pythagoras and Pythagorean Philosophy*. Grand Rapids, MI: Phanes Press, 1987.

Hansen, Chad. *A Daoist Theory of Chinese Thought: A Philosophical Interpretation* Oxford: Oxford University Press, 1992.

Hart, James. "The Discussion of the *Wu-Yi* Bells in the *Kuo-Yü*." *Monumenta Serica* 29 (1970/71): 391–418.

Harper, Donald. *Early Chinese Medical Literature: The Mawangdui Medical Manuscripts*. New York: Keegan Paul International, 1998.

———. "Warring States, Qin, and Han Manuscripts related to Natural Philosophy and the Occult." In *New Sources of Early Chinese History: An Introduction to the Reading of Inscriptions and Manuscripts*, ed. by Edward Shaughnessy, pp. 223–252. erkeley: The Society for the Study of Early China, 1997.

———. "The Conception of Illness in Early Chinese Medicine, as Documented in Newly Discovered 3rd and 2nd Century B. C. Manuscripts (Part I)." In *Sudhoffs Archiv* 74.2 (1990): 1–31.

Hendricks, Robert, trans. *Philosophy and Argumentation in Third-Century China: The Essays of Hs'i K'ang*. Princeton: Princeton University Press, 1983.

Horden, Peregrine. "Commentary on Part I, with a Note on China." In *Music as Medicine Medicine: The History of Music Therapy since Antiquity*, ed. by Peregrine Horden, 43–50. Burlington, VT: Ashgate, 2000.

Howard, Gregg. "Musico-Religious Implications of Some Buddhist Views of Sounds and Music in the Surangama Sutra." *Musica Asiatica* 6 (1991): 95–101.

Hsu, Elizabeth, ed., *Innovation in Chinese Medicine*. Cambridge: Cambridge University Press, 2001.

Huang, Yi-long, and Chang Chih-ch'eng. "The Evolution and Decline of the Ancient Chinese Practice of Watching for the Ethers." *Chinese Science* 13 (1996): 82–106.

Huainan honglie jijie 淮南鴻烈集解. See Liu Wendian 劉文典, ed.

James, Jamie. *The Music of the Spheres: Music, Science, and the Natural Order of the Universe*. New York: Copernicus Books, 1995.

Jiang, Yimin. "*Große Musik ist tonlos*": *Eine historische Darstellung der frühen philosophisch-daoistischen Musikästhetik*. Europäische Hochschulschriften XXXVI.135. Frankfurt: Peter Lang, 1995.

Jin shu 晉書. Beijing: Zhonghua shuju, 1993.

Jingmenshi bowuguan 荊門市博物館. *Guodian Chumu zhujian* 郭店楚幕竹簡. Jingmen: Wen Wu, 1998.

Johnson, Mark. *The Body in the Mind: The Bodily Basis of Meaning, Imagination, and Reason*. Chicago: University of Chicago Press, 1987.

Karlgren, Bernhard. *Grammata Serica Recensa*. Stockholm: Museum of Far Eastern Antiquities, 1957.

Kawano Akimasa 川野明正, *Chūgoku no "tsukimono": Kanan chihōu no kodoku to jujutsuteki denshō* 中国の「憑き物」華南地方の蠱毒と呪術的伝承. Tokyo: Fūkyōsha, 2005.

Kern, Martin. "Tropes of Music and Poetry: From Wudi (r. 141–87 BCE) to ca 100 CE." In *China's Early Empires*, ed. by Michael Nylan and Michael Loewe, 480–91. Cambridge: Cambridge University Press, 2010.

———. "The Odes in Excavated Manuscripts." In *Text and Ritual in Early China* ed. by Martin Kern. Seattle: University of Washington Press, 2000.

———. "*Shi Jing* Songs as Performance Texts: A Case Study of 'Chu Ci' (Thorny Caltrop)." *Early China* 25 (2000): 49–111.

———. "Religious Anxiety and Political Interest in Western Han Omen Interpretation: The Case of the Han Wudi Period (141–87 B.C.)." *Studies in Chinese History* 10 (2000): 1–31.

———. "A Note on the Authenticity and Ideology of *Shih-chi* 24, 'Yue shu,'" in *Journal of the American Oriental Society* 119.4 (1999).

———. *Die Hymnen Der Chinesischen Staatsopfer: Literatur Und Ritual in Der Politischen Repraesentation Von Der Han-Zeit Bis Zu Den Sechs Dynastien* Stuttgart: Steiner, 1997.

Kinney, Anne Behnke. *Representations of Childhood and Youth in Early China*. Stanford: Stanford University Press, 2004.

Knoblock, John. *Xunzi: A Translation and Study of the Complete Works*. 3 vols. Stanford: Stanford University Press, 1988–1994.

Lakoff, George and Mark Johnson, *Philosophy in the Flesh: The Embodied Mind and its Challenge to Western Thought*. New York: Basic Books, 1999.

Lam, Joseph. *State Sacrifices and Music in Ming China: Orthodoxy, Creativity, and Expressiveness*. Albany: State University of New York Press, 1998.

———. "Female Musicians and Music in China." In *Women and Confucian Cultures in Premodern China, Korea, and Japan*, ed. by Dorothy Ko et al., pp. 97–122. Berkeley: University of California Press, 2003.

Lai, T. C., and Robert Mok. *Jade Flute: The Story of Chinese Music*. New York: Schocken Books, 1981.

Laozi zhuyi ji pingjie 老子註譯評介, see Chen Guying 陳鼓應, ed.

Legge, James. *The Chinese Classics: With a Translation, Critica and Exegetical Notes, Prolegomena, and Copious Indexes, vol. 5 [The Ch'un Ts'ew with The Tso Chuan]* (Hong Kong: Hong Kong University Press, 1960).

Lewis, Mark. *Sanctioned Violence in Early China*. Albany: State University of New York Press, 1990.

Li ji jijie 禮記集解. Vols. 1–3. See Sun Xidan 孫希旦, ed.

Li, Ling 李零. *Guodian Chujian jiaodu ji* 郭店楚簡校讀記. Beijing: Beijing Daxue, 2002.

Li Ling and Keith McMahon. "The Contents and Terminology of the Mawangdui Texts on the Arts of the Bedchamber." *Early China* 17 (1992).

Li, Zehou 李澤厚, and Liu Gangji 劉綱紀. *Zhongguo meixueshi* 中國美學史. Zhonghe, Taiwan: Gu Feng Publishing Co., 1986.

Li, Wai-yee. *The Readability of the Past in Early Chinese Historiography*. Cambridge, Mass.: Harvard University Asia Center, 2007.

Liddell, H. G., and R. Scott, *An Intermediate Greek-English Lexicon*. Oxford: Oxford University Press, 1997.

Liu Wendian 劉文典, ed. *Huainan honglie jijie* 淮南鴻烈集解. Beijing: Zhonghua shuju, 1989).

Liu Zhao 劉釗. *Guodian Chujian jiaoshi* 郭店楚簡校釋. Fuzhou City: Fujian Renmin Publishing, 2005.

Lloyd, G. E. R. *Adversaries and Authorities: Investigations into Ancient Greek and Chinese Science*. Cambridge: Cambridge University Press, 1996.

————. *The Ambitions of Curiosity: Understanding the World in Ancient Greece and China* Cambridge: Cambridge University Press, 2002.

Loewe, Michael. "The Office of Music, c. 114 to 7 B.C." *Bulletin of the School of Oriental and African Studies* 36 (1973): 340–51.

Loewe, Michael, ed. *Early Chinese Texts: A Bibliographical Guide*. Berkeley: University of California Press, 1993.

Loewe, Michael, and Edward Shaughnessy, eds. *The Cambridge History of Ancient China*. Cambridge: Cambridge University Press, 1999.

Lü, Buwei. *The Annals of Lü Buwei (Lü Shi Chun Qiu): A Complete Translation and Study*. Translated by John Knoblock and Jeffrey Riegel. Stanford: Stanford University Press, 2000.

Lüshi Chunqiu jiaoshi 呂氏春秋校釋. Vols. 1 & 2. See Chen Qiyou 陳奇猷, ed.

Lü Wang 呂望. *Liu tao* 六韜 [Six Secret Teachings]. Beijing: Zhonghua shuju, 1991.

Lynn, Richard, trans. *The Classic of the Way and Virtue: A New Translation of the Tao-te ching of Laozi as Interpreted by Wang Bi*. New York: Columbia University Press, 1999.

Luo Zhufeng 羅竹風, ed. *Hanyu da ci dian* 漢語大詞典, vol. 1. Shanghai: Hanyu da ci dian chu ban, 1994.

Ma Chengyuan 馬承源, ed. *Shanghai bowuguan cang Zhanguo Chu zhushu* 上海博物館藏 戰國楚竹書, vol. 1. Shanghai: Shanghai Guji Publishing, 2001.

————. *Shanghai bowuguan cang Zhanguo Chu zhu shu*, vol. 7. Shanghai: Shanghai Guji Publishing, 2009).

Magoon, E. L., Rev. "The Religious Uses of Music." *Southern Literary Messenger* 9.4 (April, 1843): 193–197.

Major, John. *Heaven and Earth in Early Han Thought: Chapters Three, Four and Five of the Huainanzi*. Albany: State University of New York Press, 1993.

Major, John. "Notes on the Nomenclature of the Winds and Directions in the Early Han," *T'oung Pao* 65.1–3 (1979): pp. 66–80.

Makeham, John. *Name and Actuality in Early Chinese Thought* Albany: State University of New York, 1994.

Mansvelt Beck, B. J. *The Treatises of Later Han: Their Author, Sources, Contents and Place in Chinese Historiography*. Leiden: E. J. Brill, 1990.

Mencius. *Mengzi yizhu* 孟子譯注. Edited and translated by Yang Bojun 楊伯峻. Hong Kong: Zhonghua shuju, 1998.

Mizuhara Iko. "Chugoku kodai ongaku shiso kenkyu 中国古代音樂思想研究." *Toyo ongaku kenkyu* 10 (June 1965): pp. 207–31.

Mizukami Shizuo 水上靜夫. "'Gaku' ji ko '樂' 字考," *Nihon Chugoku gakkai ho* 18 (1996).

Mozi. *Mozi jiangu* 墨子閒詁. See Sun Yirang 孫詒讓, ed.

Munro, Donald. "The origin of the Concept of De." In *The Concept of Man in Early China*, 185–97. Stanford: Stanford University Press, 1969.

Needham, Joseph, Wang Ling, and Kenneth Robinson. *Science and Civilisation in China*. Edited by Joseph Needham. Vol. 4.1. Cambridge: Cambridge University Press, 1962.

Nienhauser, William H., Jr. and others, eds. *The Grand Scribe's Records: Volume Vii, the Memoirs of Pre-Han China*. Vol. VII. Bloomington: Indiana University Press, 1994.

Nylan, Michael. *The Five "Confucian" Classics*. New Haven: Yale University Press, 2001.

———. "Yin-yang, Five Phases, and *qi*." In *China's Early Empires: A Re-appraisal*, ed. by Michael Nylan and Michael Loewe, 398–414. Cambridge: Cambridge University Press, 2010.

Padel, Ruth. *In and Out of the Mind: Greek Images of the Tragic Self*. Princeton: Princeton University Press, 1992.

Peerenboom, R. P. *Law and Morality in Ancient China: The Silk Manuscripts of Huang-Lao*. Albany: State University of New York Press, 1993.

Peterson, Jens Østergård. "Which Books Did the First Emperor of Ch'in Burn? On the Meaning of *Pai Chia* in Early Chinese Sources." *Monumenta Serica* 43 (1995): pp. 1–52.

Peterson, Willard. "Making Connections: Commentary on the Attached Verbalizations." *Harvard Journal of Asiatic Studies*, vol. 42, no.1 (1982): 67–116.

Pian, Rulan Chao. *Song Dynasty Musical Sources and Their Interpretation*. Hong Kong: The Chinese University Press, 2003.

Picken, Laurence E. R. "The Shapes of the *Shi Jing* Song-texts and Their Musical Implications." *Musica Asiatica* I (1977): 85–109.

Pines, Yuri. "Intellectual Change in the Chunqiu Period: The Reliability of the Speeches in the *Zuo zhuan* as Sources of Chunqiu Intellectual History." *Early China* 22 (1997): 77–132.

Pinker, Steven. *The Blank Slate: The Modern Denial of Human Nature*. New York: Viking, 2002.

Plaks, Andrew. *Ta Hsüeh and Chung Yung (The Highest Order of Cultivation and On the Practice of the Mean)*. New York: Penguin Books, 2003.

Poo, Mu-chou. *In Search of Personal Welfare: A View of Ancient Chinese Religion*. Albany: State University of New York Press, 1998.

Puett, Michael. "Violent Misreadings: The Hermeneutics of Cosmology in the *Huainanzi*." In "Special Issue: Reconsidering the Correlative Cosmology of Early China," pp. 29–47. *Bulletin of the Museum of the Far Eastern Antiquities* 72 (2000).

———. "The Ethics of Responding Properly: The Notion of *Qing* in Early Chinese Thought." In *Emotions in Chinese Culture*, ed. by Halvor Eifring, pp. 37–68. Leiden: Brill, 2004.

———. *To Become a God: Cosmology, Sacrifice, and Self-divinization in Early China*. Cambridge, Mass.: Harvard University Asia Center for the Harvard-Yenching Institute, 2002.

———. *The Ambivalence of Creation: Debates Concerning Innovation and Artifice in Early China*. Stanford: Stanford University Press, 2001.

Qiu Qiongsun 丘瓊蓀. "*Lidai yuezhi lüzhi jiaoshi* 歷代樂志律志校釋. Beijing: Zhonghua shuju, 1964.

Queen, Sarah. *From Chronicle to Canon: The Hermeneutics of Spring and Autumn, According to Tung Chun-shu*. Cambridge: Cambridge University Press, 1996.

———. "Dong Zhongshu he Huang Lao si xiang," *Dao jia wen hua yan jiu* 3 (1993): 256–59.

Rickett, Allyn. *Guanzi: Political, Economic, and Philosophical Essays from Early China, a Study and Translation*, Revised ed., vol. 1. Boston: Cheng and Tsui Company, 2001.

Roth, Hal. "Some Methodological Issues in the Study of the Guodian *Laozi* Parallels." In *The Guodian Laozi: Proceedings of the International Conference, Dartmouth College, May 1998*, ed. by Sarah Allan and Crispin Williams. Berkeley: Society for the Study of Early China and the Institute of East Asian Studies, University of California, 2000.

———. *Original Tao: Inward Training and the Foundations of Taoist Mysticism*. New York: Columbia University Press, 1999.

Sawyer, Ralph (with Mei-chün Sawyer), trans. *The Seven Military Classics of Ancient China*. Boulder: Westview Press, 1993.

Schaberg, David. *A Patterned Past: Form and Thought in Early Chinese Historiography*. Cambridge, Mass.: Harvard University Asia Center, 2001.

———. "Appendix: Orality and the Origins of the *Zuo Zhuan* and *Guoyu*." In *A Patterned Past: Form and Thought in Early Chinese Historiography*, 315–24. Cambridge, Mass.: Harvard University Asia Center, 2001.

———. "Social Pleasures in Early Chinese Historiography and Philosophy." In *The Limits of Historiography*, ed. by Christina Kraus. Leiden: Brill, 1999.

———. "Song and the Historical Imagination in Early China," *Harvard Journal of Asiatic Studies* 59.2 (1999): 305–61.

Schwartz, Benjamin. *The World of Thought in Ancient China*. Cambridge, Mass.: Harvard University Press, 1985.

*Shanghai bowuguan cang Zhanguo Chu zhushu*上海博物館藏 戰國楚竹書. See Ma Chengyuan 馬承源, ed.

Shaughnessy, Edward. "From Liturgy to Literature: The Ritual Contexts of the Earliest Poems in the *Book of Poetry*." *Hanxue yanjiu* 漢學研究 13.1 (1994): 133–64.

Shi jing 詩經. See Cheng Junying and Jiang Xianyuan, *Shijing zhuxi*.

Shirakawa, Shizuka 白川靜. *Kanji no sekai*, vol. 2 漢字の世界 (Tokyo: Heibonsha, 1976.

Sima Qian 司馬遷. *Shi ji* 史記 10 vols. Beijing: Zhonghua shuju, 1992.

Sivin, Nathan. *Granting the Seasons: The Chinese Astronomical Reform of 1280, with a Study of Its Many Dimensions and a Translation of its Records*. New York: Springer, 2008.

———. *Science in Ancient China: Researches and Reflections*. Brookfield, Vermont: Variorum, Ashgate Publishing, 1995.

———. "State, Cosmos, and the Body in the Last Three Centuries B. C." *Harvard Journal of Asiatic Studies* 55.1 (1995): 5–37.

Sivin, Nathan, and Geoffrey Lloyd. *The Way and the Word: Science and Medicine in Early China and Greece*. New Haven: Yale University Press, 2002.

Slingerland, Edward. *Effortless Action: Wu-Wei as Conceptual Metaphor and Spiritual Ideal in Early China* Oxford: Oxford University Press, 2003.

Slingerland, Edward, trans. *Confucius: Analects*. Indianapolis: Hackett Publishing Company, 2003.

Smith, Kidder. "Sima Tan and the Invention of Daoism, 'Legalism,' Et Cetera." *Journal of Asiatic Studies* 63.1 (2003): 129–56.

"Special Issue: Reconsidering the Correlative Cosmology of Early China." *Bulletin of the Museum of Far Eastern Antiquities* 72 (2000).

So, Jenny F. "Music in Late Bronze Age China." In Jenny F. So, ed. *Music in the Age of Confucius*. Washington, D. C.: Freer Gallery of Art and Arthur M. Sackler Gallery, 2000.

Sun Xidan 孫希旦, ed. *Liji jijie* 禮記集解. Beijing: Zhonghua shuju, 1998.

Sun Yirang 孫詒讓, ed. *Mozi jiangu* 墨子閒詁. Taipei: Huaqu shuju, 1987.

Sun Zuoyun 孫作雲. *Shijing yu Zhoudai shehui yanjiu* 詩經與周代社會研究. Beijing: Zhonghua Shuju, 1966.

Tian Qing 田青. *Zhongguo gudai yinyue shihua* 中國古代音樂史話. Shanghai: Shanghai wen yi chu ban she, 1984.

Unschuld, Paul. *Medicine in China: A History of Ideas*. Berkeley: University of California Press, 1985.

Van Norden, Bryan, ed. *Confucius and the Analects: New Essays*. Oxford: Oxford University Press, 2002.

Van Zoeren, Steven. *Poetry and Personality: Reading, Exegesis, and Hermeneutics in Traditional China*. Stanford: Stanford University Press, 1991.

Vankeerberghen, Griet. *The Huainanzi and Liu An's Claim to Moral Authority*. Albany: State University of New York Press, 2001.

Waley, Arthur, trans. *The Book of Songs*. New York: Grove Press, 1960.

Wang, Aihe. *Cosmology and Political Culture in Early China* Cambridge: Cambridge University Press, 2000.

Wang Liqi 王利器, ed. *Fengsu tongyi jiaozhu* 風俗通義校注. Beijing: Zhonghua shuju, 1981.

Wang Xiaoyu 王孝魚, ed. *Zhuangzi jishi* 莊子集釋. Taipei: Wanjuan lou, 1993.

Wang Zichu 王子初. *Zhongguo yinyue kaoguxue* 中國音樂考古學. Fuzhou: Fujian jiaoyu chubanshe, 2003.

Watson, Burton, trans. *The Complete Works of Chuang Tzu*. New York: Columbia University Press, 1968.

Wu, Hung, "Art and Architecture of the Warring States Period." In *The Cambridge History of Ancient China*, ed. by Michael Loewe and Edward Shaughnessy. Cambridge: Cambridge University Press, 1999.

Wu Kuang-ming. *On Chinese Body Thinking: A Cultural Hermeneutic*. Leiden: Brill, 1997.

Wu Yu 吳璵, ed., *Shangshu duben* 尚書讀本. Taipei: Sanmin Publishing, 1985.

Xiao, Yumin 蕭裕民. "*Zhuangzi lun 'yue' jianlun yu 'xiao yao' zhi guanxi* 莊子論樂兼論與逍遙之關係." *Hanxue yanjiu* 23, no. 2 (2005): 1–33.

Xie Bingying 謝冰瑩 et al., eds. *Xinyi sishu duben* 新譯四書讀本, *Zhong yong xinyi* 中庸新譯. Taipei: Sanmin shuju, 1991.

Xiong Gongzhe 熊公哲, ed. *Xunzi jinzhu jinyi* 荀子今註今譯. Taipei: Shangwu Publishing, 1990.

Xu Shen 許慎. *Shuo Wen jiezi zhu* 說文解字注. Edited by Liu Dongmei. Shanghai: Shanghai shu dian, 1992.

Yu Jiaxi 餘嘉錫. "*Liji Yueji yu Shiji Yueshu*" 禮記樂記與史記樂書. In *Yueji lunbian* 樂記論辯, ed. Zhao Feng 趙澐, ed., 56–67. Beijing: Renmin yinyue, 1983.

Yan Changyao 顏昌嶢, ed. *Guanzi jiaoshi* 管子校釋. Changsha: Yuelu shushe, 1996.

Yang Bojun 楊伯峻. *Chunqiu Zuozhuan zhu* 春秋左傳注. Beijing: Zhonghua shuju, 1995.

———. *Mengzi yizhu* 孟子譯注. Hong Kong: Zhonghua shuju, 1998.

———. *Lunyu yizhu* 論語譯注. Hong Kong: Zhonghua shuju, 1984.

Yang, Xiaoneng. *Golden Age of Chinese Archaeology: Celebrated Discoveries from the People's Republic of China.* New Haven: Yale University Press, 1999.

Yates, Robin, trans. *Five Lost Classics: Tao, Huang-lao, and Yin-yang in Han China.* New York: Ballantine Books, 1997.

Yung, Bell. *Cantonese Opera: Performance as Creative Process.* Cambridge: Cambridge University Press, 2009.

Yung, Bell, Evelyn Rawski, and Rubie Watson, eds. *Harmony and Counterpoint: Ritual Music in Chinese Context.* Stanford: Stanford University Press, 1996.

Zhanguo ce, vols. 1 and 2. Shanghai: Shanghai guji, 1998.

Zhao Feng 趙澐, ed. *Yueji lunbian* 樂記論辯. Beijing, Renmin yinyue, 1983.

Zhongyang yinyue xueyuan zhongguo yinyue yanjiusuo 中央音樂學院中國音樂研究所, eds. *Zhongguo gudai yinyue shiliao jiyao, part I.* 中國古代音樂史料輯要第一輯. Beijing: Zhonghua shuju, 1962.

Zhongyang yinyue xueyuan zhongguo yinyue yanjiusuo中央音樂學院中國音樂研究所, eds. *Zhongguo gudai yinYue shumu* 中國古代音樂書目. Beijing: Yinyue chubanshe, 1961.

Zhouyi zhushu 周易注疏. Taipei: Taiwan xuesheng shuju, 1984.

Zhu Wenwei 朱文瑋 and Lü Qichang 呂琪昌. *Xian-Qin yuezhong zhi yanjiu* 先秦樂鐘之研究. Taipei: Nantian 1994.

Zhuangzi jishi 莊子集釋. Vols. 1 & 2. See Wang Xiaoyu 王孝魚, ed.

Index

Page numbers in **bold** indicate major discussions of particular topics.